Transformation, Development, and Regionalization in Greater Asia | 11

The Series

Transformation, Development, and Regionalization in Greater Asia

is edited by

Prof. Dr. Christoph Schuck
Department of Philosophy and Political Science
TU Dortmund University

Matthias Heise, M.A.
Department of Philosophy and Political Science
TU Dortmund University

Sylvia Yazid

Indonesia's Civil Society in the Age of Democratization

NGO-Responses on the Issue of Labor Migration

Die Deutsche Nationalbibliothek lists this publication in the Deutsche Nationalbibliografie; detailed bibliographic data is available on the Internet at http://dnb.d-nb.de.

Zugl.: Monash University, Australia, School of Political and Social Inquiry, Faculty of Arts, Diss., 2011

ISBN 978-3-8487-0697-6

1. Edition 2013

Acknowledgements

The publication of this book is made possible by the support from Professor Dr. Christoph Schuck and his team at the Department of Philosophy and Political Science, Faculty of Human Sciences and Theology at TU Dortmund University and the funding from the Gambrinus Fellowship of Dortmunder Volksbank, Germany. This book is based on my Ph.D. thesis, written in the School of Political and Social Inquiry, Monash University, Australia. The completion of the research would not have been possible without the remarkable support from my supervisors, Associate Professor Susan Blackburn and Dr. Penelope Graham. I am also grateful for the inputs from Dr. Michael Janover, Professor Ken Young, Professor Greg Barton, Professor Amarjit Kaur, Associate Professor Nicola Piper, and Professor Kathryn Robinson whose feedback and suggestions have helped me in shaping the research and writing this book. For the preparation of the manuscript, I would like to acknowledge the immense support from Matthias Heise, M.A., and the assistance from Julia Dumin.

I am greatly in debt to my respondents. They are Anis Hidayah, Wahyu Susilo, Alex Ong, Salma Safitri, Thaufiek Zulbahary, Risma Umar, Asma'ul Khusnaeny, Tati Krisnawaty, Damos D. Agusman, Tatang B. Razak, Ferry Adamhar, Syafruddin Setiabudi, Jumhur Hidayat, Ade Adam Noch, Ramiany Sinaga, Lisna Poeloengan, Nursyahbani Katjasungkana, Tuti L. Soetrisno, Albert Y. Bonasahat, Riana Puspasari, Riwanto Tirtosudarmo, Lisa N. Humaidah, Indra Piliang, Cynthia Gabriel, Irene Fernandez, Ridwan M. Sijabat, Geni Achnas, and many others whose knowledge and experience I have benefited from.

My candidature was made possible with the funding from the Australian Development Scholarship. For that, I thank the AusAID staff in Jakarta, Canberra, and Melbourne. To pursue my study and the fellowship, I had to be absent from the Department of International Relations, Parahyangan Catholic University, Bandung. I thank my colleagues, the faculty, and the staff for their support and understanding. For the continuous encouragement to expose myself to the international world, I thank Professor Bob S. Hadiwinata and Dr. Pius S. Prasetyo. I am also deeply grateful for the friendship of Aknolt Kristian Pakpahan, Kathrin Rucktäschel, Elisabeth S. Dewi, Riesa Fiana, Aquarini Prabasmoro, Illiah, and Gracia Girsang.

To my heart and soul, my husband Gumelar Rahayu, our son Chaska Rashadel Gumelar, and our daughter Nayla Amabel Gumelar, I could not ask for better companions in making my intellectual journey.

This book is dedicated to the brave Indonesian women who leave their families and homes in search of a better living abroad and all parties that have relentlessly made the efforts to protect these women along the way.

Content

List of Figures and Tables

FIGURES

TABLES

Glossary of Terms

Advokasi	Advocacy
Aksi	Action/protest
Apjati	*Asosiasi Perusahaan Jasa Tenaga Kerja Indonesia*, Indonesian Workers Service Companies' Association
ASEAN	Association of Southeast Asian Nations
Badan Legislasi	Legislation Body
BNP2TKI	*Badan Nasional Penempatan dan Perlindungan Tenaga Kerja Indonesia*, National Authority for the Placement and Protection of Indonesian Overseas Workers
Buruh migran perempuan	Women migrant workers
Calo	Sponsor or broker or middleman
CARAM Asia	Coordination Action Research on AIDS and Mobility Asia
CEDAW	Convention on the Elimination of All Forms of Discrimination against Women
Draft akademis	Academic draft/script
DPR	*Dewan Perwakilan Rakyat*, House of Representatives
Ecosoc	A Jakarta-based NGO focusing on the issues of migrant workers, the urban poor, and malnutrition and hunger
Fatayat	The young women's wing of the Indonesian Muslim mass organization *Nahdlatul Ulama*
FOBMI	*Federasi Organisasi Buruh Migran Indonesia*, Federation of Migrant Workers' Organizations
Foker	*Forum Kerja untuk Keadilan Pekerja Rumah Tangga Migran*, Forum for Justice for Migrant Domestic Workers
GPPBM	*Gerakan Perempuan untuk Perlindungan Buruh Migran*, Women's Movement for the Protection of Migrant Workers
HRW	Human Rights Watch
ICRMW	International Convention on the Protection of the Rights of All Migrant Workers and Members of Their Families
ILO	International Labor Organisation
IMF	International Monetary Fund
INFID	International NGO Forum on Indonesian Development
JKP3	*Jaringan Kerja Prolegnas Pro Perempuan*, National Network on Pro-Women National Legislation Program
Komisi	Commission
Komnas Perempuan	*Komisi Nasional Anti Kekerasan Terhadap Perempuan*, National Commission on Violence against Women
Komunitas	*Community*, A term used for the branch of Solidaritas Perempuan

Kontrak politik	Political contract
Kopbumi	*Konsorsium Pembela Buruh Migran Indonesia*, The Consortium for the Defense of Indonesian Migrant Workers
LBH	*Lembaga Bantuan Hukum*, Legal Aid Institute
LIPI	*Lembaga Ilmu Pengetahuan Indonesia*, Indonesian Institute of Science
LSM	*Lembaga Swadaya Masyarakat*, Self-reliant Community Institutions
Mahkamah Konstitusi	Constitutional Court
MFA	Migrant Forum in Asia
Mitra	Partner
MoFA	Ministry of Foreign Affairs
MoMT	Ministry of Manpower and Transmigration
MoSA	Ministry of Social Affairs
MoU	Memorandum of Understanding
MPR	*Majelis Permusyawaratan Rakyat*, People's Consultative Assembly
Muslimat	The women's wing of the Indonesian Muslim mass organization *Nahdlatul Ulama*
Musyawarah	Consultation
Musyawarah komunitas	Community forum
New Order Era	*Orde Baru*, The era under Soeharto's presidency, 1965-1998
NGO	Non-Governmental Organization
NOVIB	*Nederlandse Organisatie voor Internationale Ontwikkelingssamenwerking,* a Dutch NGO
NU	*Nahdlatul Ulama*, Indonesian Muslim mass organization
Ops Nyah	Get Rid Operation
Panitia Kerja	Working committee
Panitia Khusus	Special committee
PDI-P	*Partai Demokrasi Indonesia Perjuangan*, Indonesian Democratic Party of Struggle
Pekerja rumah tangga mi-gran	Migrant domestic workers
Pelita	*Pembangunan Lima Tahun*, Five-year Development Plan
Perserikatan	Association
PJTKI	*Perusahaan Jasa Tenaga Kerja Indonesia*, labor agencies
PKB	*Partai Kebangkitan Bangsa*, National Awakening Party
POEA	Philippine Overseas Employment Administration
PPTKIS	*Pelaksana Penempatan Tenaga Kerja Indonesia Swasta*, Migrant Worker Placement Private Organizer
Prolegnas	*Program Legislasi Nasional*, National Legislation Program
RANHAM	*Rencana Aksi Nasional Hak Asasi Manusia*, National Plan of Action on Human Rights

Rapat Paripurna	General meeting
RDPU	*Rapat Dengar Pendapat Umum*, Public Hearing Meeting
Reformasi	Reform
Reformasi Era	Reform Era, The era after the New Order Era ended in 1998
RUU	*Rancangan Undang-undang*, Bill
SBMI	*Serikat Buruh Migran Indonesia*, Indonesian Migrant Workers Union
Serikat buruh migran	Migrant worker union/association
SMoWE	State Ministry of Women's Empowerment
SOM	Senior Official Meeting
SP	Solidaritas Perempuan
UNIFEM	United Nations Development Fund for Women
Yayasan	Foundation

1. Non-Governmental Organizations and the Issue of Indonesian Women Migrant Workers: An Introduction

This book investigates the activism of non-governmental organizations (NGOs) concerned with Indonesian women who work overseas in the informal sector, mostly as domestic workers. This particular group of migrant workers has become a focus for activism in Indonesia due to their growing number, vulnerability to abuse, poor working conditions, and frequent exclusion from labor laws and policies. Thus, this book aims to assess the roles of Indonesian NGOs in promoting the rights of Indonesian women migrant workers by examining how they attempt to influence the government's policies on labor migration. In doing so, it focuses on two particular NGOs: *Solidaritas Perempuan untuk Hak Asasi Manusia* (SP) or Women's Solidarity for Human Rights, a women's NGO established during the New Order Era which was the first to take up this issue at the beginning of the 1990s, and Migrant CARE or Indonesian Association for Migrant Workers Sovereignty, a relatively younger migrant worker NGO established during the Reform Era with a high media profile. In making a case study of these NGOs, the aim is also to capture the shift in their activism in response to dynamic changes in the Indonesian policy context, particularly the transition from the New Order to the *Reformasi* (Reform) Era.

Although migration occurs in virtually all parts of the world, authors like Munck and Piper have pointed out that significant flows occur more within southern regions like Asia.[1] Nevertheless, most research on the issue of labor migration has focused on conditions in the receiving countries, meaning western countries or the more developed or industrialized countries in Asia. Except for the ones covering the Philippines, who are usually referred to as a success story in the protection of their migrant workers, studies focusing on the sending countries are still quite limited. Therefore, this book aims to contribute to the existing body of research on labor migration by looking at the activism of NGOs concerned with the issue of women migrant workers in Indonesia as a sending country.

In Indonesia, some of the efforts made by the post-New Order governments include passing Law No. 39/2004 on The Placement and Protection of Indonesian Workers Overseas, Indonesia's first law that specifically regulates labor mi-

1 Cf. Munck 2009, Piper 2009.

gration,[2] and signing bilateral agreements (Memoranda of Understanding or MoUs) with receiving countries such as the one signed in 2006 with Malaysia on the Recruitment and Placement of Indonesian Domestic Workers.[3] On April 12, 2012, the Indonesian parliament has finally ratified the 1990 United Nations International Convention on the Protection of the Rights of All Migrant Workers and Members of Their Families (ICRMW). At the time this book was written, the parliament and the government were still in the process of revising Law No. 39/2004. It is expected, mostly by migrant workers' advocates, that the new law would adopt the principles of the ICRMW. However, since this book focuses on the first decade of the Reform Era, the discussions will be primarily on the main policies made during this period. Therefore, I have chosen Law No. 39/2004 and the 2006 MoU with Malaysia as case studies to examine the involvement and influence of NGOs in the policy-making process.

While a significant proportion of this book examines how NGOs deal with the state, it goes beyond merely discussing NGO-state relationships. Based on the twin assumptions that NGOs conduct their activities within a political space framed by other actors and that NGOs can actually negotiate and expand this particular political space, it examines how they engage with other influential actors. The starting point is that NGOs' roles within the migration system are determined by the nature of their relationships with the key actors involved (i.e. state institutions, international organizations, recruiting agencies, and other local and international NGOs), along with their unique organizational characteristics, the way they embrace and frame the issue, and the approaches they use in conducting their activities.

Furthermore, with the understanding that a policy is highly influenced by the dynamic of its environment, the topic is sited in the context of Indonesia's changing political, economic, and social conditions. The late 1990s saw significant national and international changes influencing the policy environment. Domestically, the end of the authoritarian New Order Era in 1998 and democratization efforts led to a relatively more open and accommodative policy environment in Indonesia. Since then, the country has been going through a dynamic reform period under various governments in a relatively short period.[4] Changes happen-

2 Prior to this law, the highest policy instrument that regulated labor migration from Indonesia was a ministerial decree.

3 This MoU is widely known as the MoU on the informal sector.

4 Since the *Reformasi* Era began, Indonesia has had four presidents. Habibie, as the vice-president when Soeharto stepped down, took over without adequate legitimacy. Abdurrahman Wahid was considered as a democrat but criticized for his "laid back" approach and money politics scandals. Megawati, the daughter of Indonesia's first president Soekarno, became president with strong support from the grassroots but was criticized for failing to fulfill her promises to improve the economy. Susilo Bambang Yudhoyono has a

ing outside Indonesia have also significantly shaped the policy environment, including that of labor migration. The economic crisis that hit many countries in East Asia in 1997 forced receiving countries, including Malaysia, to adjust their policies, including those on labor migration. Furthermore, greater attention was paid to the subject of labor migration at regional and international levels as reflected in the moves made by regional and international organizations such as the International Labour Organization (ILO), the United Nations Development Fund for Women (UNIFEM), and the Association of South East Asian Nations (ASEAN). Therefore, the discussion is framed by the changing contexts at the national and international levels which have strongly influenced the government's policies, particularly those on labor migration. It attempts to understand how changes in the policy environment affect NGO activism in Indonesia, how NGOs respond to these national and international changes, and to what extent they utilize the opportunities brought by the changes.

This book is concerned with four main issues. The first issue is that of Indonesian women working in the informal sector, mostly as domestic workers in Malaysia. According to the data from the Department of Manpower and Transmigration, the number of Indonesian female workers placed in Malaysia through official channels, both in formal and informal sectors, was 111,418 in 2007, 140,658 in 2008, and 61,374 in 2009.[5] There is no official record available on the exact number of those working as domestic workers but the general assumption is, as asserted by Safitri,[6] that 70 percent of Indonesian migrant workers are women and 90 percent of them work as domestic workers. This group has characteristics which differentiate them from other migrant workers. The temporary, contract-based and informal nature of their work has differentiated them from other migrant workers. Moreover, the fact that they work in isolation in households, considered a private sphere, makes them vulnerable to abuses. Unfortunately, these conditions are not adequately recognized in most labor legislation and policies, whether in sending or receiving countries.[7]

This leads to the second issue of concern, the activism of Indonesian NGOs that are concerned with women migrant workers. This book aims to examine the

military background and was the first president to be directly elected following constitutional reform. In 2009, Yudhoyono was re-elected for his second term. He was labeled "an institutionalist" for responding to most issues by creating new institutions or task forces. Toward the end of his presidency, he has been busy dealing with issues within his party, Partai Demokrat.

5 Cf. Depnakertrans 2010. It needs to be noted that the official data at most Indonesian government's websites tends to be irregular and inconsistent in terms of availability, structure and accuracy.

6 Interview with Safitri, Salma on June 6, 2007, Jakarta.

7 Cf. Hugo 1992, Yamanaka and Piper 2005.

NGOs' efforts in influencing Indonesian government to significantly address the particular problems faced by this group of migrant workers. In doing so, this book contributes to the documentation and analysis of their activities, particularly those aimed at influencing policies on labor migration. Although the issue of female labor migration has been embraced by various types of NGOs, this book limits the analysis by looking at the activities of two NGOs, a women's NGO and a migrant worker NGO, for two main reasons. *Firstly* because the issue of women migrant workers was initially embraced by a women's NGO, followed later by migrant worker NGOs. *Secondly* because an analysis of the issue of women migrant workers needs to consider their identities both as women and as migrant workers. This book aims to understand the similar or different approaches, resources, and activities of each type of NGO and identify their challenges and opportunities in participating in the policy process.

The third issue is the transnational nature of labor migration. Because the whole process of migration crosses national boundaries, involving recruitment in and departure from the sending countries, employment in and repatriation from the receiving countries, and arrival back in sending countries, its analysis needs to take into account the various environments, authorities, jurisdictions, governments, regulations, and laws involved. This book is concerned with how the NGOs have been responding to the challenge this complexity poses. One of the NGOs' key responses is their effort to extend their activities to the regional and international level. Realizing their limitations and the need for support, most prominent Indonesian NGOs, including the two researched, have engaged in national, regional, and international networks. Thus, central to the discussion is the NGOs' involvement in transnational advocacy networks, which, according to Keck and Sikkink, "includes those relevant actors working internationally on an issue, who are bound together by shared values, a common discourse, and dense exchanges of information and services".[8] Since both NGOs researched have responded by extending their activities to the regional and international level, the question then is how the NGOs have benefited from such transnational activism.

The fourth issue is the dynamics of relationships between NGOs and other actors. In conducting their activities, NGOs interact with various actors at various levels. This book aims to document the negotiation, contestation, and/or cooperation between each type of NGO and actors, not only the elements of the state, but also regional and international institutions, local and international NGOs, the media, and recruiting agencies. The main question on this issue is how the NGOs' transnational activism affects their efforts to influence policies on labor migration.

8 Keck and Sikkink 1998, p. 2.

The issues above are framed by the contexts of a globalizing world and a democratizing Indonesia. Consequently, this research requires a multi-level analysis which accommodates the multi-level nature of the issue and the efforts made to address them. The concept of transnational activism advanced by authors like Keck and Sikkink[9] and Piper and Uhlin[10] will be used to link up the various levels of NGOs' activism.

1.1 NGOs in a Democratizing Indonesia

This book focuses on the first decade of the period after 1998, known as the *Reformasi* Era, which is seen by many as a period in which Indonesia underwent a democratic transition. In identifying the changes that may signify a transition process, this book does not cover all aspects of democratization; rather, it concentrates on one aspect commonly considered an indicator of a democratization process: the increased participation of civil society in the making of public policy. It is further focused by specifically examining the position and role of NGOs concerned with the issue of women migrant workers within the policy cycle.[11]

One of the main features of the New Order in Indonesia was its ability to maintain its existence for an extended period, 32 years, through utilization of what Hadiz[12] called "coercive power" and "a complex system of patronage". Opposition to the state through civil society activism was repressed on the grounds that it endangered national unity and that it was not part of Indonesian culture.[13] In addition, as argued by Beittinger-Lee, Indonesian civil society was weak, with a gap between the educated, politically active, urban-based middle classes and the rural population, which made it easier for the state to suppress dissent through intervention and manipulation.[14] Nevertheless, she continued, voices in opposition did not totally disappear because those with grievances and criticisms of the government formed organizations like NGOs.

9 Cf. ibid.

10 Cf. Piper and Uhlin 2004b.

11 The term policy cycle is used to refer to a process which is commonly drawn as a continuous cycle and in its simplest form involves input, process, and output. According to Howlett and Ramesh 2003, p. 13, a policy cycle involves: agenda-setting, policy formulation, decision-making, policy implementation, and policy evaluation. The result of the evaluation is then used to start a new cycle. This concept is used as a guideline for the analysis in this book because, in practice, this cycle is likely to occur not in a linear manner, and each country has its own mechanisms for making and implementing policies.

12 Cf. Hadiz 2005, p. 122.

13 Cf. Wessel 2005, p. 10.

14 Cf. Beittinger-Lee 2005, p. 96.

A quite comprehensive study of Indonesian NGOs during the New Order Era was conducted by Eldridge. He observed that at the beginning of the 1990s NGOs gained importance in Indonesia due to the demand for a more "equitable" and "participatory" social and economic development and for NGOs to promote democratic values and processes.[15] Since the late 1990s, both from inside and outside Indonesia, initially it was hoped that there would be rapid and far-reaching democratization. However, a few years into the *Reformasi* Era period, many started to express their doubts as to whether transformation toward a democracy really was occurring in Indonesia since transparency, accountability, rule of law, and social justice were yet to be established,[16] and the first presidencies after Soeharto were short, problematic, and much criticized. Nevertheless, there were efforts to create a more open and democratic political environment. Responding to demands for reform, Habibie launched a formal democratization process. More political parties were established[17] and by June 1999 parliamentary elections were conducted, followed by a session of the People's Consultative Assembly or *Majelis Permusyawaratan Rakyat* (MPR) to elect a president and vice-president. During the short presidencies of Abdurrahman Wahid and Megawati Soekarnoputri, the center devolved more power to regional governments. In 2004, the first direct presidential election was conducted, resulting in the inauguration of Susilo Bambang Yudhoyono's first term as president. When he was re-elected in 2009, Yudhoyono became the first Indonesian president to be elected for a second term after the New Order ended. In this context of democratization, the discussion in this book centers on understanding how these governments have managed labor migration, particularly that of women, and how much civil society involvement they have allowed.

In general, post-New Order Indonesia has seen an increase in civil society participation in the political arena. One of the main forms of this participation was what Clear described as "gathering information about Indonesian politics and providing policy alternatives through nongovernmental channels".[18] According to her, NGOs were seen as a significant source of and support for new ideas related to political reforms. At the same time, Clear observed that, with the more open political atmosphere, international donors were more interested in funding Indonesian institutions.[19]

15 Cf. Eldridge 1995, p. 1.

16 Cf. Clear 2005, p. 157, Hadiz 2005, p. 121.

17 From three parties during the New Order to 48 participating in the 1999 election. Cf. Hadiwinata 2003, p. 114.

18 Clear 2005, p. 172.

19 However, as argued by Beittinger-Lee 2005, p. 103, increased funding by foreign agencies also brings new risks for NGOs, mainly related to their "authenticity", or as viewed by others their "legitimacy" and "independence".

As argued by Keck and Sikkink, an understanding of domestic political context or what they call "opportunity structure" is crucial for an analysis of the emergence and development of transnational activism.[20] According to them, this opportunity structure can be assessed by comparing citizens' access to political institutions or by identifying changes in formal and informal political power relations. In relation to this, this book examines the access of NGOs', as part of civil society, to policy-making institutions, and identifies whether there are changes in the way they interact. It also asks how the reforms have affected NGO activism both domestically and transnationally. An examination of the policy environment of the Reform Era is made not only to assess the NGOs' relationship with the relevant actors but also to determine whether the NGOs have identified a window of opportunity to enhance their influence on the policy process, and if so, how they utilize the changes as part of their strategy to achieve their aims.

1.2 Labor Migration of Indonesian Women

One of the subjects that have received considerable attention in studies on labor migration is its feminization, due to the significant increase in the number of women working outside their countries in the past few decades. Besides this rapid growth, the increasing attention paid to the migration of women to work overseas, particularly in the informal sector, is also due to factors such as its micro- and macro-economic significance and its problematic nature. Problems such as unpaid salary and undocumented[21] status may apply to both male migrants who work in plantations, building sites, or factories and female migrants who work as domestic workers. However, for women domestic workers, the condition is often worsened by abuses and confinement.

Despite the limited and unreliable records of labor migration, particularly of the undocumented kind, there are attempts to compile statistical data on Indonesian labor migration and estimate the numbers of Indonesian women migrating to

20 Cf. Keck and Sikkink 1998, p. 7.

21 Various terms are used to refer to migrant workers whose migration is problematic. The more common terms used by academics and activists are "undocumented" or "irregular" migrants. The term "illegal migrants" is commonly used by the government, particularly that of the receiving country. Different terms are used due to the varied views about what causes the migration problems and how it affects the migrants' status. Those against the use of the term "illegal migrants" argue that these workers are not illegal as human beings. At a certain point in their migration, they may not hold the proper documents required, but in many cases it is not the workers' fault. A possible case is that a domestic worker had to run away from her abusive employer but, since her passport is held by the employer or the agent, she becomes undocumented.

work abroad.[22] Although the period and variables used may differ, the data shows an upward trend in the number of women migrant workers. Currently, there are almost 4 million documented Indonesians working overseas and around 70 percent of them are women.[23]

As with other types of migration, women's decisions to migrate are highly influenced by conditions in both sending and receiving countries, also known as "push-pull" factors. The main push factors in sending countries like Indonesia are usually the inability of these countries to accommodate the growing labor force and the significant contribution of migrant workers' remittances to the national income. According to the data recorded by the National Authority for the Placement and Protection of Indonesia Overseas Workers or *Badan Nasional Penempatan dan Perlindungan Tenaga Kerja Indonesia* (BNP2TKI), the remittances for 2003-2008 in billion USD are: 1.67, 1.88, 2.93, 3.42, 5.84, and 6.71.[24] The continuously increasing amount of remittances for Indonesia is also displayed in Table 1.1.[25] The table shows that remittances have grown from 0.1 percent of the GDP in 1990 to 1.3 percent in 2008 and have been at an even higher level in some years. The remittances amount to only around 1 percent of the In-

22 Cf. Hugo 1992, Komnas Perempuan and SP 2003, Yamanaka and Piper 2005, Depnakertrans 2010. As presented in the work of Yamanaka and Piper 2005, p. 8, the number of Indonesia's unskilled female migration was 12,018 in 1983 and reached 85,696 in 1993. The proportion of women in total outflows also increased from 48.4 percent to 66.0 percent. The data in the work of Hugo 1992, p. 184, which focuses on the number of female Indonesians who worked in Brunei, Hong Kong, Malaysia, and Singapore also shows an increase from 329 in during 1984-1985 to 5,807 by 1989-1990. Data compiled by the National Commission on Violence against Women (*Komnas Perempuan*) and SP 2003, p. 9, shows how the number of Indonesian female migrant workers increased from 3,817 in 1974-1979 to 972,198 in 1999-2002. More recent data from the Department of Manpower and Transmigration, Depnakertrans 2010, shows that Indonesia in 2001 sent 272,428 women workers overseas, and 345,922 in 2008. It needs to be noted that the source of this data is mainly the Ministry of Manpower and Transmigration (MoMT), meaning it reflects those who migrate through the official channels and are processed by the ministry. These numbers do not include those who migrate "illegally".

23 This is the official number of Indonesians migrating to work abroad. As mentioned in various studies, if those migrating "illegally" are included, the number may exceed 6 million.

24 Cf. BNP2TKI 2010.

25 Cf. The World Bank 2010. These are only the officially tracked remittances, transferred through the banking system. The data shows that there is a significant increase in remittances from 2004 to 2005. Wahyu Susilo (Interview with Susilo, Wahyu on February 11, 2010, Jakarta) suggested that, rather than indicating a significant increase in the flow of remittances into Indonesia, the statistic possibly indicates that more remittances went through official channels and were recorded since 2005. It is believed that the number may be higher since the banking system has not been able to identify and record all the remittances sent through official channels and the data do not include income brought into the country by the migrant workers in cash form.

donesian GDP, but it has been claimed by many, including the government, that migrant workers' remittances are the second biggest contributor to Indonesia's national income, after oil and gas.

Table 1.1: Indonesian Workers' Remittances

Year	Remittance in million USD	Percent of GDP
1990	166	0.1
1991	130	0.1
1992	229	0.2
1993	346	0.2
1994	449	0.3
1995	651	0.3
1996	796	0.4
1997	725	0.3
1998	958	1.0
1999	1,109	0.8
2000	1,190	0.7
2001	1,046	0.7
2002	1,259	0.6
2003	1,489	0.6
2004	1,866	0.7
2005	5,420	1.9
2006	5,722	1.6
2007	6,174	1.4
2008	6,795	1.3

Source: Data from the World Bank[26]

As for the pull factor in receiving countries, it has mainly been labor shortages in certain occupations. As observed by Yamanaka and Piper, in countries like Singapore, Malaysia, Hong Kong, Taiwan, Korea, and Japan, better educated women have shifted to managerial and professional occupations.[27] Therefore, more workers are needed to fulfill traditional feminine roles such as taking care of the household, the children, and the elderly. The solution is to acquire domestic workers from neighboring countries such as the Philippines, Indonesia, Vietnam, Pakistan, and Bangladesh. Although domestic workers are poorly paid by receiving country standards, they earn considerably more than they would at home. As

26 World Bank 2010.
27 Cf. Yamanaka and Piper 2005, p. 3.

an illustration, in 2009, the average salary for domestic workers in Indonesia was around 40 AUD per month, while the initial salary for Indonesians working as domestic workers in Malaysia was between 140 AUD and 175 AUD.[28] Since the working conditions are similarly poor, whether it is in Indonesia or in the receiving countries, the significant salary difference has further motivated Indonesian women to migrate. Given that the economic disparity between countries, particularly within the Asia region, is unlikely to diminish in the near future, the flow of migration between the less and the more developed countries will continue.

Another factor that has drawn attention to women migrant workers is the menial nature of their work. As asserted by Young and Chant, compared to men, migrant women have more limited access to jobs because most of those who migrate are unskilled or semi-skilled.[29] This has limited their choice of work to low-status and poorly paid employment in the informal and service sectors. In most cases, they are forced to do 3Ds (dirty, degrading, and dangerous) work on temporary and short-term contracts.

While women workers' rights are frequently violated, labor migration policies have failed to protect them. Most labor migration policies are general in nature, lacking special consideration of the conditions women employed as domestic workers are facing. They only regulate the formal sector, while the majority of women migrant workers are in the informal sector. Domestic workers are even more vulnerable because households are usually considered as private space, not covered by public policies. As argued by Yamanaka and Piper, since domestic work is usually considered as "an extension of unpaid 'service' naturally assigned to women according to traditional gender roles", this type of work is not considered as a "legitimate form of labor" by most labor laws.[30] Moreover, their employment conditions are largely determined by their employers.[31] The temporary contract-based employment also makes women migrant workers "disposable": they can be hired and fired at minimal cost.[32] The fact that these conditions generally apply to Indonesian women's labor migration is one of the reasons why the book has been written: to contribute to the body of literature that argues for the protection of the rights of Indonesian women migrant workers.

28 Cf. Antara News, November 23, 2009, Antara News, September 13, 2009. It needs to be noted that one of the factors that make Indonesian domestic workers quite popular in Malaysia is their low salary. As a comparison, in 2008, the salary rate for domestic workers from Vietnam in Malaysia was already around 265 AUD, and 495 AUD for those from the Philippines. Cf. Caraka, August 2008.

29 Cf. Young 2006, p. 21, Chant 1992, p. 204.

30 Cf. Yamanaka and Piper 2005, p. 16.

31 Cf. Ball and Piper 2006, p. 219, Loveband 2006, p. 78.

32 Cf. Choi 2006, p. 151.

1.3 Arguing for NGO Activism on the Issue of Women Migrant Workers

Apart from the NGOs' own potential and strengths, as in other cases calling for greater involvement of non-state actors, the main argument for their having a bigger role is the failure of state and market mechanisms. Thus, the following sections briefly identify what has and has not been done by some key actors concerning labor migration. The assumption is that the failure of these other actors, or at least their inability to adequately address the issues faced by Indonesian women migrant workers, gives legitimacy to the involvement of NGOs in the management of labor migration in Indonesia.

1.3.1 The State and the Management of Labor Migration

One of the main debates on globalization concerns the role of the state. Kenichi Ohmae's work in 1995 has triggered a series of globalization studies on topics such as "the erosion of state sovereignty", "the hollowing out of the state", or "the decline of the state". Authors like Kerr and Sweetman argue that governments' ability to protect their citizens' rights and address various problems is declining.[33] On the other hand, Gills maintains that the state, with its central role, might be able to deal with the negative impacts of globalization.[34] As also argued by Young, the marginalization of the state's role continues to be debatable.[35] In most cases, a government's political and economic considerations and interests continue to be the major factors that determine the making and implementation of public policies. On issues like labor migration, despite their failure to provide adequate protection for the migrant workers, governments have continued to play the main role, particularly when it comes to regulating the process. However, government failure or underperformance in managing labor migration creates loopholes that allow and provide legitimacy for the more active participation of non-state actors.

It needs to be noted that the earlier international labor migration from Asian countries was conducted with minimum involvement by governments. As observed by Yamanaka and Piper, although international labor migration began in the 1970s, it only started to emerge as a policy concern in many Asian receiving countries in the 1980s, when governments started to manage and regulate it.[36]

33 Cf. Kerr and Sweetman 2003, p. ix.
34 Cf. Gills 2002, p. 26.
35 Cf. Young 2006, p. 19.
36 Cf. Yamanaka and Piper 2005, p. 7.

Since then, the policies of sending and receiving countries have clearly reflected their main views and interests on labor migration. Despite receiving countries' dependency on foreign workers to solve their labor shortage problems, most receiving countries have adopted highly restrictive policies towards migrant workers. According to Yamanaka and Piper, this is usually based on the argument of protecting the balance of the society from the "mass invasion" of migration.[37] Consequently, protection of migrant workers' rights in receiving countries' labor laws is limited by the higher priority of protecting the employment of their own citizens. As for the sending countries, their policies are aimed at maximizing earnings, often at the expense of disregarding governments' mandate to protect their citizens.[38]

Through time, despite the various problems faced by Indonesian women migrant workers, government responses have been far from adequate and appropriate. Government policies are criticized for being based more on the state's interest rather than migrant workers' interests, thus aimed more at facilitating the process than protecting the migrant workers.[39] Furthermore, until 2004, labor migration was regulated through ministerial decrees and government regulations[40] which were criticized for being weak, and contradictive, and could not comprehensively address the issues faced by migrant workers.[41] In 2002, after the crisis in Nunukan,[42] the government took the initiative of introducing a bill on the Protection of Indonesian Migrant Workers and their Families. Law No. 39/2004 on the Placement and Protection of Indonesian Workers Overseas was eventually passed in October 2004 and has since then been highly criticized by migrant labor advocates for not providing adequate protection for migrant workers. The government also made bilateral agreements with some receiving countries. However, according to the National Commission on Violence against Women or *Komisi Nasional Anti Kekerasan Terhadap Perempuan* (*Komnas Perempuan*) and SP, these agreements are weak, largely due to the "unequal power relations" between sending and receiving countries.[43] Nevertheless, government efforts to improve the laws, set up systems for managing labor migration, sign bilateral agreements with receiving countries, and participate in re-

37 Cf. ibid., p. 13.
38 Cf. Ball and Piper 2006, p. 223.
39 Cf. Piper and Iredale 2003, p. 21.
40 These decrees and regulations can be viewed at www.nakertrans.go.id.
41 Cf. Ford 2005, p. 9.
42 The crisis happened when the government of Malaysia decided to conduct a massive deportation of Indonesian undocumented migrant workers. These workers entered Indonesia through Nunukan, a border town in East Kalimantan, and many had to camp there because they did not have the resources to go on to their area of origin. The Indonesian government was criticized for failing to manage this repatriation flow.
43 Cf. Komnas Perempuan and SP 2003, p. 43.

gional and international arrangements should be acknowledged as attempts to improve the management of labor migration, regardless of the motivation and results.

Inputs and influences for policy-making and implementation can come from non-state actors both from inside and outside the country but since the dominant role of the state in the management of labor migration will persist, a more reasonable aim will be to determine what other forces can do to cooperate with, influence, and possibly monitor the state. Thus, in this book, an understanding of the relationship and interaction between NGOs and the government will support the analysis of NGOs' influence on the process of making and implementing policies on labor migration.

1.3.2 Regional and International Instruments

Protection and promotion of the rights of migrant workers are also expected to come from the documents signed and ratified by sending and receiving countries in the context of their membership in regional and international organizations. An established body of literature has reviewed the existing regional and international human rights instruments that can be used to promote the rights of migrant workers. This literature emphasizes that one of the major obstacles is the fact that many countries involved in labor migration practices are hesitant in adopting the international conventions and addressing this issue at the regional level.[44]

The major international instrument that aims to ensure protection and respect for the rights of migrant workers and their families is the 1990 United Nations ICRMW which came into force on July 1, 2003. Although this convention is seen by many as a significant step in the protection of the human rights of migrants,[45] there are issues that prevent its full implementation. The major issue is the low ratification rate, as most countries involved in the practice of labor migration have yet to ratify this convention and translate its principles into national laws on labor migration. Until 2004, when Indonesia passed its law on labor migration, apart from the Philippines, which had passed The Migrant Workers and Overseas Filipinos Act of 1995, none of the sending countries had a migrant worker bill that included human rights.[46] Based on their investigation on a sample of countries, Piper and Iredale identified the obstacles to ratifying the con-

44 Cf. Piper and Iredale 2003, Yamanaka and Piper 2005, Ball and Piper 2006.

45 Cf. Piper and Iredale 2003, p. 5.

46 Cf. ibid., p. 16. Although Indonesia has ratified the ICRMW in 2012, at the time this book was written, the parliament and the government were still in the process of revising Indonesia's first law on labor migration. However, it was the view of migrant workers' advocates that the bill has yet to accommodate the principles of ICRMW.

vention, which included:[47] the failure of many governments to immediately investigate the clauses for the legal implications of ratifying; the concern of sending countries that, since they are also employing foreign workers (usually skilled workers or experts from developed countries), the ratification will force them to comply with a higher standard of workers' rights compared to the existing one for local workers; the shift in governments' priorities towards counter-terrorism efforts and national security since September 11, 2001, which made them focus more on anti-trafficking issues; sending countries' fear of losing markets by being "too demanding" and "rights conscious"; the combined interests of recruitment agencies, employers, and government officials which do not include the protection of migrant workers' rights; and NGOs' lack of resources to campaign for the ratification. Therefore, they argued, there needed to be external assistance which might take the form of local, regional, and global campaigns for the ratification of ICRMW by NGOs.[48]

At the regional level, human rights was considered a taboo topic for quite a long time. Ball and Piper observed that migration received little attention in the region until the financial crisis of 1997, which highlighted the urgency of addressing irregular labor migration problems and the ineffectiveness of isolated policies.[49] Even so, they asserted that Asian governments have been reluctant to discuss labor migration issues at regional forums, and although these governments have individually ratified international human and labor rights conventions, there is no guarantee of "universal, consistent or actual implementation". Ball and Piper believe that factors such as different ministerial policies, the sensitivity of the issue, the intention to preserve national sovereignty, and the interest of maintaining labor market 'flexibility' have prevented the development of a regional approach.[50]

The rather late attention toward labor migration and the continued reluctance to deal with this highly sensitive issue at a regional level is reflected in the policies of Asia-Pacific key regional bodies. According to Ball and Piper, none of them – ASEAN, the South Asian Association for Regional Cooperation

47 Cf. ibid., pp. 49-55.

48 Cf. ibid., p. 54.

49 Cf. Ball and Piper 2006, p. 220.

50 Cf. ibid., p. 221. Regional initiatives which have attempted to deal with specific aspects of migration include: the Bangkok Declaration on Irregular Migration, adopted by ministers and representatives from 18 governments in Bangkok in April 1999; the Intergovernmental Asia-Pacific Consultation on Refugees and Displaced Persons and Regional Ministerial Conference on People Smuggling, Trafficking in Persons, and Related Transnational Crime (Bali Process); the establishment of the Global Commission in International Migration (GICM) by UN Secretary Kofi Annan in December 2003; and a ministerial level meeting among Asian labor-sending countries in April 2003 initiated by the governments of Sri Lanka and Indonesia in Colombo.

(SAARC), and the Asia Pacific Economic Cooperation (APEC) forum – has migration as an integral element of its mandate.[51] They argue that, in the case of APEC, the narrow definition of APEC's central concerns and its status as an umbrella organization for countries with widely differing circumstances and national interests have made it difficult to bring the issue of migrant workers to the fore.[52] Also, since APEC is based on a government-private sector partnership, it is difficult for other social forces to challenge, which means minimal or no NGO involvement. As for ASEAN, its members in 2007 signed a declaration on the protection and promotion of the rights of migrant workers, but to date there has been no agreement or instruments among ASEAN members which significantly bind the member countries to take necessary steps in protecting migrant workers.

The above conditions have created space for and motivated NGOs to conduct regional and international campaigns urging governments to ratify existing international instruments and formulate bilateral and regional agreements which provide better protection for migrant workers and mechanisms to address the issues they are facing. Therefore, this book is concerned with how NGOs conduct these campaigns, considering that they are dealing with governmental organizations which allow extremely limited involvement of non-state actors. How do the NGOs access them and what have been the results?

1.3.3 Labor Unions and Migrant Workers' Organizations

NGOs' involvement in the issue of women migrant workers is also legitimized by the fact that, although women migrant workers are part of the labor force, in most cases, both in sending and receiving countries, they are not members of trade unions. Several studies have shown how trade unions have focused more on local labor issues and marginalize migrant labor issues. Ford, for example, argued that the significance of NGOs' activism on the issue of migrant workers is gained from the constant exclusion of migrant workers from both industrial relations mechanisms and trade union movements in either the sending or the receiving countries.[53] This is to a great extent due to the foreign status of migrant workers, the temporary and informal nature of their work, and the private nature of their workplace in the case of women working as domestic workers. Sentiments toward migrant workers are also determining factors. In sending countries the common reason for excluding migrant workers from trade unions is that, by

51 Cf. ibid.
52 Cf. ibid., p. 222.
53 Cf. Ford 2006b.

working abroad, migrant workers are better off than local workers,[54] and in receiving countries, migrant workers are considered a threat to the local workers' interests and jobs.[55] Ford and Piper suggest in their works that the gap left by the trade unions has been filled by other civil society organizations, including NGOs, one of which in Indonesia's case was the first civil society organization to take up the issue of women migrant workers.[56] As argued by Ford, the fact that unions were weakened by strong state control during the New Order has allowed NGOs to step in.[57]

The absence of migrant worker unions or associations or any other form of migrant workers organizing themselves had provided further legitimacy for NGO activism on the issue, which in Indonesia began in the 1990s with activities like case handling and, through time, developed to include policy advocacy. While Ford observes that, since 1998, trade unions have started to take over the labor movement from labor NGOs,[58] NGOs working on the issue of migrant workers continue to dominate activism on behalf of migrant workers, even when migrant workers have started to organize themselves. This is partly due to the NGOs' strength in knowledge and reputation, which derives from their years of experience and the fact that the existing migrant workers unions or organizations are relatively new and have not yet reached the point where they can take over the role from NGOs.

During the *Reformasi* Era, there has been a tendency for trade unions to include the rights of migrant workers. Ford gave the example of Indonesian trade union bodies such as the Confederation of All Indonesian Trade Unions or *Konfederasi Serikat Pekerja Seluruh Indonesia* (KSPSI), which have formed migrant labor divisions.[59] Nevertheless, the few unions that embrace the issue of foreign workers tend to focus more on those employed in the formal sector with long-term contracts, marginalizing women migrant workers who are mostly on short-term contracts in the informal sector. As again confirmed by Piper, the informal, temporary, and non-citizen status of women migrant workers in receiving countries has excluded them from trade unions.[60] This tendency to discriminate between formal and informal sector workers, which Ford[61] called "sectoral apartheid", has further hampered the effort to promote better protection of women migrant workers through laws, regulations, and official mechanisms. As for In-

54 Cf. Piper 2005c, p. 93.
55 Cf. Ford 2006b, p. 301.
56 Cf. Ford 2006b, Piper 2005c.
57 Cf. Ford 2004, p. 106.
58 Cf. Ford 2009, p. 205.
59 Cf. Ford 2004, p. 111.
60 Cf. Piper 2010, p. 109.
61 Cf. Ford 2006b, p. 304.

donesia as a sending country, it can be argued that unions cannot be expected to shift their focus significantly from the national scene, especially when the list of labor problems that need to be addressed is still very long.

The recent trend in Indonesia is for migrant workers to establish their own associations, many assisted by NGOs. Although they use the word *serikat* or union in their names, it is still debatable whether they truly function as unions or whether they are more like NGOs. Part of this book looks into how NGOs, which adopted the migrant labor issue earlier and have been key civil society actors on this issue, deal with the emergence of new players such as migrant workers' organizations.

1.4 Structure of the Book

This book covers the situation from shortly before 1998, when the reform occurred, until late 2009. However, for the purpose of providing background information and comparison, some material may date back to the 1990s when Indonesian NGOs first adopted the issue of migrant workers, and to the 1970s when Indonesians first migrated to work abroad. Also, with the ongoing nature of the issue, some key developments until 2012 are also included in certain parts of the discussions.

This book is divided into ten chapters. The first two chapters provide the necessary practical and theoretical background for the analysis of the topic. The first chapter has already introduced the theme of the book by highlighting the significance of NGOs activism on the issue of Indonesian women migrant workers. It is then followed by Chapter 2, which briefly canvasses existing themes in the literature relating to the topic, showing the position of this book within this literature and its contribution towards the advancement of each theme.

After these two introductory chapters, the book is divided into three parts. The first part of those, consisting of Chapters 3, 4, and 5, provides the contextual information needed for the analysis. In discussing the main problems faced by Indonesian women migrant workers, Chapter 3 is structured to show the interconnectedness of the problems and the stakeholders involved. It aims to answer the questions: What are the problems that need to be addressed? When and why do they occur? And who is involved? Chapter 4 mainly aims at identifying and examining the efforts that have been made by the state in regulating and managing Indonesian labor migration. Although most elements of the government tend to concur on the involvement of other stakeholders, particularly NGOs, there are differences within the government about what type of pressure they are more responsive to and how they respond. Thus, rather than just making an inventory of all the rules and regulations on labor migration, this chapter addresses the questions: What are the main efforts made by the state through its institutions? Why did they make those efforts or what are the factors that influence their decisions? Chapter 5 concerns NGOs in Indonesia. The first part of the chapter briefly compares the roles and positions of Indonesian NGOs before and after the 1998 *Reformasi*. The questions asked here are: How have the changes brought by the democratization process during the Reform era affected the activism of Indonesian NGOs, particularly those working on the issue of migrant workers? Have the NGOs merely been allowed more freedom to speak or have they really been listened to and involved in the governance process? The rest of this chapter focuses on NGO activism on the issue of women migrant workers by addressing the questions: How did Indonesian NGOs concerned with the issue of women migrant workers begin to take up the issue? How do they try to organize themselves? How do they adapt to the new political context? This is also where the two NGOs researched, SP and Migrant CARE, are introduced.

The second part, consisting of Chapters 6 and 7, concentrates on NGOs' responses toward democratization. Chapter 6 examines the NGOs' efforts to influence a domestic policy: Indonesia's first law on migrant workers, Law No. 39/2004 on the Placement and Protection of Indonesian Workers Overseas. In examining their involvement in the policy-making process, this chapter also assesses the relationship between the government and the NGOs during the process. Examining the extent to which the NGOs are involved in policy-making and the state of the relationship between the government and civil society, in this case NGOs, is considered one of the ways to assess the process of democratization in Indonesia. Chapter 6 attempts to establish whether there have been any changes since 1998 in the way the NGOs and the state interact and why; how much space there was available for NGO involvement in the policy-making process; the differences and similarities in the way the two NGOs conduct their activities to influence the policy-making process, including the stakeholders that they interact with; and whether the NGOs have been able to secure a significant role in influencing policies. Chapter 7 concentrates on the NGOs' activities conducted after the law was passed. It aims to determine how the NGOs continue their work in the new context of Indonesia's labor migration system regulated by a law. This chapter also gauges to what extent the NGOs have reflected on their experience so far and utilize the lessons learned to strengthen their future activism.

The third part, consisting of Chapters 8 and 9, focuses more on the NGOs' responses toward globalization. Chapter 8 examines the NGOs' efforts to influence a foreign policy: the 2006 MoU between the governments of Indonesia and Malaysia on the Recruitment and Placement of Indonesian Domestic Workers. It examines the NGOs' involvement in the MoU formulation process and assesses the relationship between the government and the NGOs during the process.

Besides asking the questions posed in Chapter 6, this chapter also takes into account the bilateral nature of the policy instrument and the transnational nature of the issue of women migrant workers and the NGOs' activism. The assumption is that these factors significantly affect the form and extent of NGOs' involvement in the process. Thus, in this chapter and the following one, the discussion of NGOs' transnational activism is central to the analysis of how NGOs link their national and international work on the issue of women migrant workers. Chapter 9 covers the NGOs' activities since the passing of a policy instrument, this time the MoU between Indonesia and Malaysia. This chapter concentrates more on the NGOs' transnational activism and investigates how the NGOs researched have been taking up the opportunities and overcoming the challenges brought by globalization. Like in Chapter 7, the main interest in this chapter is about finding out what lessons the NGOs have learned and how they are going to use them to strengthen their influence in changing the existing policy.

This book is then concluded in Chapter 10 by summarizing the NGOs' responses to democratization and globalization in the context of their activism on the issue of women migrant workers, determining whether they have managed to carve an influential role, and finally assessing whether there has been any strategy emerging from their experience so far.

This book analyzes the involvement of Indonesian NGOs in the process of making one domestic and one foreign policy on migrant workers. While this book does not aspire to generalize the roles of NGOs in the Indonesian political system, by examining the involvement of NGOs as a part of civil society in the public policy process, it does aim to contribute to the assessment of the democratization process in Indonesia. More specifically, it aims to understand and explain how NGOs concerned with the issue of migrant workers conduct their activism in a democratizing country like Indonesia.

This book is concerned with changes, both nationally and internationally, affecting Indonesia during the transition from the New Order to the Reform Era. Rather than adding to a well-established body of literature which discusses NGOs as agents of change,[62] it focuses more on how NGOs are affected and respond to the changes around them. Authors like Eldridge, Hadiwinata, and Sakai have pointed out that while the Reform Era allowed the NGO sector to grow and gave them more freedom, it also brought challenges for them.[63] There is a change in the environment and power structure, and NGOs are facing competition from new players such as the newly established political parties and migrant workers organizations. At the same time, expectations and demands for NGOs to play a more significant role have also risen, along with increased scrutiny of

62 Cf. Gumay 2002, Hadiwinata 2003, Eldridge 2005, Antlöv et al. 2006.
63 Cf. Eldridge 2005, Hadiwinata 2003, Sakai 2002.

their accountability. Thus, it is important for NGOs to have the ability to adapt to the changes around them, which is being examined in this book through analysis of the two NGOs selected as case studies. The analysis is also aimed at assessing whether the NGOs have been able to overcome the challenges and utilize the opportunities brought about by the wider changes.

This book gains importance from its analysis of the NGOs' involvement in the policy-making process. As part of democratization in Indonesia, civil society actors have been allowed more involvement in the policy process. Public hearings, workshops, seminars, and audiences have become common terms used to describe the decision-makers' efforts to gather inputs from the public. Nevertheless, the change toward a more accommodative attitude to NGO involvement is still uneven among the state institutions. Thus, this book is concerned with whether the NGOs have been able to engage with influential actors who allow them access to significantly influence the making and implementation of policies. The assumption is that the question should no longer be whether civil society is involved in the policy process or not, but more about the extent to which their voices are reflected in the policies. In this context, this book is intended to contribute to the evaluation of the democratization process in Indonesia.

This book also highlights the significance of NGOs as transnational actors. Authors like Lyons and Piper have emphasized the importance of transnational activism for the issue of migrant workers.[64] In practice, NGOs concerned with the issue of migrant workers, including Indonesian NGOs, have also commonly expressed the need for them to be involved in international networks. The NGOs' main reason for this expansion is to strengthen their activism at home, particularly in putting pressure on the government. Thus, this book is concerned with how the NGOs have been conducting their transnational activism and whether this has actually strengthened their activism at home.

Finally, this book is focused on the work of NGOs on the issue of Indonesian women migrant workers, particularly those working in the informal sector as domestic workers. A very large group of migrants that continues to grow in number still faces various problems and remains marginal in policies on labor and migrant workers. As long as this condition remains, any research into better ways of addressing the issue is crucial for the promotion of their rights.

With the aim of achieving the objectives above, this book intends to answer the main questions of: How do Indonesian NGOs concerned with the issue of women migrant workers influence government policies on labor migration in the changing context of democratizing and globalizing Indonesia? How far they have gone and how far can they go?

64 Cf. Lyons 2004, Piper 2005c, 2010.

2. NGOs and Labor Migration Policies in the Context of Democratization and Globalization: A Review of Literature

In discussing the work of NGOs on a complex and cross-border issue such as labor migration, which involves a substantial number of stakeholders with their vested interests and concerns various aspects of the life of migrant workers and their surroundings, this book relates to research on various themes. On the topic of labor migration, a significant number of literature on labor migration, particularly that focusing on the region of Asia, has identified the problems faced by migrant workers and shown how the management of labor migration has generally failed to protect them which leaves a gap filled by NGOs.

As for the topic of non-governmental organizations, most of the well-established body of work on NGOs has used development NGOs as the object of their studies.[1] This book is intended to enrich the growing literature on human rights activism by NGOs, a more specialized area of study, by focusing on the NGOs' efforts to influence government policies on labor migration in Indonesia as a sending country. Thus, a better understanding of the context is gained from literature which discusses NGOs in Indonesia, particularly looking at the development of NGO activism in this country and the NGOs' relationship with key actors. The basis for understanding the process of making public policy and the interaction between actors involved is taken from literature on public policy. It is then used to analyze the position and role of NGOs in a public policy-making process. The analysis is enriched by the concept of political space to examine whether the political environment is conducive for greater NGO involvement in the policy process. Within the literature which has looked at the work of NGOs on the subject of labor migration, this book contributes through its specific analysis on how the NGOs attempt to influence labor migration policies within a democratizing sending country like Indonesia.

As stated earlier in the introduction, this book focuses on a period in which both democratization and globalization significantly affect virtually all aspects of life in Indonesia, including policy-making. Therefore, the two concepts set the context of this research. A number of studies have argued for the importance of NGOs in pushing for a democratization process to commence and also in accelerating the process.[2] This book focuses more on how NGOs respond to the new

1 Cf. Eldridge 1995, Riker 1995c, Hulme and Edwards 1997, Riker 1998, Edwards and Hulme 2002, Bebbington et al. 2008.

2 Cf. Hadiwinata 2003, Antlöv et al. 2006.

environment fashioned by the process. Also, focusing on the first decade after the democratization process began in Indonesia, and by assessing the extent to which NGOs as part of the civil society are involved in the policy process, this study is also intended to be a form of evaluation of what has been achieved, in a limited scope concerning labor migration. On the topic of NGOs and globalization, rather than merely discussing how local NGOs are affected by the wave of globalization, this book aims to go further by examining how the NGOs have actively responded to the new opportunities globalization creates and overcome the challenges it brings. Also, in an attempt to link the domestic and global contexts, this book is using the concept of transnational activism to explain why the NGOs have been expanding their activism across the state's border and how that move affects their domestic activism.

2.1 Labor Migration in Asia

Existing studies have examined labor migration from various angles with the general themes of management of labor migration, problems faced by migrant workers, violations of migrant workers' rights, and strengths and weaknesses of existing national policies and international conventions. Also, there is an extensive body of literature that provides general overviews of labor migration in Asia. A historical understanding of the development of labor migration in Southeast Asia can be obtained from the work of Kaur, who has documented labor transformation in the context of globalization.[3] Globalization, transformation, and change is also the main theme in the works of authors like Young, who looks into changes in the management of the migration of service workers in the Asia-Pacific, who are predominantly women working as domestic workers,[4] and Cohen, who identifies the changes in the division of labor and migratory patterns brought by globalization.[5] The works of Piper and her colleagues provide insights on labor migration in Asia on a range of issues such as political and gender aspects of labor migration, feminization of labor migration, empowerment of migrant workers, NGOs' involvement, the rights of migrant workers, trafficking, and evaluation of existing policies.[6] The above body of literature provides background information for understanding the issues concerning labor migration in Asia, including that of Indonesians.

3 Cf. Kaur 2004.
4 Cf. Young 2006.
5 Cf. Cohen 2006.
6 Cf. Piper 2002, 2003, 2004a, 2004b, 2005a, 2005b, 2005c, Yamanaka and Piper 2005, Ball and Piper 2006, Piper 2006.

Works on intra-Asia labor migration have extensively documented conditions and efforts made in receiving countries, where abuses and violations of migrant workers' rights often occur. The book edited by Debrah (2002), for example, provides insights on how migrant workers are perceived in receiving countries in the Asia-Pacific through evaluations of the states' policies.[7] However, a more comprehensive understanding of the issue would require analysis of the various instances at every stage of the migration process. Authors like Hugo and Anggraeni have specifically examined Indonesian labor migration.[8] Hugo's work shows the changes in the levels and patterns of movement of Indonesian women migrants, both internally and internationally, and discusses how their migration is different from that of men, while Anggraeni describes the experience of Indonesian women who work as domestic workers overseas and discusses government policies and efforts made by stakeholders, including NGOs. It is apparent that problems occur even at the initial stage of labor migration (i.e. predeparture), and they continue to exist even after the repatriation of the migrant workers. This book contributes to this growing work on sending countries by focusing on the efforts made by the NGOs to influence the labor migration policies of a sending country.

2.2 NGOs in Indonesia

There are various ways of defining NGOs and categorizing them. In Indonesia, as explained by Eldridge, various terminologies have been used, whether based on the size of the organization – big NGOs or BINGOs and little NGOs or LINGOs – or based on political considerations – self-reliant community institutions (*Lembaga Swadaya Masyarakat*) or non-governmental organizations (*Organisasi Non-Pemerintah*).[9] In this book, with no intention of over-simplifying the complex world of NGOs and in agreement with Eldridge, who defined NGOs as non-party and non-profit organizations,[10] an NGO is understood as an organization which is neither created by the government and part of it or the private sector, does not conduct profit-seeking activities, and is not a union. The last factor is significant to differentiate between NGOs and migrant worker associations (*serikat buruh migran*) or organizations which, although frequently considered as "unions" of migrant workers, operate more like NGOs. Unlike unions, NGOs do not depend financially on membership fees. Because NGOs' funding com-

7 Cf. Debrah 2002.
8 Cf. Hugo 1992, Anggraeni 2006.
9 Cf. Eldridge 1995, pp. 12-15.
10 Cf. ibid., p. 3.

monly comes from donor or funding organizations, instead of being accountable to members, NGOs' accountability is more directed toward their donors. Consequently, while unions work directly for their members, as their beneficiaries, NGOs promote their perception of the interests of a particular group that they are concerned about and are influenced by their donors.

Although there has been more literature that examines NGOs' work on issues like environment and human rights, the majority of studies on NGOs continue to assess their work on development issues. An example is the book edited by Bebbington et al., which is based on papers presented at the fourth Manchester NGO conference in 2005.[11] Although this book mainly focuses on NGO efforts in promoting "development alternatives", some of the points made are also applicable to other types of NGOs. For example, the changing context and the challenges that development NGOs have been facing, which were discussed in Michael Edwards' chapter on the development of NGOs in the last one and a half decades,[12] generally apply to the most types of NGOs. Due to the dominance of literature on development NGOs, the similarities in the way development and human rights NGOs work, and the fact that more NGOs concerned with legal and human rights issues are also directing their attention toward development issues and vice versa, this book has benefited from borrowing some concepts and arguments from the existing analyses of development NGOs.

2.2.1 Development of NGO Activism in Indonesia

Most works on NGOs in Indonesia include a brief history of the development of NGOs in this country. Ford, for example, stated that service delivery oriented NGOs had operated in Indonesia since the 1950s and that in the 1980s and 1990s a new wave of more politically focused NGOs emerged.[13] According to her, national and international changes like the end of Cold War, the economic liberalization in the mid- to late 1980s, and the period of political openness in Indonesia allowed NGOs to do more than providing basic services and adopt a more direct and confrontational approach in achieving their agenda.

Through time, NGOs in Indonesia have continuously adapted their activism to the existing political environment. The work of Eldridge, which is frequently referred to by researchers on NGOs in Indonesia for example, shows how NGOs

11 Cf. Bebbington et al. 2008. This book includes chapters written by Michael Edwards and David Hulme, two prominent scholars who not only initiated the first conference but who have also consistently made NGOs a major part of their work.

12 Cf. Edwards 2008.

13 Cf. Ford 2004, p. 106.

tried to adapt to the existing political environment during the New Order.[14] NGOs' adaptation is again discussed on Eldridge's later work, in which he described the evolution of NGOs after the New Order Era.[15] According to him, Indonesian NGOs have gained greater freedom of expression and association, and social, cultural, and intellectual space.[16] They have also managed to develop networking capacities that enabled them to engage in policy dialogue with relevant authorities and utilize public advocacy to place new issues such as the environment, public health, consumer rights, the status of women, and human rights on the political agenda. Aspinall has also looked at the transformation of civil society in Indonesia.[17] One of the changes that he identified is the emergence of a more "variegated and energetic" NGO sector.

Nevertheless, although more opportunities have been opened for NGOs since 1998, as argued by Eldridge, in practice formal controls over NGOs still exist to some extent, NGOs are still dependent on aid, and they frequently collaborate with those they criticize; a contradiction which, according to him, could be justified based on NGOs' need to survive.[18] A stronger opinion comes from Aspinall, who argued that the 1990s Indonesian civil society was weaker than that of the 1960s.[19] He believes that three factors contribute to the emergence of the "limited civil society" in Indonesia: changes in the international setting, changes in economic structures and the dynamics of class conflict, and the evolution of the state both in the way it structures civil society and in the perception of the state by civil society. Aspinall further argued that the emergence of civil society requires a civil state. A rather different observation come from Sakai who argued that although state control seemed to be strong during the Suharto regime, it was also inconsistent, creating a space for NGOs to operate, and this has not changed much since the regime ended.[20] This book, like those of Eldridge, Aspinall, and Sakai, is also concerned with the changes occurring both inside and outside Indonesia. Certainly the changes have significantly affected Indonesian civil society, including the NGOs. As to whether civil society and state are weaker or stronger, and how this "changed" the ways civil society and state interact with each other, those are questions to be addressed in this book. It investigates how NGOs view and adapt to the post-New Order policy environment. This question becomes significant because, although the policy environment seems to be more

14 Cf. Eldridge 1995.
15 Cf. Eldridge 2005.
16 Cf. ibid., pp. 164-65.
17 Cf. Aspinall 2004.
18 Cf. Eldridge 2005, pp. 152 and 166.
19 Cf. Aspinall 2004.
20 Cf. Sakai 2002, p. 161.

open, many NGOs are still expressing frustration about their efforts to influence government policies.

2.2.2 NGOs' Relationships with Other Actors

This book is also concerned with the complex relationship between NGOs and other actors, particularly the state. Existing studies have looked into the relationship between NGOs and states, or NGOs and donors, or the more complex relationship among the three of them. The work of Hulme and Edwards maps through diagrams and matrices the complex relationship between NGOs (North and South), states, and donors in the context of development and democratization.[21] The relationship between NGOs, states, and international agencies is also the focus of Rumansara's work, which uses the International NGO Forum on Indonesian Development (INFID) as an example of network-building efforts in discussing NGOs' advocacy activities.[22] Focusing on the subject of labor migration, Ford examines the relationship between Indonesian migrant labor NGOs, migrant worker organizations, and trade unions, both in practice and in literature.[23] Within this theme of NGOs' relationships with other actors, this book intends to establish whether a wider national and transnational network built by NGOs with other actors, combined with a more open policy environment and more accommodative state institutions, translate to a more enhanced NGO involvement in the policy process.

Since this book is focused on NGOs' efforts to influence policy-making processes, the discussion is inevitably centered on the relationship between NGOs and the policy-makers who constitute elements of the state. A focus on NGO-state relationships is taken by Riker whose works have shown the correlation between the mode of interaction between governments and NGOs and the existing type of policy environment, whether it is an environment where NGOs are highly controlled by the government or one where the government is accommodative and cooperative towards NGOs.[24] In line with Riker's arguments, this book emphasizes the importance of examining both the policy environment and the mode of interaction between the government and the NGOs at the period discussed. Combined with the examination of existing political space, it will help determining the NGOs' influence on policies concerning labor migration.

21 Cf. Hulme and Edwards 1997.
22 Cf. Rumansara 1996.
23 Cf. Ford 2004.
24 Cf. Riker 1995a, 1995b, 1995c.

Analysis of the work of the NGOs in this book is based on the assumption that NGOs are significantly influenced by the environment surrounding them, including the actions of other actors. An understanding of how they operate within the existing political space and negotiate or expand that space will help to explain the roles they are playing in the management of labor migration in Indonesia. Analyses of the context in which NGOs operate and interact with other actors, also known as political space, can be found in the works of Riker and Shigetomi.[25] Riker defines political space as "the arena in which non-state actors may undertake initiatives independently vis-a-vis the state".[26] According to him, this political space is sensitive and ever-changing because all actors, including NGOs, generally attempt to shape it in accordance with their interests. While NGOs' actions are determined by the available political space, they are also trying to extend that space. Usually NGOs expand their space by influencing the parameters drawn by the existence and power of other actors, particularly the state.[27] Riker explains the strategies that could be employed by NGOs in expanding their political space, which involve both strengthening the NGO sector and convincing the government of the significance of NGOs.[28] In assessing NGOs' roles in the management of labor migration in Indonesia, a part of this book examines the efforts made by Indonesian NGOs in shaping their political space and the strategies they use.

The end of the New Order does not necessarily translate to stronger civil society. Most analysts consider it having been difficult for the NGOs to take a stronger role and claim the political space available, due to the repression they have experienced for an extended period of time during the New Order era. This book investigates whether there are other causes, besides past repression, that have made it difficult for NGOs to take a significant role and expand their political space.

2.3 NGOs and the Policy-Making Process

There are several studies that have included examination of certain aspects of Indonesian government's policies on labor migration in particular periods of time. The chapters in the book edited by Irewati, for example, have examined government policies on illegal labor migration to Malaysia and their implementation.[29]

25 Cf. Riker 1995a, Shigetomi 2002. Shigetomi goes further to include economic space and combines it with political space.
26 Riker 1995a, p. 23.
27 Cf. Riker 1995a, Shigetomi 2002.
28 Cf. Riker 1995b, pp. 124-25.
29 Cf. Irewati 2003.

This book is not a detailed analysis of the government policy documents. Instead, it examines the participation of NGOs in policy processes relating to one domestic and one foreign policy instrument: Law No. 39/2004 on The Placement and Protection of Indonesian Workers Overseas, and the 2006 MoU between the governments of Indonesia and Malaysia.

For the purpose of understanding the policy process, this book borrows the concept of "policy cycle" from public policy studies. Although, in practice, a policy process does not always occur in a segregated and sequential manner, in conducting a policy study, the public policy-making process is commonly simplified by breaking it into stages which occur in a sequence, involving: agenda-setting, when problems come to the attention of governments; policy formulation, when policy options are formulated within the government; decision-making, when the government chooses an action or a non-action; policy-implementation, when policies are put into effect; and policy evaluation, when the results of policies are monitored by state and societal actors.[30] The result of this evaluation may become a new set of policy problems and solutions to start a new cycle. This concept is used in this book to identify at which stages of the policy cycle NGOs play significant roles and to what extent their activities influence the policies. Nevertheless, since the policy cycle concept only provides a general framework for analysis: a better understanding of Indonesian government policies requires an examination of how policies are made in Indonesia and who are the main actors involved, which will be discussed in more detail in Chapters 6 and 8.

As for the NGOs, their non-governmental nature has automatically excluded them from the formal policy-making process. However, since democratization requires the government to involve civil society in policy-making, there is an opening for a degree of NGO involvement there. This book examines how the form of NGO involvement is negotiated in a democratizing Indonesia. With the changes brought by the *Reformasi*, Indonesian NGOs need to re-define their role so that they can make the best use of the opportunities. Hadiwinata argued that, in the post-Soeharto era, NGOs have played important roles, *firstly* in easing the effects of the 1997 economic crisis on the poor, and *secondly* in sustaining political reform and democratization.[31] This book relates more to the second role. The extent to which NGOs are able to be involved in and influence the policy-making process and the state of their interactions with other stakeholders, particularly the decision-makers, may be used as indicators to assess the democratization process in Indonesia.

30 Cf. Howlett and Ramesh 2003, p. 11.
31 Cf. Hadiwinata 2003, pp. 251-53.

2.4 NGOs and the Issue of Migrant Workers

A continuously growing number of publications on labor migration have highlighted the failure of states in managing labor migration, pointed out the efforts made by civil society organizations, such as NGOs, to promote the rights of migrant workers, and therefore argued for their greater prominence. However, most of these studies are on NGO activism in the receiving countries or their regional initiatives through networks. An exception is the Philippines, as several studies have included discussions of NGO activism in the Philippines as a sending country, which is commonly considered to be a success story: they have pressured their government to implement comprehensive labor migration policies at home and to make agreements with the receiving countries to protect their rights during the process of working abroad.[32] As for Indonesia, there is still ample room for studies which specifically investigate NGO activism on the issue of labor migration. In so doing, this book contributes by looking at the roles of NGOs in influencing the policies on labor migration in Indonesia as a sending country.

Works on NGOs and labor migration can be categorized based on the area or level that they cover in their analysis. A growing and quite established body of literature has studied NGO activism in receiving countries. The work of Gurowitz reviews the increase of civil society activity and migration in Southeast Asia through the examination of activism on behalf of migrant workers in Malaysia.[33] She also identifies the opportunities and constraints for conducting the activism. Yamanaka and Piper discuss the conditions in of a number of receiving countries and their policies, and examine the civil society activism in each country.[34] They then discuss some good practices from the Philippines, as a sending country, which signifies the importance for sending country NGOs to conduct activism both inside and outside their country. Furthermore, through the discussion of the NGOs' role in supporting the implementation of the ICRMW, they draw attention to the rise of a transnational advocacy network in the region. Analysis of NGOs' roles at various levels can be found in the work of Ball and Piper.[35] Besides providing a picture of the regional dynamics of migrant workers' rights recognition in the Asia-Pacific, this work also emphasizes the need for bilateral and multilateral cooperation and transnational activism by NGOs. The literature mentioned above has mostly covered efforts made in receiving countries and at the regional and international levels. This book contributes to this body of work by examining the efforts that come from the sending countries, but

32 Cf. Piper 2005c, Yamanaka and Piper 2005.
33 Cf. Gurowitz 2000.
34 Cf. Yamanaka and Piper 2005.
35 Cf. Ball and Piper 2006.

whereas Yamanaka and Piper have discussed the Philippines, the focus of this book is Indonesia. It highlights the activism of NGOs from a sending country which, in conducting their activities, have made attempts to go global by engaging with regional and international actors and getting involved in networks at both levels. Thus, a part of this book looks at how Indonesian NGOs conduct their transnational activism, specifically by relating to regional and international arrangements and utilizing existing regional and international mechanisms to support their national activities. The aim is to examine whether the NGOs' efforts to make their activism more transnational have actually supported and strengthened their efforts to influence the management of labor migration at the national level. In other words, have they succeeded in bringing their transnational activism home?

The NGOs' activities, whether conducted at the national, regional, or international level, ultimately aim at influencing the Indonesian government's policies on labor migration. Works by authors like Ford, and reports made by national institutions and NGOs like *Komnas Perempuan* and SP and international institutions such as the ILO and Human Rights Watch (HRW) have investigated policies toward Indonesian migrant labor and/or efforts made by NGOs.[36] In this context, by taking case studies of two NGOs and two policy instruments, this book examines the link between the two topic areas by specifically taking a close look at how Indonesian NGOs attempt to influence the government's policy-making process.

This book is also concerned with the NGOs' efforts to adapt to their current environment. The literature reviewed shows how NGOs, through time, have changed or shifted their activities in response to changes in their environment. Yamanaka and Piper, for example, argue that the lack of adequate domestic laws that protect migrants has encouraged Asian activists to use international conventions instead.[37] They also see a shift in NGO activism from providing services and supporting migrants to a more political role.[38] This book seeks to confirm whether these shifts are actually occurring in Indonesia, which relates to the aim of determining whether Indonesian NGOs have adapted to the changes occurring around them.

A major writer on the subject of Indonesian migrant workers and efforts to promote their rights is Michele Ford, whose works have captured the general condition of labor migration from Indonesia. Ford wrote a country study which provides a general overview of Indonesian labor migration by covering its political, economic, and social issues, and documents the main migrant labor organi-

36 Cf. Ford 2002, 2004, 2005, 2006a, Komnas Perempuan and SP 2003.
37 Cf. Yamanaka and Piper 2005, p. 32.
38 Cf. ibid., p. 22.

zations (NGOs) and unions, their activities and the relationships among them.[39] In her other work, Ford examines the activism of migrant labor NGOs, migrant labor associations, and unions in Indonesia.[40] Ford has also listed some important decrees and regulations.[41] It is her view that Indonesian government policies on labor migration have been interventionist and that, until the passing of Law No. 39/2004, labor migration was regulated through ministerial decrees and other government regulations which are weaker policy instruments.[42] In this work, Ford maps the key players active on the subject of labor migration, which includes migrant labor organizations, NGOs, networks, and unions. She gives a picture of the relationships between them, which are characterized by both cooperation and competition. Through the case studies, this book aims to look deeper into the relationships between actors by finding out the challenges in building joint efforts between the stakeholders addressing the issues concerning women migrant workers. Therefore, although this book takes NGOs as a departing point, it also provides the perspectives of other influential stakeholders, particularly those with whom the NGOs claimed to have worked or interacted with.

2.5 Democratization, Globalization, and NGOs' Transnational Activism

This book is focused on the period from the late 1990s to the late 2000s, at a time when democratization and globalization had striking impacts on Indonesia. Thus, the analysis on NGO activism is framed by these two related contexts. The terms globalization and democratization have been defined in various ways. A quite general way of defining globalization, as recognized in the work of Gills, is to perceive it as "a process through which interdependence and interconnectedness among societies becomes further extended and intensified on a world wide scale".[43] Gills also pointed out the common perception that globalization is a multifaceted process occurring in all areas of life. Similarly, Grugel defined globalization as a rapidly expanding process of connecting societies through markets and new technologies.[44] While accepting the notions commonly associated with globalization such as interdependence, interconnectedness, multifaceted, and involving all areas of life, this book agrees with Gills and Piper and Uh-

39 Cf. Ford 2005.
40 Cf. Ford 2004.
41 Cf. Ford 2005.
42 Cf. ibid., pp. 8-9.
43 Gills 2002, p. 14.
44 Cf. Grugel 2004, p. 30.

lin, who question the notion of the weakening of the state due to globalization,[45] particularly since this book concerns policy-making where the state has sole authority.

Munck argued that migration, as a global issue, has been studied from the receiving countries' perspective, and he suggested the adoption of a Southern perspective to create a holistic global approach towards migration and development.[46] To say that there is an absence of Southern perspective would be misleading, particularly within the literature of labor migration, but there should be a balance between the perspectives of receiving and sending countries. Thus, Munck is right to say that the topic of migration cannot be studied in isolation.[47] Comparing the data on international migration, Munck noted that more migration occurs within the Southern part of the globe, which reflects the uneven process of globalization.[48] In a similar note, Piper stated that the global phenomenon of labor migration tends to occur more within regions from low-income to middle- or high-income countries and referred to Asia as an example.[49] In Indonesia's case, although initially Indonesians migrated to work in the Middle East and many are still choosing to go there, the number of those choosing to work in neighboring countries such as Malaysia is increasing, mainly because of the proximity and the expectation that there will be fewer language and cultural barriers. This has been one of the reasons for focusing on the migration of Indonesian women to work in Malaysia in this book.

Related to the more regional than global trend, authors like Piper and Uhlin have argued for the use of the term "transnational" instead of "global" for the reason that it is quite rare for the cross-border interactions to actually become global.[50] The interactions tend to be more regional with differences between them. While accepting this viewpoint, this book uses the term "globalization" to describe the context of the topic where information and activities can virtually cross state borders and to emphasize the wide scope of labor migration, which, in Indonesia's case, can reach areas like the Middle East. Another reason is that, although it appears to be patchy, NGOs seem to have always aimed for global action and impacts. However, the concept of transnational activism is utilized to explain how NGOs link their activities at the domestic and international levels and, in agreement with Piper and Uhlin,[51] the term "transnational" is used in a

45 Cf. Gills 2002, Piper and Uhlin 2004a.
46 Cf. Munck 2009, p. 2.
47 Cf. ibid.
48 Cf. ibid., p. 4.
49 Cf. Piper 2009, p. 61.
50 Cf. Piper and Uhlin 2004a, p. 5.
51 Cf. ibid.

quite general manner to include both global and regional cross-border interactions.

As for democratization, Gills sees it as a counter-trend to the neo-liberal economic globalization and defines it as "a process of broadening inclusion", which requires "significant changes in the composition of power, allowing the inclusion of a broad spectrum of social forces into the state, or giving them access to influencing the state policy decision-making process".[52] According to Gills, the social forces include workers, whether organized, unorganized, or marginalized, such as women, children, and migrant labor. This book particularly assesses whether all relevant stakeholders are actually included in the political process. Also, this book goes beyond identifying changes within formal political institutions to also include an analysis of civil society's informal political activism, which, according to Piper and Uhlin,[53] constitutes a broader definition of democratization.

Covering the period between 1990 and 2001, Hadiwinata's work focuses on discussing various aspects of Indonesian NGO activism during the period of transition toward a more democratic political system, the early years after 1998.[54] It is still debatable whether the transition process has concluded and Indonesia has actually reached the democratic stage. Thus, by concentrating on the decade after 1998, this book is still positioned within a "transition period", assuming that, while to a certain degree democracy has been adopted into state governance in Indonesia, adjustments are still occurring.

According to some studies, Indonesian NGOs' advocacy work emerged during the 1990s along with the adoption of issues such as democratization and human rights.[55] As noted by Sakai, after the Cold War ended, industrialized countries put more emphasis on human rights and democratization issues in allocating their official development assistance (ODA) and private investments.[56] Thus, due to their dependence on foreign investment and financial assistance, countries like Indonesia had to pay more attention to these issues and avoid repressing NGOs to maintain international confidence. It can be said then that democratization is spread through globalization when financial assistance and foreign investment require recipient countries to be democratic or at least to move in that direction. In the process, democratization gives freer rein to many of the forces of globalization when actors like NGOs are given more freedom to move, including expanding their activism beyond the border of the state. At the same time, studies have also shown that NGOs engage in transnational activism because of lack of

52 Gills 2002.
53 Cf. Piper and Uhlin 2004a, p. 12.
54 Cf. Hadiwinata 2003.
55 Cf. Riker 1998, Sakai 2002.
56 Cf. Sakai 2002, p. 172.

domestical political space. In the transition period of democratization, NGOs could be frustrated by the slow pace of the process or the unchangeable bureaucracy. This usually stimulates efforts to search for alternatives such as expanding their activism. In other words, being active from the inside out is often a strategy to trigger and speed up the democratization process.

Most literature on democratization and NGOs highlights the potential of NGOs as actors within civil society to help trigger the process of democratization.[57] Through their campaigns and political education at the grassroots level, NGOs have contributed to the creation of conditions that assist a democratization process to occur in previously authoritarian states. Thus, NGOs as part of civil society and social movement are frequently associated with and regarded as actors that can foster democratization. Hadiwinata, for example, claimed that Indonesian NGOs' efforts to promote democracy since the early 1990s contributed to the end of the New Order era.[58] He argued, that by familiarizing ordinary people with the idea of people's sovereignty (*kedaulatan rakyat*), the NGOs prepared them to immediately embrace the transition to a more democratic political system when the reform occurred in 1998. Antlöv et al. have also stated that, without the voluntarism and commitment of NGOs and other elements of Indonesian civil society, the transition would have been "longer" and "bumpier".[59] The NGOs used as case studies in this book may not be among those that triggered the process of democratization. Nevertheless, their effort to influence policies on migrant workers is seen as a way to maintain and advance the process of democratization and to ensure that the transition process goes well.

This research uses the concept of transnational activism to bridge the domestic realm of democratization and the international realm of globalization. As stated by Piper and Uhlin, when NGOs begin to expand their focus beyond the domestic arena to cross the state borders, transnational activists networks materialize.[60] They further argue that the transnational nature of an activism may derive from its transnational focus, actors, methods and strategies, targets, and the activists' transnational views.[61] In agreement with this argument, "transnational" is made an important concept for this book for at least the three following reasons. *Firstly*, the migration itself is transnational in nature, crossing national boundaries and involving at least two countries, sending and receiving ones.[62] Thus, it needs a transnational initiative to regulate the migration flow. *Secondly*, the strongly in-

57 Cf. Hadiwinata 2003, Jemadu 2004.
58 Cf. Hadiwinata 2003, p. viii.
59 Cf. Antlöv et al. 2006, p. 150.
60 Cf. Piper and Uhlin 2004a, p. 3.
61 Cf. ibid., p. 5.
62 In some cases, such as the migration to Middle Eastern countries, it involves a third country as a transit point.

terrelated problems occur in different jurisdictions, what makes them quite complex and requires transnational efforts to address them. *Thirdly*, for the above reasons and also due to their frustration with the government, Indonesian NGOs have taken the initiative to expand their activism by joining regional and international networks to build pressure on the government from the outside. Thus, part of this book looks into the NGOs' involvement in traditional advocacy networks, which, according to Keck and Sikkink, involve "relevant actors working internationally on an issue, who are bound together by shared values, a common discourse, and dense exchanges of information and services"[63] and which Jemadu defines as "functional and complementary interactions of various international and national NGOs, which aim to accomplish common objectives".[64]

An emphasis on transnational political activism can be found in the work of Nicola Piper. Ball and Piper, for example, emphasize the importance of transnational activism, which, according to them, is "the key to articulating concerns and formulating strategies in multiple political arenas".[65] Piper and Uhlin argued that transnational activism can be triggered by both a more and less democratic domestic condition.[66] According to them, when the political system at home is more democratic, activists tend to shift their activism across the state border. On the other hand, the decision to conduct transnational activism may also be made as a way to build pressure on a more authoritarian political system from the outside, an approach identified as a "boomerang pattern" by Keck and Sikkink.[67] They argue that, when the channels between states and other domestic actors are blocked, actors such as NGOs tend to bypass the state to search for international allies, such as the media and other activists, in building pressure on the domestic policy elites by opening space for the issues to develop outside the country and echo them back into the country.[68] As stated by the NGO activists interviewed for this book, their main reason for expanding their activism abroad is mainly because they feel that they have exhausted all strategies to influence the government from the inside.

Nevertheless, transnational activism should not occur at the expense of the national one. In fact, it is important for sending countries' NGOs to balance their activism inside and outside the country. As argued by Grugel, the transnational politics should complement rather than replace the national ones.[69] The success story of the Philippine NGOs' activism in improving the conditions of their mi-

63 Keck and Sikkink 1998, p. 2.
64 Jemadu 2004, p. 152.
65 Ball and Piper 2006, p. 229.
66 Cf. Piper and Uhlin 2004a, p. 13.
67 Cf. Keck and Sikkink 1998, pp. 12-14.
68 Cf. Keck and Sikkink 1998, pp. 200-02.
69 Cf. Grugel 2004, p. 37.

grant workers abroad has proven this. Yamanaka and Piper believe that the success of Filipinas' activism in receiving countries is determined by related activism at home and the linkage that exists between them.[70] Although regional and international environments are becoming more accommodative to the issue of migrant labor, activism at the regional and international levels needs to be coupled with equally strong activism at home. Thus, this book is concerned with whether the Indonesian NGOs' efforts to extend their activism abroad through transnational activism have assisted them in strengthening their national activism and influence on government policies.

Piper has further argued for the importance of adopting a transnational and transinstitutional perspective and approach in addressing issues concerning temporary economic migration.[71] In relation to this, this book looks into the transinstitutional NGOs' networking efforts by first identifying the regional and international partners that the NGOs have been working with, because it is believed that while the NGOs may have preference in choosing who to work with, the relationship is also largely determined by their access to networks and which stakeholders are willing to cooperate. Then, this book determines the extent to which the NGOs and their partners have been able to coordinate their work which is needed for their activism to significantly affect the government's policies on labor migration.

In utilizing the transnational activism concept, it is important to recognize a number of principles as put forward by authors like Grugel, who argues that the space for civil society is highly influenced by other actors, including the state, the national and transnational activisms are highly connected, and the state remains the central actor.[72] Thus, this book is not based on a view that suggests that NGOs should replace the state's role in making policies on migrant workers, but rather argues for a cooperative engagement between them.

2.6 Conclusion

This chapter has briefly reviewed a number of publications in the areas related to this book. The purpose was to position this book within this body of literature and to identify how this work can build on and contribute to it. This book examines the role of Indonesian NGOs in promoting the rights of women migrant workers. It is focused on their efforts to influence government policies and framed by the changing context of democratization and globalization in Indone-

70 Cf. Yamanaka and Piper 2005, p. 29.
71 Cf. Piper 2010.
72 Cf. Grugel 2004, pp. 38-39.

sia. By concentrating on Indonesia, it intends to augment the limited number of works on efforts made in sending countries. Nevertheless, the activism of Indonesian NGOs on the issue of migrant workers is not studied in isolation because this book also examines their efforts to make their activism more transnational in order to strengthen their work at home.

After the New Order era ended, changes occurred at almost all levels, on all aspects and in various areas, making the environment and the pattern of relationships among actors more complex. Thus, this book is concerned with how the NGOs respond to these changes, particularly how they have adapted to the new policy environment. While acknowledging the changes, it also questions whether the policy environment during the Reform era has actually allowed NGOs to significantly influence the policy-making process.

In analyzing the NGOs' efforts, this book has benefited from the existing literature on state-NGO relationships. However, the analysis is extended to also include examination of the way the NGOs use their relationship with other actors to influence their relationship with the government. The aim is to establish whether the NGOs' wider national and transnational network, combined with a more open policy environment, translates to enhanced participation by NGOs in the migrant labor policy process. Furthermore, rather than just documenting how the NGOs conduct their activism within the new political space, this book investigates whether they have attempted to shape the political space and environment and, if so, whether it has resulted in them having a stronger role in the policy process.

In the context of policy-making, this book aims to document how NGO involvement is negotiated in a democratizing Indonesia. With the opportunities brought by the *Reformasi* in Indonesia, there is a chance for a redefinition of the NGOs' role, which is not solely determined by the NGOs themselves but rather by the existence and actions of other key actors. Thus, this book puts emphasis on the examination of the relationship between NGOs and other stakeholder, and the way they perceive each other.

Most literature on Indonesia post-New Order has praised NGOs as one of the driving forces of reform and democratization. Rather than viewing NGOs in this light, this book is more concerned with how they are affected by and respond to the democratization process. The analysis of NGOs' involvement in policy-making and their ability to significantly influence that process is also intended as a way to assess the democratization process in Indonesia.

It has also been well argued that with the wave of globalization and the transnational nature of labor migration, NGOs also need to make their activism more transnational. On the assumption that one of the NGOs' main purposes in conducting transnational activism is to strengthen their activism at home, the discussion of the NGOs' regional and international activism in this book is aimed at determining whether their national activism has actually benefited from efforts to extend their activism abroad, particularly in terms of influencing Indonesian government policies on labor migration.

As mentioned at the beginning of this chapter, this study benefits from views from work on various themes. Among the writers in the area researched, a few names are referred to quite often in this book, such as Michele Ford and Nicola Piper. Since they have produced quite extensive work on the subject, this book frequently deals with, confirms and sometimes challenges their views. It agrees with a number of Ford's and Piper's arguments. In fact, some of the arguments in this book are built based on theirs. Both authors have argued for the NGOs to conduct transnational activism which is commonly conducted through transnational networks. A significant part of this book looks into the transnational activism of the NGOs as their response to the wave of globalization and the transnational nature of the issue, and assesses the actual benefit of doing so.

Finally, this book is intended to contribute to the work on NGOs and labor migration as a documentation and analysis of how two Indonesian NGOs establish their roles in the labor migration system through their efforts to influence the government's domestic and foreign policies within a democratizing and globalizing Indonesia.

3. The Problematic Migration of Indonesian Women Migrant Workers

The purpose of this chapter is to provide an overview of the problems faced by Indonesian women migrant workers. It addresses the questions: What are the problems that need to be addressed? When and why do they occur? And who are the stakeholders involved? The chapter starts with a brief description of how migration has transformed in Asia, with a section focusing on the migration of Indonesian women overseas for employment. It then goes on to discuss typical problems faced by Indonesian women migrant workers at each migration stage. Detailed discussion of the problems faced by women migrant workers, including those from Indonesia, can be found in the extensive body of literature on this subject.[1] This chapter only covers some of the common problems which set the stage for the analysis in subsequent chapters of efforts to address them.

3.1 Transformation of Migration in Asia

3.1.1 The Rise of Labor Migration within the Region

Labor mobility can be traced quite far back in history. In Asia, it became particularly apparent during the colonial era when labor was moved from one place to another to work on construction projects and in plantations and mines. To a certain degree, this earlier form of migration within colonial territories was less restricted than today and migrants tended to move permanently, which led to settlement in the destination areas.[2] During the post-independence era of economic development, earlier bodies of research on Asian labor migration focused more on internal migration, which mainly involves labor migration from rural to urban areas. Since the 1980s, the trend shifted more toward labor migration between Asian countries, and by the early 1990s almost all countries in the region were involved in the sending and receiving of migrant workers.[3] Affected by various factors and changes occurring in the region, transnational migration, including

1 Cf. Jones 2000, Chin 2002, Komnas Perempuan and SP 2002, 2003, HRW 2004, Hugo 2005, Pigay 2005, Piper 2005c, Anggraeni 2006, Kaur 2007.

2 Cf. Kaur 2006, p. 2.

3 Cf. Yamanaka and Piper 2005, p. 2.

that in Asia, has gone through transformations.[4] Migration goals have shifted more towards economic purposes, where more people migrate to seek employment. Asian states have also started to be involved in the migration process by regulating it through policies. The form of migration has shifted from permanent toward temporary migration, with migrants working on contract arrangements, preventing them from settling in the destination countries. Two types of migrants exist, skilled and semi- or unskilled, whereat movement is easier for the former. A disturbing development is the increased undocumented movement of people through smuggling and trafficking. More important for this research is the significant increase in the number of women migrating to work abroad. As noted by Ball and Piper, the economic booms of the 1980s and 1990s led to increased demand in some countries for short-term contract workers for the service sector, which leads to the growing number of women migrating to work in entertainment and domestic service, a phenomenon known as the feminization of labor migration.[5]

By the 1990s, labor migration had become a significant element of Asian countries' economic system and international relations. As an illustration, by the mid-1990s, almost a quarter of Singapore's and Malaysia's labor force consisted of foreign migrant workers.[6] Analyses of the causes of this continuous and increasing flow of migrant labor usually refer to the disparities existing in sending and receiving countries as one of the driving forces. Social changes that accompanied economic development in receiving countries have caused their domestic labor force to move away from physically demanding types of work with poor pay and working conditions. At the same time, foreign workers, mostly from countries with lower living standards, poor economic performance, and high under- or unemployment rates like Indonesia and the Philippines, have fewer objections to these types of work[7] and thus became a timely solution for labor shortages in receiving countries. In other words, demand for labor in receiving countries is met by supply of excess labor in sending countries.

To some extent, labor migration offers economic benefits for both states and individuals. It could be viewed as a solution to labor shortages in receiving countries, low national income and high unemployment in sending countries, and economic problems of the migrant workers and their families. Consequently, as observed by Piper and Iredale, more players are entering the international labor migration arena.[8] However, as they point out, this has led to greater supply than

4 Cf. Ford 2004, p. 100, Hugo 2005, p. 54, Yamanaka and Piper 2005, p. 11, Cohen 2006, p. 163, Kaur 2006, p. 2.
5 Cf. Ball and Piper 2006, p. 214.
6 Cf. Kaur 2006, p. 6.
7 Cf. ibid., p. 9.
8 Cf. Piper and Iredale 2003, p. 15.

the demand for migrant labor, which disadvantages migrant workers because their rights are frequently sacrificed in an attempt to maintain employment competitiveness. Labor migration, which was considered as a solution for the challenging economic conditions of both the state and its people, has rapidly turned into a source of problems.

3.1.2 Migration of Indonesian Women to Work Overseas

As for most other countries in Asia, Indonesia's organized labor migration was triggered by changes in the 1980s. Ford considers Indonesia's decision to liberalize its economy in the mid-1980s to have significantly affected women's work in Indonesia.[9] According to her, decreased opportunities in agriculture and increased competition in the informal sector caused women from rural areas to increasingly migrate to urban areas and even abroad, mostly to work in domestic service.[10] Also in the 1980s, the Indonesian government decided to start developing its overseas labor contract program, mainly consisting of women employed as domestic workers in the Middle East and Malaysia.[11] Since then, Indonesia has set and included targets for sending workers overseas in its five-year economic development plans.

It is not only the women migrant workers and their families who benefit from their employment abroad. With their new spending powers, women migrant workers have made important contributions to the economies of their villages by creating demand for goods and services. This explains the growth of small businesses like telecommunication kiosks, transportation, banking, and many others in some origin villages in Indonesia.[12] Local and national media have also profiled a number of returning migrant workers who have successfully gathered some capital during their employment abroad to start a business when they return to their origin areas. Nationally, migrant workers' contribution to the national economy through their remittances is acknowledged by giving them the title "*pahlawan devisa*" (foreign exchange heroes).

Despite the limited and unreliable records on labor migration, particularly of the undocumented type, a general indication of the trend for Indonesian workers' placement overseas can be found in the gender-categorized data presented in Table 3.1.

9 Cf. Ford 2002, p. 90.
10 Cf. ibid., p. 93.
11 Cf. Piper and Iredale 2003, p. 21.
12 Cf. Komnas Perempuan and SP 2003, p. 10.

Table 3.1: Placement of Indonesian Workers Overseas (1994-2012)

Year	Sex		Total
	Male	Female	
1994	42,833	132,354	175,187
1995	39,102	81,784	120,886
1996	228,337	288,832	517,169
1997	39,309	195,944	235,253
1998	90,452	321,157	411,609
1999	124,828	302,791	427,619
2000	137,949	297,273	435,222
2001	55,206	239,942	295,148
2002	116,786	363,607	480,393
2003	80,041	213,824	293,865
2004	84,075	296,615	380,690
2005	149,265	325,045	474,310
2006	138,040	541,960	680,000
2007	152,030	544,716	696,746
2008	148,545	496,186	644,731
2009	103,126	529,046	632,172
2010	124,601	451,202	575,803
2011	205,054	376,027	581,081
2012	78,929	109,130	188,059

Source: National Authority for the Placement and Protection of Indonesian Overseas Workers[13]

Table 3.1 shows that the number of Indonesians migrating to work overseas is quite fluctuative.[14] The political relationship between Indonesia and the receiving country at a particular time significantly influences the fluctuation of these numbers. The table also shows that the number of female migrant workers is generally higher than the male one, confirming the feminization trend in labor migration.

13 BNP2TKI 2013.

14 Although further research is needed to verify, based on the trend it can be assumed that the downturns tended to occur following a change of policy and/or economic conditions in the receiving countries. A sharp fall from 1996 to 1997, for example, can be associated with the Asian economic crisis and, as explained later in this chapter, the significant fall from 2002 to 2003 was highly related to the changes in Malaysia's immigration policy. Another declining trend, particularly of female workers from 2009 to 2012 was due to the moratoria imposed by the Indonesian government on the placement of domestic workers in Malaysia and Saudi Arabia through official channels, as responses to cases faced by Indonesian women migrant workers in these countries.

In terms of destination, migration of Indonesian workers has reached various corners of the world. So far, the biggest numbers are concentrated in two regions, Asia and the Middle East. Table 3.2 shows the numbers of Indonesian migrant workers in these two regions, categorized by type of work (formal and informal) and gender (male and female).[15]

Table 3.2: Placement of Documented Indonesian Workers Overseas (2001-2008) in Two Major Regions

Year	Region of Place- Place- ment	Formal Sector			Informal Sector		
		Male	Female	Total	Male	Female	Total
2001	Asia-Pacific	55,349	31,584	86,933	675	129,947	130,622
	Middle East	22	240	262	10,269	110,649	120,918
2002	Asia-Pacific	96,780	22,549	119,329	1,160	117,835	118,995
	Middle East	1,140	904	2,044	17,631	222,286	239,917
2003	Asia-Pacific	64,518	24,313	88,831	707	20,184	20,891
	Middle East	774	465	1,239	13,739	168,792	182,531
2004	Asia-Pacific	68,022	47,284	115,306	497	45,167	45,664
	Middle East	609	312	921	14,930	203,848	218,778
2005	Asia-Pacific	134,503	58,356	192,859	2,789	101,643	104,432
	Middle East	2,104	1,911	4,015	9,869	163,135	173,004
2006	Asia-Pacific	107,991	63,472	171,463	6,364	148,984	155,348
	Middle East	113,050	64,518	177,568	25,242	477,190	502,432
2007	Asia-Pacific and U.S.			124,827			114,933
	Middle East and Africa			177,568			502,432

15 Complete data available at www.nakertrans.go.id.

2008	Asia-Pacific and U.S.	126,710	139,605
	Middle East and Africa	8,506	175,211

Source: Department of Manpower and Transmigration[16]

Various comments can be made on Table 3.2. *Firstly*, the way the data is collected, categorized, and presented on the official website of Department of Manpower and Transmigration changes frequently, making it rather difficult to draw comparison and conduct analysis of the trend.[17] *Secondly*, the data in this table – and most of the data used in this research – is mainly taken from the government's website. Thus, it only represents those who migrate through official channels, not including those who migrate illegally and those who migrate to countries that do not have bilateral agreements or MoUs with Indonesia on placement of migrant workers. As stated by Ford, the "two faces" of Indonesian female labor migration are those who migrate through authorized government programs and those who migrate "illegally" in order to avoid the problems posed by official channels.[18] This lack of reliable and comprehensive data may further affect the effectiveness of the policies and efforts made in addressing the particular problems faced by each group of migrant workers. *Thirdly*, more men are working in the formal sector and more women in the informal sector, usually in domestic service. The fact that the informal sector is commonly not covered by labor laws has made women migrant workers more vulnerable and less protected. *Fourthly*, after 2002 the placement of migrant workers in the informal sector in Asia dropped significantly. This may be due to the mass deportation from Malaysia which was followed by tighter entry control by the Malaysian government, appeals in Indonesia to stop the placement of Indonesian workers in Malaysia[19]

16 Department of Manpower and Transmigration 2010.

17 As can be seen in table 3.2, for 2007 and 2008 the regional grouping was changed to Asia-Pacific and U.S. and Middle East and Africa, and the data was only divided into sectors. For 2008, there is a separate gender-based categorization of data for each region: Asia-Pacific and U.S.: 87,050 male and 179,265 female, and Middle East and Africa: 17,066 male and 166,651 female, but it was not integrated with the sectoral categorization.

18 Cf. Ford 2002, p. 92.

19 After enacting a new immigration act in 2002, the Malaysian government deported thousands of undocumented migrant workers and made it more difficult for migrant workers to (re-) enter Malaysia. The deported migrant workers had to camp in Nunukan, a border area on the island of Kalimantan, with poor living conditions because most of them did not have enough money to pay for their transport home. Since there was no mechanism available to respond to a mass deportation of migrant workers, conditions in the camp got

and, as reflected in Table 3.1, since 2009, the moratoria on the placement of Indonesian domestic workers imposed by the government of Indonesia.

Within the region of Asia, the largest flow has been to Malaysia, followed by Singapore. As observed by Hugo, toward the end of the 1990s, the countries of destination have extended to include Hong Kong and Taiwan.[20] In some Asian receiving countries, particularly Malaysia, Indonesian female domestic workers have also increasingly replaced the Filipinas, who formerly dominated the domestic worker market. Hugo believes that this is due to the higher wages demanded by Filipina domestic workers, the efforts of the Indonesian labor agents and recruiters to promote their workers, and the efforts of the Indonesian government to expand its labor market. As an illustration, Table 3.3 shows the number of workers from the top six sending countries, taken from a table on the number of foreign workers in Malaysia for 2003-2006.

Table 3.3: Foreign Workers in Malaysia from the Six Main Sending Countries (2003-2006)

No.	Sending Countries	Period				
		2003/1/1 to 2003/12/31	2003/11/1 to 2004/10/31	2005/7/1 to 2006/6/30	2006/1/1 to 2006/12/31	2006/7/1 to 2006/06/30
1.	Indonesia	718,688	729,544	1,192,846	1,174,013	1,176,463
2.	Nepal	109,030	145,035	197,921	213,551	226,225
3.	India	63,035	75,123	136,756	138,313	143,308
4.	Myanmar	48,104	60,153	95,409	109,219	119,365
5.	Vietnam	70,137	73,318	93,740	10,751	114,406
6.	Bangladesh	94,204	55,981	64,738	62,669	67,756

Source: Indonesian Embassy in Kuala Lumpur[21]

This table shows that Indonesian workers significantly outnumber other foreign workers in Malaysia. Each year, at least 70 percent of foreign workers in Malaysia are Indonesian. Although the Philippines, one of the major sending countries in Asia, also have their citizens working in Malaysia, it does not appear in the top six of this list. This may be because workers from the Philippines are now more skilled and more rights-conscious, demanding higher wages and preferring

worse each day, causing the death of a number of people. The crisis itself and the harsh public response in Indonesia, insisting the government to stop the placement of Indonesian migrant workers in Malaysia, may have temporarily discouraged Indonesians from migrating to Malaysia.

20 Cf. Hugo 2005, p. 61.

21 Indonesian Embassy in Kuala Lumpur 2007.

to work in countries with better working conditions. Meanwhile, Malaysia is quite notorious for poor treatment of migrant workers and high demand for cheap labor. Hence, the majority of Indonesian migrant workers, with their limited skills and willingness to accept low working standards and low wages, have more opportunities in Malaysia. In fact, many recruitment agencies have promoted Indonesian domestic workers for their low wages and willingness to work seven days a week without extra cost.[22] The data should also be read while bearing in mind that Malaysia is a well-known market for informal and semi- or unskilled workers where most male migrants are employed in construction or plantations and most female migrants as domestic workers. The research conducted by HRW reveals that for many Indonesian women migrant workers, particularly for first-timers, Malaysia is considered as a stepping stone which will provide them with experience and qualifications to obtain better paid jobs in the Middle East, Singapore, or Hong Kong.[23] Domestic work is often chosen because it suits women with limited or no skills,[24] because it does not require an initial processing fee, and because with accommodation provided by the employer, the women domestic workers expect to save more money.

As mentioned before, one of the driving forces for labor migration is the economic and social development in the destination countries, which causes their workers to abandon certain types of menial jobs. In the case of women, the shift is highly related to the changing status and roles of women in the destination countries when women manage to get higher educational status and gain better-paid work. They then tend to leave their role as "caretaker" of the family and look for women who are willing to take over this role. Moreover, policies of both sending and receiving countries also contribute to the increased number of female migrant workers. Kaur has highlighted the correlations between the increased number of women who decide to work abroad, receiving countries' gender-selective policies, and the emergence of a "gender-specific employment niche".[25] The dominance of women in the flow of migrant workers to countries like Malaysia, Singapore, Hong Kong, and Taiwan is a good illustration of this situation. On a similar note, Hugo has also pointed out three elements that con-

22 Cf. Komnas Perempuan and SP 2003, p. 12. In 2012, Anis Hidayah from Migrant CARE found an advertisement in Malaysia stating "Indonesian maids now on SALE". Similar practice was also found in Singapore, which illustrates how Indonesian women migrant workers are often considered as cheap laborers, as compared to those from other countries, such as the Philippines.

23 Cf. HRW 2004a, pp. 13-14.

24 Although prior to working overseas as domestic workers Indonesian women are required to undergo training, domestic work is generally considered as a type of work that requires minimum or no skills.

25 Cf. Kaur 2006, p. 10.

tribute to the increased significance of the flow of women out of Indonesia to work as domestic workers.[26] The first element is the state's changed attitude toward labor migration, from merely regulating people's movement to exploring new markets for its workers, particularly after the 1997 financial crisis increased the significance of migrant workers' remittances for the national economy. The second element is the growth and increased activities of the migration industry, which involves, among others, labor recruiters, travel providers, and training providers. Female labor migration has become a lucrative business, motivating those involved in it to continuously expand the market and increase the labor supply. The third element is the role of social networks. The "pioneer" women migrants with their "success stories" tend to motivate and assist the movement of other women related to them.[27] Their relatively higher wages overseas have attracted more women to follow their steps.[28]

Major events that occurred in Indonesia at the end of the 1990s – the end of the New Order Era and the financial crisis – have affected the labor migration flow. Ford noted that, while the number of women seeking employment abroad after the financial crisis tended to increase, receiving countries like Malaysia – also affected by the crisis – took the initiative of repatriating illegal migrant workers to safeguard their domestic labor market.[29] Despite the fluctuation of the migration flow, as the number of Indonesian women working overseas continues to increase, the problems they are facing remain, and even become more complex.

3.2 Problems Faced by Indonesian Women Migrant Workers

Established bodies of literature, reports made by a number of organizations,[30] and coverage in the mass media extensively document the problems faced by In-

26 Cf. Hugo 2005, pp. 69-70.

27 A similar pattern can also be found in the migration of women from rural areas to work as domestic workers in Indonesia's urban areas.

28 As a comparison, in 2009, the average monthly salary of domestic workers in Indonesia was around 40 AUD, while in Malaysia a first timer received around 140 AUD to 175 AUD. In other receiving countries they earn even more, around 575 AUD in Hong Kong, 259 AUD in Singapore, 580 AUD in Taiwan, 199 AUD in Saudi Arabia, and 430 AUD in Kuwait. Cf. Antara News, September 13, 2009, November 23, 2009.

29 Cf. Ford 2002, p. 104.

30 This section relies heavily on the reports made by U.S.-based organizations, Human Rights Watch 2004a and by *Komnas Perempuan* and SP 2002, 2003, which have comprehensively documented the problems faced by Indonesian women domestic workers at every stage of their migration to work in Malaysia.

donesian women migrant workers at all stages of their migration process.[31] The work of Anggraeni, for instance, has provided an in-depth study of the problems faced by Indonesian women domestic workers throughout their migration process.[32] These problems are interconnected: a wrong-doing or violation at one stage will most probably cause problems later. As argued by Hugo, the premature return of some Indonesian women migrant workers reflects their bad experiences.[33] This section will briefly canvas the common problems faced by women migrant workers and the stakeholders involved, divided by stages ranging from pre-recruitment to the aftermath of working abroad, as illustrated in Figure 3.1.

Figure 3.1: Stages of Working in Malaysia for Indonesian Women Migrant Workers

Recruitment
Pre-Departure
Departure/Transit
Arrival
Pre-Recruitment
Influenced and determined by:
- Policies in Indonesia
- Policies in Malaysia
- Bilateral/Multilateral Agreements
- Regional and International Arrangements and Mechanisms
Employment
After Working Abroad
With Problems
Without Problems
Returning

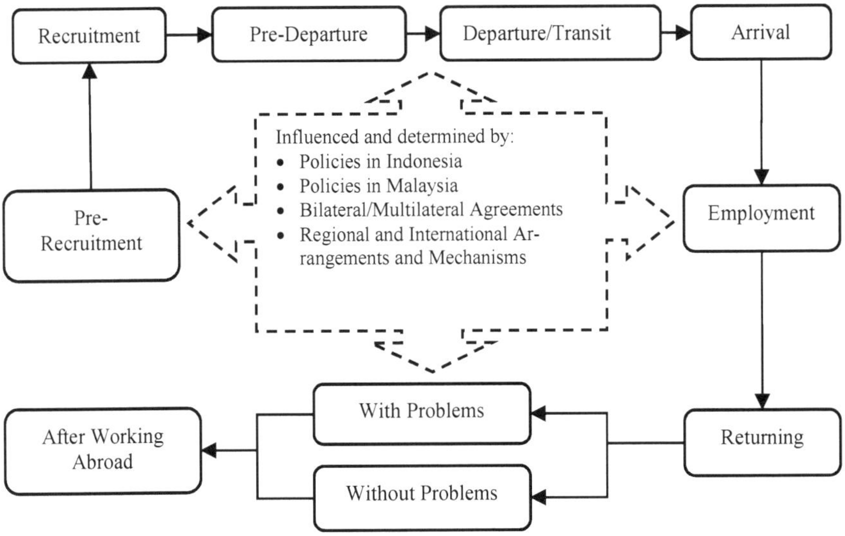

Source: Figure composed by author

31 A table in the report by *Komnas Perempuan* and SP 2003, p. 31, shows the continuously increasing migrant worker cases in Sukanto Police Hospital in Jakarta from 2000 to June 2003. A table on the website of the Department of Manpower and Transmigration 2010 shows the types and number of cases faced by Indonesian migrant workers abroad. Although the data is not gender disaggregated and does not include those who choose not to report their cases, it reflects the range and the significant number of problems faced by migrant workers.
32 Cf. Anggraeni 2006.
33 Cf. Hugo 2005, p. 73.

Although this diagram specifically deals with the migration process to Malaysia, the process of migration described generally applies to most Indonesian women migrating to work overseas, particularly as domestic workers.

3.2.1 Pre-Recruitment

Analyses of problems faced by women migrant workers commonly divide the migration stages into pre-departure, during employment, and post-employment abroad. Only a few discuss the period before prospective women migrant workers meet the recruiters or even embrace the idea of working overseas. This is actually the stage where some of the main roots of the problems exist and need to be addressed. Most Indonesian villages traditionally depend on agriculture. Unfortunately, in some areas land has become unproductive due to environmental destruction or the villagers may have lost ownership of their lands for various reasons. Poverty and unavailability of income generating jobs are the main issues because they are powerful factors that motivate people to seek alternative sources of income. One of the seemingly easy ways out is to seek employment abroad in the informal sector, which usually requires minimum skills. If adequately paid jobs are available locally, presumably people will be less tempted to seek jobs somewhere else. Nevertheless, since working as domestic workers in Indonesia, for example, is as risky and as unprotected[34] as doing the same job overseas, many would opt to work overseas where they are paid at least three times higher.

The next issue is low educational level. Poorly educated people are more likely to accept any type of work offered without considering the risks entailed. They also tend to be less informed and to avoid paper work and bureaucracies. Since the poor and remote areas are usually not reached by official sources of information, they are least likely to receive the appropriate information on working overseas or they will only get information from those who are willing to come to these areas, which in most cases are individual recruiters. A poor area inhabited by unemployed, low educated, and un- or ill-informed people of working age is a common and easy target for unscrupulous individual recruiters.[35] In fact, in some instances, recruiters at the village level are the ones who introduce the idea of

34 Considering that until 2012 Indonesia is yet to pass a law on the protection of domestic workers.

35 As further explained in the next section, individual recruiters become dangerous when they operate in remote areas, away from the monitoring coverage of authorities and/or migrant workers' advocates, and take advantage of the people's lack of knowledge about the migration process and its requirements.

migrating to the rural women.[36] There are concerns that these local recruiters may provide false information for the sake of their business interests, and with the lack, if not absence, of official information dissemination there is a high risk that more women will be "tricked" into migrating in a way that endangers them.

3.2.2 Recruitment

Semi- or un-skilled women in rural areas rarely have direct access to employment abroad.[37] As described in the previous section, this is where individual recruiters play significant roles. The network of recruiters or middlemen, usually known as *calo* or sponsors or brokers, operate in villages, looking for potential migrants to be sent to local or national recruitment or labor agencies, also known as *Perusahaan Jasa Tenaga Kerja Indonesia* (PJTKI) or *Pelaksana Penempatan Tenaga Kerja Indonesia Swasta* (PPTKIS). These recruiters usually receive commission from labor agencies based on the number of workers they can recruit.[38] As a result, to reach their target, they frequently ignore certain requirements for overseas employment such as minimum age. With the absence of regulations that can protect prospective migrant workers from local recruiters' bad practices, they continue to collect fees without actually assisting the migration process, give loans with high interest, fake documents, trade migrant workers, and even commit sexual harassment.[39]

In the Indonesian migration system, official employment for domestic workers should be obtained through licensed labor agencies.[40] Prospective migrant workers may come directly to these labor agencies or may be taken by individual recruiters as mentioned above. In 2004, a report by HRW described the issues concerning many labor agencies.[41] HRW stated that there were at least four hundred licensed labor agencies in Indonesia, not including those operating illegally, and they operate with minimum monitoring from the government. According to this organization, establishing agencies to recruit or supply domestic workers is not very difficult in Indonesia and Malaysia. The main requirements are only that the company is legally registered and has a stipulated amount of funds. In terms of service quality and staff qualifications, no guidelines exist. In Indonesia, the Ministry of Manpower and Transmigration (MoMT) issues labor agencies with

36 Cf. Hugo 2005, p. 70.
37 Cf. Kaur 2006, p. 15.
38 Cf. HRW 2004a, p. 26.
39 Cf. Komnas Perempuan and SP 2003, p. 15.
40 In practice, there have been Malaysian employers who personally come to Indonesia to hire domestic workers.
41 Cf. HRW 2004a, pp. 21-22.

licenses which are rarely reviewed or renewed. Although licenses will be suspended or cancelled if the agency cheats workers or breaks any regulations, with the weak monitoring system it is difficult to identify or penalize such agencies. Even suspended agencies can continue their operations by establishing new companies.

3.2.3 Pre-Departure

Fees

Although poverty in sending countries is one of the push factors of migration, Kaur argued that those who migrate to work abroad are not necessarily the poorest among the poor, since they still need to have a substantial amount of money to fund their migration.[42] Semi-skilled and unskilled workers have to meet various costs which may include agency fees, insurance fees, a bank guarantee and a one way air ticket.[43] However, according to HRW, unlike those who migrate to work in plantations, factories, and construction, women who migrate as domestic workers do not have to pay the fees in advance.[44] Moreover, many prospective women migrant workers live far from government offices which deal with the migration process, have low educational level, and are not experienced in dealing with complex bureaucracies.[45] Thus, dealing with local recruiters is often preferable because they take care of all the requirements, even the letter of permission from family or husband. However, for their service, recruiters often ask for fees from prospective migrant workers and they even provide loans with high interest to cover the service fees.

The common practice is to have the first four or five months of the migrant workers' salary deducted which leads to the migrant workers receiving little or no payment for their work. This can be dangerous because there are cases where the salary deduction is prolonged to the point that the women receive almost nothing. The situation can be even worse for those who migrate illegally because they have to pay large initial fees to the labor agencies, which are usually borrowed from local agents, moneylenders, families, or friends. In most cases, they will have to pay high interest rates, which trap them in debt. In short, in both arrangements there is a great possibility that the workers return home financially disadvantaged.

42 Cf. Kaur 2006, p. 6.
43 Cf. ibid., p. 15.
44 Cf. HRW 2004a, p. 23.
45 Cf. Nagib 2001, p. 13.

Medical Check-Up

Receiving countries like Malaysia usually make it mandatory for migrant workers to have medical check-ups before entering, usually for pregnancy, HIV/AIDS, malaria, and tuberculosis.[46] If conducted properly, medical check-ups may be useful in helping to determine the appropriate working conditions and workload for a particular worker. An informative medical record can also be useful in case of emergencies. However, there are instances when the result of medical check-up is used as a basis to deny entry to a country or cancel employment, and, as mentioned before, it is also used as an excuse to charge the prospective migrant workers extra fees. Migrant workers' advocates have also criticized how the check-ups are conducted and how the result is treated. Workers are not usually told what they are tested for or what the results are.[47] Instead, results which should be treated as confidential personal information are given directly to the labor agencies.[48]

Training Centers

One of the government requirements for Indonesian citizens going overseas as domestic workers is to undergo pre-departure training. Responsibilities to conduct this training are given to the business sector. More established labor agencies usually have their own training facilities. Those who do not will contract out. Training usually covers skills such as housekeeping, childcare, and language skills.[49] Unfortunately, not all the curricula are well-developed, the quality of the training is often low, and not all training centers are well-equipped. Nagib explained that if the labor agencies choose to conduct proper training with complete material, it will require more time and cost.[50] This will affect their ability to respond to labor demand and they will be less preferred by prospective migrant workers, compared to labor agencies with shorter training programs. Thus, many labor agencies tend to "simplify" the training to meet their placement quota.

While the prospective women migrant workers undergo training, the labor agencies take care of requirements such as medical check-ups, passports, temporary employment visas, insurance, and approval from the MoMT.[51] At the same time, these workers are being selected by receiving countries' agents, usually on

46 Cf. Komnas Perempuan and SP 2002, p. 21, HRW 2004a, p. 22.
47 Cf. Komnas Perempuan and SP 2002, p. 22.
48 Cf. HRW 2004a, p. 23.
49 Cf. Komnas Perempuan and SP 2002, p. 21, HRW 2004a, p. 24.
50 Cf. Nagib 2001, p. 24.
51 Cf. HRW 2004a, p. 24.

the basis of their biodata.[52] There are regulations that limit the length of stay in the training centers, which is up to three months.[53] However, there are cases where prospective women migrant workers have to stay much longer than that, waiting for their documents or the availability of employment. The lengthy waiting period often leads to deeper debt entrapment.[54] While in the training centers, there are daily needs which are not covered by the agencies. To meet these needs, the women usually borrow money from the agencies. Each day the debts get higher, contributing further to their salary deduction.

The women migrant workers' suffering is often worsened by poor conditions in some training centers. As observed by HRW, many are overcrowded and some do not provide adequate or any sleeping facilities, while food and water and toilets and showers are limited or in poor condition.[55] The MoMT has set minimum standards for space, food and sanitation but since monitoring is infrequent or lacking, this situation persists.

Issues have also arisen from the way these women are treated while they are in the training centers. Those who become ill often do not receive proper treatment.[56] HRW has documented how women are verbally, physically and sexually abused in the training centers.[57] There are cases where women are sexually abused or raped by the staff, or where they have to give sexual favors in exchange for faster placement. Also, women in the training centers are usually restricted from leaving the facilities. According to HRW, labor agencies' excuses for limiting the women's freedom of movement are to avoid pregnancies and rape, and to prevent them from getting lost.[58] Obviously, it is also related to profit safeguarding. Since the business of supplying domestic workers is highly competitive, labor agencies need to have a ready supply of workers, and they will not get paid unless the workers are recruited. Their payment will come from their commissions and deductions from the workers' salaries. After investing a substantial amount of money in preparing these workers, they will not want to lose their investment. Also, the labor agencies' enormous power over the prospective women migrant workers during the pre-departure stage is often abused by telling the women to work as maids in local households while waiting for their placement, claiming it as part of the training program.[59] Some women are paid for doing this, but frequently their wages are taken by the agencies.

52 Cf. Nagib 2001, p. 17.
53 Cf. ibid., p. 38, Komnas Perempuan and SP 2002, p. 10.
54 Cf. Komnas Perempuan and SP 2002, p. 10.
55 Cf. HRW 2004a, p. 33.
56 Cf. Komnas Perempuan and SP 2003, p. 18.
57 Cf. HRW 2004a, pp. 34-35.
58 Cf. ibid., pp. 32-33.
59 Cf. HRW 2004a, p. 35.

Although there are labor agencies which can be considered as well-equipped and well-managed, the bad practices of some have created a negative image for labor agencies. As discussed further in Chapter 7, this has put the relationship between NGOs and labor agencies continuously at odds.

Documents and Requirements

The Indonesian official labor migration system is known for its long process, high cost, and complex requirements.[60] These are seen as obstacles by Indonesian labor agencies. To compete with other agencies, including those from other sending countries, Indonesian labor agencies need to be responsive to labor demands. Consequently, to maintain their competitiveness and profit, many agencies have conducted practices which violate the existing laws and regulations.

Commonly, the documents required for migrating to work overseas from Indonesia are passport, working visa, fiscal waiver,[61] tickets, and insurance.[62] Unfortunately, the process for getting these documents is long and complicated. One document is a prerequisite for another and the actual process for each document usually takes longer than the officially stated time. Thus, short cuts are usually taken by giving bribes to the institutions in charge.

Another common practice is altering documents to meet certain requirements from the receiving countries such as minimum and maximum age: many labor agencies have altered passports and other documents to change the women's age, name, and/or address.[63] Some labor agencies also falsify migrant workers' competency test certificates.[64] In conducting these practices and to speed up the paperwork processes, labor agencies usually have to provide bribes and pay unofficial fees to the authorities.[65] Thus, while some labor agencies provide these "services" for free, many are charging the women extra fees.

Prospective migrant workers may be aware from the very beginning that some parts of their migration process have contravened the regulations, risking their legal status. However, many of them are not aware of this. As an example, in order to speed up the process, applications are made out for the workers to receive

60 Cf. ibid., p. 25.
61 Since 2011, this document is no longer needed because the government of Indonesia abolished the fiscal tax for Indonesians going abroad.
62 Cf. Nagib 2001, p. 27.
63 Cf. HRW 2004a, p. 29. Age alteration occurs to make the women appear older or younger than their actual age.
64 Cf. Nagib 2001, p. 26, HRW 2004a, p. 25.
65 Cf. Komnas Perempuan and SP 2003, p. 18.

short-term visitor visas, instead of two-year temporary employment visas.[66] This may increase the women migrant workers' possibility of becoming "illegal" or undocumented, if they are not informed of this arrangement and continue to stay for the full length of their employment, which is usually one or two years.

A consequence of the long process and complex requirements is the increased number of people seeking employment through unscrupulous agents, who usually promise them shorter waiting periods and bypass training and health requirements. For these workers, the risk of abuse will be higher and redress is less likely because governments from both sending and receiving countries usually refrain from addressing labor rights violations for this type of migrant worker.[67] Moreover, under Malaysian immigration law they are subject to arrest, detention, and deportation.

Lack of Information

Indonesian domestic workers may also face problems due to their lack of information. They may not know what kind of information they need to obtain, and the sources of this information, or in many cases the information itself is not disclosed to them. Many of the women migrant workers have minimal information about their labor agents. They usually cannot recall the name of the agencies, the address, and whether the agencies are licensed or not.[68] As I found out through my conversations with some of the abused Indonesian women domestic workers accommodated at the shelter in Indonesia's Embassy in Kuala Lumpur in 2007, many of them only knew the first name of their agents. This makes it difficult to make the agencies accountable when the women face problems during their employment.

Women migrant workers often enter the migration process with limited knowledge of what will happen. According to HRW, there are cases where labor agents give vague or no information about the duration of training, salary, workload, and where to go and what options there are available for the migrant workers in the case of abuses or other problems.[69] The agents focus more on making sure that the workers will not run away, and that they will obey their employers and work hard. Various advocacy groups have long argued for the inclusion of sessions on migrant workers' basic rights as human beings, workers, and women

66 Cf. HRW 2004a, pp. 26-27.
67 Cf. ibid., p. 27.
68 Cf. ibid., p. 28.
69 Cf. HRW 2004a, p. 27.

in the training curriculum.[70] Unfortunately, lack of information remains one of the major issues in the migration system that needs to be addressed.

3.2.4 Departure/Transit

The common practice is that, after being prepared by Indonesian labor agencies, prospective migrant workers are selected by Malaysian labor agencies and/or employers. Domestic workers are selected from their written "biodata" forms which include their personal information, skills, and photograph.[71] Discrimination exists during this selection process. Indonesian women domestic workers are not only promoted and selected by Malaysian labor agencies based on their skills, but also on characteristics like age, weight, height, complexion, marital status, and number of children.[72] In this manner, as argued by migrant labor rights advocates, women domestic workers are considered more to be tradable goods, rather than human beings.

The transit process from Indonesia to Malaysia is also loaded with problems. As mentioned before, after being recruited and trained, there is no guarantee that the migrant workers will immediately depart. There are also cases where workers are transported by boat, instead of by plane as promised, which is not only more inconvenient but can also be more dangerous.[73]

3.2.5 Arrival

Upon arrival, Malaysian labor agencies and employers often demand that the migrant workers' health should be re-tested because they do not trust Indonesian documents. There are instances where prospective migrant workers, who have been proclaimed healthy in Indonesia, received the opposite result in the destination countries, indicating differences in medical standards in both countries.[74] For Malaysia, those who are tested positive for pregnancy, HIV/AIDS, tuberculosis, malaria, leprosy, sexually transmitted infections, or drug use are not allowed to enter and are immediately deported.[75] To make matters worse, they rarely get a proper explanation about the health test result and the diseases that they might have.

70 Cf. Komnas Perempuan and SP 2002, p. 21.
71 Cf. HRW 2004a, p. 24.
72 Cf. ibid., p. 30.
73 Cf. ibid., p. 24.
74 Cf. Komnas Perempuan and SP 2003, p. 29.
75 Cf. HRW 2004a, p. 22.

3.2.6 Employment

Some women migrant workers are fortunate enough to get good, attentive, and generous employers. These women bring their success stories home and motivate more women to work overseas. Unfortunately, this is not always the case for Indonesian women migrant workers. Generally, semi- or unskilled women migrant workers have to live and work in distressing conditions, doing '3D' (dirty, dangerous, and degrading) work.

Malaysia became a popular destination for Indonesian migrant workers partly due to its proximity to home and the similar culture and language to Indonesia. Hence, it is assumed that it will be easier for Indonesian women migrant workers to adapt in Malaysia and it is considered to be a "friendlier" place to work. However, the problems faced by Indonesian women migrant workers in Malaysia have proven the contrary. The following are some of the common problems faced by Indonesian women migrant workers during their employment in Malaysia.

Violations of Labor Rights

Employment of foreign domestic workers in Malaysia is usually based on two-year work contracts. However, as documented by HRW, many of them are only shown the employment contract briefly and not given time to read or discuss the content of the contract with other more informed parties so that they can fully understand the content before signing it.[76] This frequently puts them in a disadvantaged situation because, in many cases, the contract – which is supposed to be a legal document that can be used as an instrument to protect their rights as workers – rarely includes the job description, workload, working hours, and overtime payment. Some contracts may allow domestic workers to have one day off per week, but if employers are willing to pay, they can make them work for seven days a week. Two issues that migrant workers advocates have been campaigning on are the rights of the migrant workers to practice their religion and to have a day off. Although some contracts allow domestic workers to practice their religion, there are many cases where Muslim domestic workers are not allowed to pray five times a day or fast during the month of Ramadan.[77] As for working hours, according to HRW, working hours for Indonesian domestic workers in Malaysia are long, typically 16 to 18 hour days, seven days a week with enormous workloads, which usually include cooking three meals a day, cleaning the

76 Cf. ibid., p. 28.
77 Cf. ibid., p. 45.

house, taking care of children, washing cars, doing the laundry by hand, and ironing.[78] Rest time is usually short or none is given. Those who are also taking care of the family's children often have to be "on call" 24 hours a day. Moreover, many women migrant domestic workers have to live in distressing conditions where they have to sleep in inadequate space, or share it with a male, and receive insufficient meals.[79]

Employers and labor agents interviewed by HRW about giving domestic workers rest time or a day off claimed that domestic workers do not know how to rest and they might run away, get impregnated or bring strangers into the house.[80] Thus, most domestic workers are forbidden to leave the house unless with the employers or instructed by them, and they are often not allowed to make contact with friends, families, or even neighbors. There are cases where Indonesian domestic workers are locked in the premises.[81] Such restrictions imposed on domestic workers obviously violate their rights and isolate them socially, which may lead to loneliness and depression.[82] Most importantly, it will be difficult for them to seek help in the case of abuse or other emergencies.

A common strategy used by employers to prevent domestic workers from running away or to cheat them out of their full salary is to give them their salary only at the end of the two-year contract, with the excuse of helping them to save money by depositing their salaries into a saving account.[83] By this means, if the domestic workers left before completing their contracts or if the employers do not pay them even until they have to leave due to visa expiration, it would be difficult for them to claim their salaries. In other cases, some domestic workers did not receive the salary they deserved because they were not able to calculate their actual full payment or their employers made deductions for daily supplies, medicines, and phone calls.[84]

78 Cf. ibid., pp. 38-39.

79 Cf. Komnas Perempuan and SP 2003, p. 19.

80 Cf. HRW 2004a, p. 39.

81 In many of these cases, the domestic workers waited until their employers left for a few days before trying to escape from locked apartments by making ropes out of sheets and climbing out of high windows. During my visit to the Indonesian Embassy in Kuala Lumpur in 2007, I met two Indonesian domestic workers who tried to escape this way: Ceriyati, who tried to escape from a 15th floor apartment in June, and Parsiti, who tried to escape from a 17th floor apartment in August. Their cases were widely covered by the media, and Migrant CARE was actively advocating these cases and using them in their campaigns to urge Indonesian and Malaysian governments to improve protection of Indonesian women migrant workers.

82 Cf. HRW 2004a, p. 41.

83 Cf. ibid., p. 42.

84 Cf. ibid., p. 43.

Abuse

Abuse of domestic workers can exist in various forms. The distressing living and working conditions previously explained are some of the common forms of abuse faced by Indonesian domestic workers working overseas. In addition, women domestic workers are verbally abused through insults and threats and vulnerable to sexual harassment, assault, or rape by employers and male migrant workers.[85]

Many women domestic workers tend to force themselves to endure abuse and decide not to run away. According to HRW, this is usually due to the threats made by the employer and to the fact that they still need to pay off their debt while hoping to eventually receive their withheld salaries.[86] As reported by HRW, it is difficult for women domestic workers to report abuse, obtain help, and escape due to confinement, lack of information about or access to institutions that could provide assistance, and regulations that require domestic workers' passports to be held by the employers.[87] Moreover, those who decide to report harassment and abuse are immediately sent back to Indonesia, some without receiving their salaries.

After experiencing abuse, women domestic workers rarely have immediate access to medical treatment. They first need to leave the abusive workplace, either by running away or by being picked up by the police based on reports made by neighbors.[88] They are then taken to hospitals or the Indonesian embassy's shelters to be treated. However, the treatment is quite limited: there is no psychological counseling service available at the embassy.

Despite the rampant abuses experienced by women domestic workers, the informal characteristics of their job and the private nature of their working place have made it difficult to monitor what is happening, and they are not protected by labor laws, which only cover those working in the formal sector.

Undocumented Status, Detention, and Imprisonment

Another risk faced by women migrant workers is undocumented status. Such status can apply to those who enter destination countries illegally through unofficial channels and without proper documents, those who overstay their visa, those who move to other jobs different from the ones stated in their visa, those who

85 Cf. ibid., pp. 47-49.
86 Cf. ibid., pp. 49-50.
87 Cf. ibid., p. 37.
88 Cf. ibid., p. 47.

work while on a non-working visa, those who were trafficked, and those whose documents are withheld by their employers. In the case of women domestic workers, many become undocumented because they run away from abusive employers who withhold their passports.[89]

Detention and imprisonment have been among the risks faced by Indonesian migrant workers in Malaysia. Some workers are turned in by employers making accusations of theft and cheating.[90] Others are detained or imprisoned for their undocumented status. The majority of detained migrant workers are arrested because they are considered illegal workers. Unfortunately, illegal status is defined quite loosely and applied to any worker who cannot produce work documents when they are arrested.[91] As argued by *Komnas Perempuan* and SP, many migrant domestic workers are not able to show valid documents because the agencies have altered their documents, their documents are withheld by their employers or agencies, or they have changed employers so that their working visas are not valid anymore.

Getting access to detention centers is difficult. However, there are reports on the conditions in detention camps in Malaysia. A report by Tenaganita, a Malaysian NGO, for example, revealed that, in the 1990s, detention centers had no clean drinking water, limited sanitation facilities, and unfit meals.[92] Later reports by migrant workers' advocates and the media indicate that there has been little improvement since then.

3.2.7 Returning

Many of the problems faced by migrant workers during their employment remain unresolved. It is even harder to find resolutions for problems such as unpaid salaries and abuses if the migrant workers have left the receiving countries. This is why many migrant domestic workers who have unresolved problems choose to stay in Malaysia, usually in the Indonesian Embassy's shelter, to wait for a resolution to their cases because if they leave Malaysia, there is usually no guarantee that they will be allowed to re-enter.[93]

89 Cf. Komnas Perempuan and SP 2003, p. 27, Hugo 2005, pp. 64-65.

90 Cf. Komnas Perempuan and SP 2003, p. 19.

91 Cf. ibid., p. 27.

92 Cf. ibid.

93 In most instances, Indonesian migrant domestic workers with problems who go into Indonesian embassy shelters are in an "imprisonment" situation. Since they have no documents, including no visas, they are not allowed to leave the embassy and this can last for months. In Nirmala Bonat's case, it was four years until her case was finally decided and she could finally go home.

For some migrant domestic workers who choose to return home, the ill-treatment continues. At most re-entry points these workers have to face further exploitation. The Indonesian government designated Terminal III at Soekarno-Hatta International Airport in Jakarta as a special terminal for migrant workers to create a one-stop service for returning migrant workers and to speed up the re-entry process.[94] However, this terminal became a place of rampant abuse of returning migrant workers with unofficial fees, sexual harassment, and forced lower currency exchange rates.[95] The returning workers were also exploited by transportation providers. To reach their home towns, they usually need land transport, and transportation providers often charged them far above the normal rate or asked for additional charges on the way. According to *Komnas Perempuan* and SP, the gap between the normal charge and "Terminal III charge" could reach more than 200 percent.[96] There have been changes made aimed at addressing the problems and eliminating bad practices,[97] but there are still reports on returning migrant workers being disadvantaged at the entry points.

Migrant domestic workers have to go through at least two medical check-ups before their employment: one before departure and another as soon as they arrive in the receiving country. In contrast, no medical examination is required when they finish their employment or when they arrive home, and the health conditions of returning migrant workers are not properly documented.[98] It is even harder to get accurate data on cases of rape and sexual abuse because most women migrant domestic workers see such abuse as a disgrace that should not be exposed to the public, which is preventing them from seeking assistance. Some of the impregnated women domestic workers choose to raise the child, but many others tend to leave or give the child away before returning to their home town.[99] For those who come home with problems such as unwanted pregnancies, unpaid

94 Cf. Komnas Perempuan and SP 2002, p. 18.

95 Cf. Komnas Perempuan and SP 2003, p. 20.

96 Cf. Komnas Perempuan and SP 2002, p. 20.

97 Over time, the management of Terminal III was changed several times and, in 2007, the responsibility of overseeing the operation of this terminal was handed over from the MoMT to the BNP2TKI. In 2009, the designated terminal for returning Indonesian migrant workers was changed to Terminal IV in Selapanjang. Migrant workers who arrived at Soekarno-Hatta International Airport were transferred by bus to a building in this Terminal IV for the purpose of recording their data. In 2010, the government announced its intention to close Terminal IV so migrant workers can enter Indonesia through any arrival terminals with other passengers. Cf. Tempo Interaktif, January 26, 2010. By the end of 2012, returning Indonesian migrant workers can exit through Terminal II like other inbound passengers. Nevertheless, the bad practices seem to continue.

98 Cf. Komnas Perempuan and SP 2002, p. 27.

99 A feature on one Indonesian TV station, Metro TV, in 2007, showed that there were women with unwanted pregnancies or babies who gave their babies to whoever wanted to care for them even when they just arrived at Soekarno-Hatta International Airport.

salaries, abuse, or HIV/AIDS, the situation is even harsher because they still have to face humiliation by village communities, families, or husbands who lack knowledge, tolerance, and understanding.[100]

The referral hospital for sick and injured returnees who come through Soekarno-Hatta International Airport is the Sukanto Central Police Hospital in East Jakarta. Between 2000 and 2003, around 70 percent of cases at this hospital were abuse-related, with the common cases treated being physical injuries such as fractures, burns, head injuries, trauma from blunt objects, open wounds, and dislocation, and psychological illnesses such as psychosis and depression.[101] Unfortunately, this hospital has been facing difficulties with unpaid bills because many agencies avoid their responsibilities of covering the migrant workers' hospital bills. Consequently, the hospital began to set limits to its services and considered rejecting migrant workers sent by recruiting agencies unknown to the hospital or being on their list of delinquent debtors.[102]

One of the requirements from the MoMT is for migrant workers to pay 15 USD of insurance fees before their departure.[103] However, the insurance scheme has been criticized by migrant workers' advocates for not being specific on matters such as maximum coverage for hospitalization and whether it covers acts of abuse. Moreover, paperwork and limited access from the migrant workers' remote home towns seem to be the reasons for not going through the claim a process, which is usually limited to one month after their return.

Many migrant workers are deported. Deportation from Malaysia has taken two forms: on-going small-scale deportations and a larger round-up, which is usually caused by a particular occurrence such as rioting by Indonesian migrants in 1998 and 2002.[104] One of the biggest deportation waves from Malaysia occurred in 2002, triggered by a Malaysian government decision that year to enact the Immigration Act No. 1154, which amended the 1959 and 1963 immigration acts to allow caning, imprisonment, and fines for those involved in illegal placement of migrant workers.[105] Malaysia then launched its anti-migrants policy and deported thousands of undocumented migrant workers. This led to a humanitarian crisis in Nunukan, a border town in Kalimantan.

100 Cf. Komnas Perempuan and SP 2003, pp. 21 and 29.
101 Cf. ibid., pp. 13 and 30.
102 Cf. Komnas Perempuan and SP 2002, p. 24.
103 Cf. HRW 2004a, p. 26.
104 Cf. Komnas Perempuan and SP 2002, p. 27.
105 Cf. Komnas Perempuan and SP 2003, p. 28. In most cases, these punishments only apply to "illegal" migrant workers.

3.3 Conclusion

Large scale migration of Indonesian men and women to seek employment abroad started in the 1970s. Remittances from these workers have significantly contributed to the country's economy and the welfare of migrant workers, their families, and communities. However, more than three decades later, the migration system is still suffering from many forms of exploitation, and levels of protection for migrant workers remain low.

Despite the various success stories of some returned migrant workers, many of them have come home empty handed and suffering from a range of problems which occur at every stage of the migration process. In fact, the government, migrant labor advocates and scholars have acknowledged that 80 percent of the problems occur even before the migrant workers leave Indonesia. In most cases, problems at home eventually lead to bigger problems during employment abroad.

This chapter has briefly described the common problems and challenges faced by Indonesian women migrant workers at every stage of their migration process and has shown the interconnectedness of the problems and the stakeholders involved. A migration system which is not well-developed and managed, not supported by comprehensive laws and regulations, and undermined by corruption, bad practices, and a lack of protective mechanisms is one of the main issues. Therefore, the next chapter will look into the efforts made by the government of Indonesia to address these problems.

4. Responding to Pressures: Government Management of Labor Migration

Through the discussion of the problems faced by Indonesian women migrant workers, the previous chapter has highlighted both the government's key role and the weaknesses of government policies. Therefore, this chapter aims to examine the government's efforts to improve the management and regulation of Indonesian labor migration. In doing so, this chapter goes beyond merely making an inventory of the rules and regulations issued by the government. It rather aims to recognize differences within the government in responding to the issues considering women migrant workers and identify the type of pressures to which the government is more responsive. The chapter sets out to answer questions like: What are the efforts made by related state institutions? And why did they make those efforts, or what are the factors that influence these decisions?

The chapter starts with an overview of the government's involvement in the labor migration process which mainly takes the form of regulating it. This section also highlights some of the main pressures that the Indonesian government has been responding to in making policies on labor migration.[1] The discussion then continues by looking at the efforts made by the main state institutions and identifying the type of pressures each institution has been responding to.

4.1 Government Involvement in the Migration Process

The government of Indonesia has not always been involved in the migration of its citizens to work abroad. As observed by Hugo, Indonesian labor migration began in a significant way in the mid-1970s, when individual entrepreneurs started sending Indonesian women to work as domestic workers in the Middle East.[2] While there are various opinions on when the government started to get involved in the migration process, it is quite clear that the state's economic interest was one of the main motivations. According to Pigay, since the first five-year development plan or *Pembangunan Lima Tahun* (*Pelita*), 1969/1970-1974/1975, the government has formally made various efforts to encourage work-related mi-

1 The major official responses – the Law No. 39/2004 on the Placement and Protection of Indonesian Workers Overseas and the 2006 MoU between Indonesia and Malaysia – will be discussed in greater depth later in chapters 6 and 8.

2 Cf. Hugo 1992, p. 181.

gration from Indonesia.[3] Other authors, however, argue that the government only began to get involved in the 1980s through the development of its overseas labor contract program, as a response to the changes in the structure of its labor market, characterized, among others, by the increased flow of rural women to urban areas and abroad to seek for employment.[4] By the second half of the 1980s, the significance of migrant workers' remittances to the state's economy was already explicitly identified in the country's fourth five-year development plan, 1984/85-1988/89.[5]

The Indonesian government's policies in the last decade on the issue of migrant workers tend to be reactions to a range of frequently contradictory pressures. On the one hand, domestic economic and unemployment pressures have caused the government to continue to promote and facilitate the sending of Indonesians to work abroad. On the other hand, issues concerning human and workers' rights, raised by migrant-worker advocates, including local and international governmental and non-governmental organizations, have forced the government to take measures to address the issue. In addition, pressures also come from events such as the Asian financial crisis, domestic reform, and mass deportations of Indonesian migrant workers from Malaysia. Nevertheless, judging from the existing policies, it seems that in, most cases, economic interest is stronger than the will to address the various problems faced by Indonesian migrant workers or, in other words, perceived national interests tend to surpass migrant workers' interests.

Market demand is also a strong source of influence on government policies. It often determines where the government directs its attention and the initiatives undertaken. As described by Jones, in the early and mid-1980s, the Indonesian government's attention was focused more on the Middle East, instead of on Malaysia, mainly because of the high flow of workers to this region.[6] In fact, in 1981, the Indonesian Manpower Supply Association (IMSA), a consortium of labor recruiting agencies, was formed and licensed by the then Ministry of Manpower to find and arrange employment for Indonesian workers in the Middle East.

As problems and cases of abuse gain more publicity, the government has also become more responsive to these publicly highlighted unfortunate events experienced by migrant workers and to pressures such as those from civil society groups, including NGOs. In 2002, after the crisis in Nunukan, there was increased pressure on the government to work on a law concerning migrant work-

3 Cf. Pigay 2005, p. 96.
4 Cf. Ford 2002, p. 90, Piper and Iredale 2003, p. 21.
5 Cf. Jones 2000, p. 18.
6 Cf. ibid., p. 17.

ers.[7] Law No. 39/2004 on the Placement and Protection of Indonesian Workers Overseas was eventually passed in October 2004.

Responding to pressures related to the violation of human and workers' rights, on several occasions the Indonesian government has expressed the intention to stop sending domestic workers abroad and start training and sending skilled and/or semiskilled workers instead. Jones documented instances when intentions to take tough measures were announced.[8] She argued that all these statements of intent were more of "a public relations ploy" because they contradicted the real situation where the demand for domestic workers in Malaysia, Singapore, and Middle East was still high and the work force in Indonesia was still dominated by unskilled workers. Up to the present, this situation remains the same. The majority of Indonesians migrating to work abroad are still semiskilled and/or unskilled women working in the informal sector, mainly as domestic workers. Also, from time to time, the government has announced intentions to ban the sending of domestic workers abroad, usually triggered by reports of exploitation or abuse of Indonesian women. The work of Robinson, through a detailed discussion on the condition of Indonesian domestic workers in the Middle East in the 1980s, has highlighted the beginning of the political debates over what she identifies as prohibition versus protection.[9] She argued that the move to send more Indonesians to Malaysia was part of a move to quell criticism of the government's failure to protect its citizens in the Middle East. To date, the government continues to resort to prohibiting and banning migration when high profile cases are taken up by the media and arouse controversy. In 2009, after rampant cases of abuse in Malaysia were again exposed in the media, the Indonesian government declared a moratorium on sending Indonesian workers there. Although it cannot be confirmed whether Indonesian workers were actually prevented from going to Malaysia, the moratorium was used as a way to put pressure on the Malaysian government to start negotiating the revision of the 2006 MoU between the two countries. Robinson pointed out how certain stakeholders, including NGOs like SP, opposed prohibition as a solution.[10] As reflected in my interviews with the NGOs researched, their stand is still against total prohibition, on the grounds that poverty is still an issue in Indonesia and the government has not been able to come up with an alternative to employment abroad.[11] Thus, while the 2009 moratorium may be intended as an instrument of pressure on the Ma-

7 Cf. Ford 2005, p. 10.
8 Cf. Jones 2000, p. 81.
9 Cf. Robinson 2000.
10 Cf. ibid., p. 70.
11 Interview with Safitri, Salma on August 2, 2007, and Hidayah, Anis on November 18, 2008.

laysian government, a prolonged moratorium without any feasible alternatives will only increase illegal migration.

Despite some weaknesses, the Indonesian government has made efforts to improve the protection of its migrant workers. As acknowledged by *Komnas Perempuan* and SP in their country reports to the UN Special Rapporteur on the Human Rights of Migrants, the government took some initiatives to protect migrant workers by issuing and introducing regulations and guidelines for the migration process, and made various efforts at the ministerial level.[12] There have also been attempts to coordinate efforts between related state institutions. For example, in 1999 the Coordinating Body for the Placement of Migrant Workers or *Badan Koordinasi Penempatan Tenaga Kerja Indonesia* (BKPTKI) was formed by the Presidential Decree No. 29/1999. Positioned directly under the responsibility of the President, it consists of the MoMT as the chair, with representatives from the Ministries of Home Affairs and Regional Autonomy, Foreign Affairs, Justice and Human Rights, Education, Finance, Transport, Religious Affairs, Health, Women's Empowerment, the Police Department, and the Governor of Bank Indonesia.[13]

In general, the government has generated a number of policies to improve the regulation and management of labor migration. Accordingly, related ministries and departments have also taken some initiatives to implement those policies. However, there are differences within the government about what type of pressures they are more responsive to and how they respond. As an example, the MoMT seems to respond more to economic and unemployment pressures, while other ministries like the Ministry of Foreign Affairs and the State Ministry of Women's Empowerment tend to respond more to rights-based pressures. There are different types of pressure on the government of varied intensity and urgency, and which pressure will get the government's immediate response is also influenced by factors such as the government's interest and political will. Since these two factors may vary greatly among state institutions and even between individual government officers and staff from the same institution, one of the challenges for those, who intend to put pressure on the government, like the NGOs, is first to identify the right type of pressure to be applied and relate this to the interest and political will of the state institution concerned. To illustrate the problem, the next section looks into the efforts made by some related state institutions to show their differing attitudes toward the issue of migrant workers and the varied pressures to which they are more responsive.

12 Cf. Komnas Perempuan and SP 2002, 2003.
13 Cf. Komnas Perempuan and SP 2003, p. 14.

4.2 Efforts Made by State Institutions

Although the responsibility to regulate labor migration from Indonesia mainly rests with the MoMT, the complexity of the issue has required involvement of other related ministries. The Ministry of Foreign Affairs with its representative offices (embassies and consulates) in receiving countries handles bilateral agreements with receiving countries, manages consular issues, and protects and assists migrant workers facing problems during their employment abroad. The State Ministry for Women's Empowerment focuses on the gender concerns of women migrant workers. The Ministry of Home Affairs issues IDs, the Directorate General of Immigration within the Department of Law and Human Rights issues passports, and the Ministry of Health conducts pre-departure medical check-ups.[14]

A range of factors can be used to determine the authority and relative capabilities of each institution in dealing with the issue of labor migration. The mandate of each institution, which is reflected in its name, is the main determining factor, placing the primary responsibility and authority for regulating labor migration on the MoMT. This ministry formulates the content of both domestic and foreign policies on migrant workers. In the case of bilateral and multilateral agreements, negotiation and signing are conducted by the officials from the Ministry of Foreign Affairs, but the substance of the agreements is mostly determined by the MoMT.

Another way to determine the relative authority and capacity of these institutions is by looking at their allocated budget. Each year, the government sets its spending priorities with the priority usually put on fields such as public service, education, economy, defense, security, and health. Government priorities are also reflected in the budgets for each institution. Table 4.1 shows the budget allocations for key governmental institutions for the subject of labor migration.

The data does not directly show the particular capacities of each institution in dealing with the issue of migrant workers. Nevertheless, the table can be used as a general indication of the financial capacity of each institution in funding their programs and activities. For example, the data shows that the State Ministry of Women's Empowerment (SMoWE) has by far the smallest budget allocation, even compared to the newly established institution, the BNP2TKI. Moreover, since, within the SMoWE, programs related to the protection of Indonesian women migrant workers are only part of its many priorities, they are only allocated a small fraction of the budget. In comparison, as an institution mandated to manage the placement and protection of migrant workers, the BNP2TKI's budget allocation is fully devoted to programs related to migrant workers.

14 Cf. Komnas Perempuan and SP 2002, p. 16, ILO 2006, p. 9.

Table 4.1: Spending of Government Institutions and the House of Representatives (DPR) (in billion IDR)[15]

Year	Government Institutions	Spending Budget
2005	Department of Foreign Affairs	3,160.0
	Department of Manpower and Transmigration	1,068.3
	Department of Social Affairs	1,661.9
	State Ministry of Women's Empowerment	85.4
	DPR	673.7
2006	Department of Foreign Affairs	3,152.8
	Department of Manpower and Transmigration	2,069.4
	Department of Social Affairs	2,221.4
	State Ministry of Women's Empowerment	116.9
	DPR	939.9
2007	Department of Foreign Affairs	3,376.2
	Department of Manpower and Transmigration	2,451.1
	Department of Social Affairs	2,766.0
	State Ministry of Women's Empowerment	143.6
	DPR	1,068.7
2008	Department of Foreign Affairs	3,707.0
	Department of Manpower and Transmigration	2,352.5
	Department of Social Affairs	3,213.5
	State Ministry of Women's Empowerment	122.9
	DPR	1,283.4
	BNP2TKI	209.7
2009	Department of Foreign Affairs	4,112.5
	Department of Manpower and Transmigration	2,949.7
	Department of Social Affairs	3,270.1
	State Ministry of Women's Empowerment	111.8
	DPR	1,752.2
	BNP2TKI	244.7

Source: Ministry of Finance[16]

In short, financially, the SMoWE has less power compared to other institutions. In addition, as a state ministry, it does not have a department, has limited resources, and thus has limited authority and capability in implementing pro-

15 Each year, there are revised versions of the State's Income and Spending Budget (*Anggaran Pendapatan dan Belanja Negara*). The data included in this table is the actual spending for each year.

16 Departemen Keuangan Republik Indonesia 2010.

grams.[17] It is important to take such information into consideration, since some NGOs have considered this ministry as one of their alternative channels into the policy process, mainly because it has been more accommodative toward them.

Obviously, factors such as the scope and range of responsibilities, the size of each institution, the number of staff and the characteristics of the ministers and heads of institutions also need to be taken into account for a more holistic study of the capacity of each institution in dealing with the issue of migrant workers. Nevertheless, in an attempt to build up a general picture of the power relations among these institutions and their efforts to address the issue of migrant workers, the following section will briefly examine some of the actions taken by key government institutions. The discussion is aimed at showing how these institutions respond to various pressures, which, in many instances, can be contradictory. Analysis of the relative authority and responses of each state institution is also crucial as a basis for assessing whether the NGOs have engaged and worked with a relatively strategic partner within the government, which can actually assist them in channeling their voice into the policy process.

4.2.1 The Ministry of Manpower and Transmigration

At present the official name of the ministry responsible for the regulation of labor migration is the MoMT, overseeing the Department of Manpower and Transmigration, and dealing with the issues of transmigration and domestic and overseas employment.[18] Besides making policies to regulate Indonesian labor migration, the MoMT also has the authority to post labor attaches at Indonesian Embassies,[19] particularly in major receiving countries, decide whether to expand the overseas labor market to new destinations, and make agreements with new receiving countries.

In terms of the labor migration process, the ministry coordinates a wide range of activities, which include, among others, making, implementing, and monitoring policies, formulating the substance of bilateral and multilateral agreements,

17 In 2009, the ministry was changed to State Ministry of Women's Empowerment and Child Protection, and then to Ministry of Women's Empowerment and Child Protection. Nevertheless, it still has limited capacities in addressing the issues faced by Indonesian women migrant workers.

18 The fields of manpower and transmigration have not always been under one ministry. They have only been combined under the Kabinet Pembangunan II (1973-1978) and III (1978-1983) in the New Order Era and under the last three cabinets, Gotong Royong (2001-2004) and Indonesia Bersatu I and II (2004-2009 and 2009-2014), in the Reform Era.

19 Unfortunately, the number and outreach of these labor attaches are still limited.

issuing licenses for labor agencies, regulating, and even managing entry points like Terminal III at Soekarno-Hatta International Airport, checking paperwork requirements, and regulating and monitoring other issues related to migration process such as pre-departure training, insurance, placement, and repatriation, and mediating conflicts between stakeholders. At the provincial level, besides the provincial offices, this department has also established technical implementation units to specifically deal with the placement of migrant workers overseas. This unit, known as the Office of Indonesian Workers Overseas Placement Service or *Balai Pelayanan Penempatan Tenaga Kerja Indonesia* (BP2TKI) conducts most of the placement activities, and labor agencies at the regional level interact with the department through these units.

Making, implementing, and monitoring policies has always been a challenging combination of tasks for most ministries in Indonesia, with criticisms particularly directed toward their weaknesses in implementing and monitoring policies. The MoMT is also responsible for conducting and monitoring the implementation of the policies it produces. However, as observed by Santoso and Pramodhawardani, the staff is generally preoccupied with administrative activities, including checking whether the migrant workers' documents filed by labor agencies have fulfilled the requirements stated by regulations.[20]

With the ministry's workload, it is doubtful that it has enough resources and time to conduct proper monitoring, particularly of labor agencies and training centers. Furthermore, according to *Komnas Perempuan* and SP, the government does not have a well-established system to monitor and evaluate the performance of labor agencies.[21] Although the MoMT from time to time has reviewed and revoked the licenses of labor agencies, the monitoring system is not well-established and the standard for revoking licenses is more related to financial aspects, rather than to protection of migrant workers.

In addition, as criticized by migrant workers' advocates, the MoMT had to carry out the functions of both the placement and protection of migrant workers, with the latter function generally marginalized. Since the ministry is also responsible for reducing domestic unemployment and underemployment rates, increased placement of Indonesian workers overseas has been given higher priority than their protection. Migrant workers advocates have criticized the policies and regulations produced by the MoMT for concentrating more on facilitating labor export and on the managerial and operational aspects of labor export, rather than

20 Cf. Santoso 2006, pp. 23-24, and Pramodhawardani 2006, p. 63.

21 Cf. Komnas Perempuan and SP 2002, p. 17. As a comparison, the Philippines, with its Philippine Overseas Employment Administration (POEA), have different types of inspections which include regular inspections, spot inspections, and regional inspections.

setting up protection mechanisms.[22] Indonesia's relationship with receiving countries has also been a higher priority compared to the protection of migrant workers. As described by Jones, in the 1980s, when there were reports of abuses of migrant workers in Saudi Arabia, the then Minister of Manpower's response was to issue a decree that required prospective migrant workers to sign a declaration stating that they would not speak to the press.[23]

Despite its tendency to focus more on the placement aspect of labor migration, the MoMT has made efforts intended to improve labor migration mechanisms. One of the main issues faced by prospective migrant workers is their inability to pay the initial fees.[24] To address this issue, the ministry has tried to assist migrant workers to get access to bank loans. In 2005, the government conducted a trial for this loan program for migrant workers departing for Taiwan.[25] Since prospective migrant workers and their family members are required to open bank accounts both in Indonesia and Taiwan, the program also aimed to assist the transfer of remittances.

The MoMT has also attempted to provide assistance through tripartite arbitration of cases of disputes such as unpaid salary, which involves the government, migrant workers, and the recruiting agency.[26] The process usually begins with negotiations between the migrant worker and the recruitment agency, and if agreement is not reached, the MoMT becomes involved as a mediator in a tripartite negotiation. However, as argued by *Komnas Perempuan* and SP, it has not been easy to access this assistance and since the tripartite agreement does not impose sanctions on unresponsive agencies, this legal channel is often disregarded by recruitment agencies.[27]

Regulation and management of labor migration has been mainly placed under the authority of the MoMT. Despite the changes in name and scope of the ministry, its policies and regulations have remained similar to the New Order Era in the way it focuses more on the placement rather than the protection aspect of labor migration. I would argue that this is due to the fact that the main demands that they need to respond to remain increasing remittances and decreasing unemployment. Thus, when there needs to be a choice between placement and protection, the first usually prevails.

A quite significant change in the system occurred after Law No. 39/2004 was passed. The law, supported by the Presidential Instruction No. 6/2006 on the Re-

22 Cf. ibid., p. 16.
23 Cf. Jones 2000, p. 18.
24 Many prospective migrant workers are trapped in debt for paying the initial fees because they borrow from illegal sources which charge high interest.
25 Cf. Poeloengan 2006, p. 27.
26 This does not apply to undocumented migrant workers.
27 Cf. Komnas Perempuan and SP 2002, p. 23, 2003, p. 45.

form Policy of Placement and Protection System of Indonesian Workers Overseas, mandated the establishment of the BNP2TKI. Until the beginning of 2007, the structure of the Department of Manpower and Transmigration included the Directorate General of Overseas Placement Development with the tasks of formulating and implementing policies on the development and placement of workers overseas.[28] After the BNP2TKI was established in 2007, the task of conducting placement of workers overseas was handed to the BNP2TKI. In other words, the BNP2TKI was assigned the operational function, allowing the ministry to concentrate more on the regulating function. However, in reality, this division of functions was difficult to implement. Different interpretation of what should be the responsibility and authority of each institution generated overlapping actions, which led to tensions between the two institutions.

4.2.2 The BNP2TKI

As a non-departmental institution, the BNP2TKI reports directly to the President and is supposed to handle the operational aspect of the placement and protection of migrant workers. The head of this institution is positioned at the same level as a minister, and Jumhur Hidayat, a former labor activist, was chosen to take this position. Most of his deputies and staff come from the former Directorate General of Overseas Employment Development. The MoMT handed over the operational tasks, 522 staff, allocated budget for 2007, and authority over the Office of Indonesian Workers Overseas Placement and Protection Service or *Balai Pelayanan Penempatan dan Perlindungan TKI* (BP3TKI).[29] As an attempt to coordinate efforts among other related government institutions, some deputies and directors in this institution were taken from institutions such as the Department of Foreign Affairs, the Department of Law and Human Rights, the Department of Health, and even the police force.[30]

There were great expectations that this institution would bring changes to the labor migration system. Less than a year after its establishment, however, migrant workers' advocates had started to criticize the institution for slow progress, corruption, and collusion practices, and for still focusing more on placement rather than protection of migrant workers. They also argue that the fact that most of the staff are from the Department of Manpower and Transmigration has made it difficult to change their perception of the issue of migrant workers. The Minis-

28 Cf. Depnakertrans 2008.
29 Cf. Depnakertrans 2007, p. 10.
30 Interview with Hidayat, Jumhur on July 30, 2007.

ter of Manpower and Transmigration for 2005-2009, Erman Suparno,[31] stated that, although the BNP2TKI is directly responsible to the President, it will coordinate with the ministry to avoid overlap.[32] Jumhur Hidayat also stated that in conducting his work, he coordinates with related ministers, including the Minister of Manpower and Transmigration.[33] Nevertheless, since the beginning of its establishment, there are already indications of overlapping actions between the the BNP2TKI and the MoMT.

It is still difficult to clearly determine the type of pressure to which this institution is more responsive. Jumhur Hidayat stated that his institution tried to give balanced attention to the placement and protection aspects of labor migration.[34] He said that the two words should be pronounced in one breath, indicating that there should not be any separation or imbalance of priorities between the two aspects. Nevertheless, while this institution has managed to improve some economic aspects of labor migration by abolishing some fees, increasing the minimum salary in some receiving countries, and black-listing errant labor agencies,[35] it has not been able to significantly improve the protection of Indonesian women workers from other types of abuses, particularly physical and sexual ones. A comprehensive protection mechanism is yet to be established and operated. Although this institution has tried to display a more accommodative attitude toward migrant workers' advocates, including NGOs, it still shows preferences on who to work with.[36]

In 2010, due to a number of factors such as the continuous tensions between the BNP2TKI and the MoMT, the bad practices conducted by its staff, and its failure to improve the protection of Indonesian migrant workers, there were already calls for the abolition of the BNP2TKI. At the time of completing this book, the BNP2TKI had not been abolished, but the tensions and overlapping actions between this institution and the MoMT continue, to the point that labor agencies began to express their concern over the division of authority between the two institutions in conducting placement of Indonesian workers.

31 Erman Suparno replaced Fahmi Idris after Susilo Bambang Yudhoyono reshuffled his cabinet in 2005.

32 Cf. Depnakertrans 2007, pp. 10-11.

33 Interview with Hidayat, Jumhur on July 30, 2007.

34 Ibid.

35 Ibid.

36 The BNP2TKI's close relationship with an Indonesian migrant workers union, SBMI, was shown in some of their statements and cooperation in conducting information dissemination programs at the provincial level (Interview with Hidayat, Jumhur on July 30, 2007). They also signed a political contract before the 2009 election, which was criticized by the NGOs (see further discussion in chapter 7).

4.2.3 The Ministry of Foreign Affairs and the Indonesian Embassy in Kuala Lumpur

Out of the seven Directorate Generals in the Ministry of Foreign Affairs (MoFA), the tasks of at least three directors were related to the issues faced by women migrant workers, namely, the Directorate of Human Rights and Humanitarian Affairs under the Directorate General of Multilateral Affairs, the Directorate of Economic and Sociocultural Affairs under the Directorate General of Legal Affairs and International Treaties, and the Directorate of Protection of Indonesian Citizens and Legal Entities under the Directorate General of Protocol and Consular Affairs.[37]

Since 1998, there have been changes within the ministry which indicate greater attention to the protection of Indonesian citizens abroad. The changes include making "improving the quality of the service and protection of Indonesian citizens abroad" one of the tasks of the MoFA.[38] In relation to this, in 2002, when the ministry restructured its organization, the position of the Director for Protection of Indonesian Citizens and Legal Entities was established with the main task of handling policies and technical standards relating to protection and legal assistance to Indonesian citizens and institutions.[39] As for the issue of migrant workers, the objectives of Indonesian foreign policy for 2004-2009 included increasing cooperation with country users of Indonesian manpower and decreasing the problems faced by Indonesian citizens and institutions abroad.

While the MoMT formulates the substance of bilateral agreements between Indonesia and receiving countries, the negotiation and establishment of agreements are handled by the MoFA. The fact that bilateral agreements concerning migrant workers are handled by the Director for Economic and Sociocultural Affairs shows that the issue is considered to be more of an economic issue than as a political one. Accordingly, the degree of urgency of this issue is considered moderate compared to other issues categorized as political. Nevertheless, the MoFA has made a range of efforts to improve the protection of Indonesian citizens abroad, which include: the establishment of Citizen Services at the Representative Offices in a number of receiving countries[40] to provide quick, cheap, and friendly services to citizens abroad; providing a same day passport service at the Indonesian Embassy in Kuala Lumpur; making bilateral agreements on the Mandatory Consular Notification which require the signing countries to notify Indonesian Representatives if there is any Indonesian who has legal matters in

37 Cf. Deplu 2010.
38 Cf. Deplu 2007.
39 Cf. ibid.
40 Singapore, Seoul, Bandar Sri Begawan, Amman, Damascus, and Doha.

that country; and, specifically for migrant workers, developing an in-flight movie, a foreign manual, or a "bible" containing information on working overseas, and a web for migrant workers which provides important information for workers leaving Indonesia.[41]

Since the end of the New Order, along with the national reform, the MoFA has undertaken its own internal reform. Improved service for the protection of Indonesian citizens overseas has become one of the main targeted changes. The ministry has also made efforts to increase its professionalism, restructure its organization, and be more open to civil society. The ministry's intention to reach out to other stakeholders can be seen in its actions such as developing forums to hear the views of NGOs concerned with the issues faced by migrant workers.[42] The ministry has also conducted and been involved in various seminars and workshops on the issue, such as conducting a seminar on "The Protection of Indonesian Migrant Workers in the Context of the UN" in Jakarta in 2003, and conducting a meeting of expert groups on "Optimizing Citizen Protection in Handling the Issue of Indonesian Migrant Workers in the Middle East" in Medan in 2007.[43]

As mandated by Law No. 39/2004, protection for Indonesian workers during their employment in foreign countries is provided by Representative Offices of the Republic of Indonesia in receiving countries. The Indonesian Embassy provides protection, assists migrant workers who have problems with their employers or agencies, provides them with temporary shelters, brokers a consultation (*musyawarah*) between employers, agencies, and migrant workers, and, when cases have to go through the courts, helps in providing lawyers by coordinating with local law enforcers.[44]

As in some other Indonesian embassies in major receiving countries, the embassy in Kuala Lumpur has a shelter built within the embassy's area. It is mostly occupied by women migrant workers who have to wait for redress, whether with the police, a court or an employer. The embassy provides their daily needs such as rice, meat, spices, cooking oil, and gas for cooking, and even personal needs such as toiletries and feminine pads.[45] The funding for operating the shelter, which mainly comes from the Departments of Manpower and Transmigration and Foreign Affairs,[46] is usually not enough to meet demand, because most of the time the shelter is overcrowded and since many cases may take a long time to

41 Cf. Menteri Luar Negeri Indonesia 2008 and interview with Adamhar, Ferry on July 6, 2007.
42 Cf. Kompas, October 30, 2004.
43 Cf. Deplu 2007.
44 Cf. Sutaat 2005, pp. 21-22.
45 Cf. Wawa 2005, p. 34.
46 Cf. ibid., p. 35.

process, some women migrant workers may have to stay at the shelter for months or even years. There are times when members of the staff of the embassy donate their own money to help migrant workers in the shelter.[47] Moreover, the embassy is neither a crisis center nor equipped as one. As argued by Sutaat and Nuryana, since the service is temporary in nature and focuses more on consular aspects, many post-abuse problems such as stress, insomnia, and trauma have not been addressed adequately.[48] The embassy's staff has tried to help by identifying and taking records of the problems faced by migrant workers and provide counseling services. Nevertheless, since they are not specifically prepared and trained to do this, the social service provided is still far from adequate.

The type of services available in Representative Offices in each city or country varies, depending on the capacities, workloads, and initiatives of the staff. As a comparison, the Indonesian Embassy in Singapore tried to assist migrant workers waiting at their shelter by employing them in the homes of staff and paying them adequately.[49] The embassy also provides training for skills like language, sewing, and beauty salon skills for both migrant workers at the shelter and for those who are still working and given days off to come to the embassy. There is also a 24 hour phone and text messaging service for migrant workers.

The Indonesian Embassy in Kuala Lumpur is a major embassy, staffed by First Secretaries, attaches (including labor attaches) and a Senior Liaison Officer from the police force.[50] Although the embassy had a corruption problem,[51] it has made attempts to improve its organization and performance including the provision of services to Indonesian citizens. On President Susilo Bambang Yudhoyono's visit in January 2008, the embassy reported the following improvements: passport processing was shortened from 41 days to three hours, service booths increased from eight to 25, the service area was equipped with an electronic queuing system, toilets, and air-conditioned waiting areas, and the number of local staff was increased from 74 to 137. The facilities of the shelter within the embassy were also improved to accommodate 70 beds and other facilities. Moreover, the embassy, through the Placement and Protection Task Force, could restore around 3.5 billion IDR (around 350,000 USD) of migrant workers' money to them, mostly related to violation by the insurance consortium. The embassy also made an effort to empower the women migrant workers staying at the shelter by employing them at the immigration service. After two years of inactivity, the embassy's website was also reactivated, providing information

47 Cf. Sutaat 2005, p. 22.
48 Cf. Sutaat and Nuryana 2005, p. 235.
49 Cf. Muchtar 2005, p. 277.
50 Cf. Embassy of the Republic of Indonesia Kuala Lumpur Malaysia 2008.
51 As widely published in the mass media the former Ambassador, Rusdiharjo, and some other former staff, were sentenced for corruption in 2008.

needed by Indonesian citizens. One factor that determined the above improvements was the implementation of a corporate culture at the embassy, which entails taking the side (*berpihak*) of Indonesian citizens, improving services so that they are easy, cheap, quick, comfortable, and friendly, and providing maximum protection by what was called "addressing problems without problems".[52]

The changes within the MoFA, including the Representative Offices in receiving countries, particularly the one in Kuala Lumpur, show improved attention toward the protection of Indonesian migrant workers overseas. Although these changes may partly be seen as the ministry's response to human rights pressures from migrant workers' advocates, including NGOs, I would argue that it is more a result of the ministry's internal reform. Many, including Ferry Adamhar, gave the credit to the leadership of Hassan Wirajuda, who was Minister for Foreign Affairs in two cabinets, from 2001 to 2009.[53] Although there were cases of corruption, particularly relating to document processing fees at the embassies, in general this ministry is more likely to respond to human rights pressures and to its perceptions of national sovereignty and interests rather than to economic pressures.

4.2.4 The State Ministry of Women's Empowerment

The Indonesian government's program for women began to be implemented in 1978 with the appointment of a Junior Minister on Women's Role (*Menteri Muda Peranan Wanita*). Since then, the responsibility for dealing with women's issues has been held by a state ministry which does not have a department, has limited resources, and only works at the policy leve,l not at the operational level.[54] Thus, in most cases it has to coordinate with other institutions in implementing policies. A quite significant change in the name of the ministry was made after 1998, when the wording "Women's Role", which was generally used during the New Order Era, was changed to "Women's Empowerment",[55] signifying a shift in the way women's position in society is perceived, from being the companion (*pendamping*) of their husbands to independent beings who have the potential to flourish by themselves. Although this change of perception can be seen as an improvement, the ministry remains a state ministry with limited resources, budget and authority, thus there is still a question of how much power it has to

52 Cf. Deplu 2007.

53 Interview with Adamhar, Ferry on July 6, 2007.

54 Interview with Setiabudi, Safruddin on June 19, 2007.

55 In the last cabinet, Kabinet Indonesia Bersatu II (2009-2014), the naming became the State Ministry of Women's Empowerment and Child Protection, and then the Ministry of Women's Empowerment and Child Protection.

actually influence policies concerning women, including those on women migrant workers.

In 2005, the SMoWE established the position of the Deputy for the Protection of Women. As explained by Safruddin Setiabudi, the then Deputy Assistant for the Protection of Women Workers, his section deals with the protection of women workers both inside and outside the country.[56] The initiative to establish a special deputy within the ministry which gives more attention to issues faced by women migrant workers came quite late, considering that Indonesian women have migrated to work abroad since the 1970s, and that since then they have been facing various problems, including those related to their status as women. The delay was highly influenced by the fact that, during the New Order Era, this ministry was expected to focus on the traditional women's roles as wife and mother.

The SMoWE has been known for its more accommodative and cooperative attitude toward civil society compared to other Ministries, particularly the MoMT. In 2003, the SMoWE conducted a pilot project with the Women's Movement for the Protection of Migrant Worker Rights or *Gerakan Perempuan untuk Perlindungan Buruh Migran* (GPPBM), a coalition of women's groups. The project aimed to improve the regulatory environment for women migrant workers, which entailed the three phases of pre-departure education and preparation, in-country support services, and post-return assistance for overseas women workers.[57]

Although the SMoWE has shown increased concern toward the issue of women migrant workers, due to their limitation as a state ministry, their influence over policies on migrant workers remains limited. Nevertheless, as discussed further in later chapters in this book, many NGOs have continued to cooperate with this ministry in conducting programs to address the issue of Indonesian migrant workers.

4.2.5 The Ministry of Social Affairs

As reflected by its relatively large budget, the Ministry of Social Affairs is quite a big ministry. It gained a good reputation from its role in addressing the humanitarian crisis that happened in Nunukan in 2002 when thousands of Indonesian illegal migrant workers were deported from Malaysia. This ministry was praised by some migrant workers advocates for its quick response to the situation. After the Nunukan crisis, the ministry set up a new division focusing on migrant workers: the Directorate of Social Assistance for Abuse Victims and

56 Interview with Setiabudi, Safruddin on June 19, 2007.
57 Cf. Komnas Perempuan and SP 2003, p. 40.

Migrant Workers, which is placed under the Directorate General of Social Assistance and Support.[58] It also cooperated with civil society groups in a pilot project to establish a crisis center in Jakarta for victims of violence, which was intended to address various problems faced by migrant domestic workers such as mental and physical health and legal issues.

Although this ministry does not have a major role in the formulation of policies on migrant workers, its institutional mandate, its rapid response toward some critical migrant workers' issues, and its initiatives in addressing some problems faced by migrant workers have highlighted its significance in efforts to protect migrant workers.

4.2.6 Other Related Ministries, the Parliament, and Regional/Local Governments

The above are ministries which are responsible for addressing the issue of migrant workers or which have special deputies or sections assigned to deal with aspects of labor migration. Other government institutions are also involved in the process of labor migration, but do not have special sections assigned to the issue. Their association with the issue occurs because, at some points in the migration process, workers and labor agencies have to deal with offices which are under the authority of these institutions.

The migrant workers are required to have IDs, which are issued by local government offices under the authority of the Ministry of Home Affairs and Regional Autonomy. Passports, visas, and other documents needed to travel and work overseas are issued by the Directorate General of Immigration under the Ministry of Justice and Human Rights. The education aspects of Indonesian citizens are overseen by the Ministry of Education. Flows of remittances through banking institutions are overseen by the Ministry of Finance and the Governor of Bank Indonesia. For their travel, migrant workers are assisted by transport providers which are regulated by the Ministry of Transport. The Ministry of Religious Affairs is usually concerned with instances such as when Indonesian women workers migrate to Islamic countries in the Middle East and/or the domestic workers have to work in households that practice a religion different from their own. Medical examinations and treatments for abused migrant workers are handled by the Indonesian hospitals under the authority of the Ministry of Health. In the case of abuses or conflicts, the Police Department may be involved.

The above institutions have their specific roles, responsibilities, and authority within the migration system. At the ministerial level, economic interest may not

58 Cf. ibid., p. 41.

be dominant. However, as shown in the cases exposed by various media and migrant workers' advocates, at the operational level there are bad practices which are frequently motivated by the economic interests of individual staff such as charging unofficial fees for the service they are providing.

Since 1998, Indonesia's House of Representatives, the Dewan Perwakilan Rakyat (DPR) has also gone through a reform process. As argued by Eldridge, after 1998 the Indonesian parliament had to leave its "rubber stamp" role behind and democratize internally.[59] The reform has brought changes to the structure of the parliament and the number of party representatives and their seats. As described further in Chapter 6 on the NGOs efforts to influence the process of making Law No. 39/2004, there are also changes in the way the parliament interacts with civil society groups and the government. Conducting public hearings and audiences and other forms of input gathering like seminars and workshops as a part of policy formulation has become a common practice in the parliament. The parliament has also shown a degree of critical scrutiny of the government's policies, and there are instances when the parliamentary commission responsible for the issue of migrant workers questions government policies and actions or non-action toward particular cases concerning migrant workers.

The significance of local/regional governments derives from the fact that they have authority in the transit and origin areas of migrant workers. Moreover, with the launching of Indonesia's decentralization policies in the late 1990s, more power has been transferred from the central to the regional governments. One of the effects of these policies is that regional governments have more authority in managing their incomes. As a result, regions with more natural resources, industries, businesses, and strategic locations have been able to develop their economies better than the others. This has created and widened the economic and social gaps between regions. For some regions migration of their people to work abroad has become an alternative solution, with remittances as their potential sources of income. With the regional autonomy policy, the roles of local governments, particularly those of origin and transit areas, have become more significant in the management of labor migration. They need to make policies which facilitate the placement and protection of migrant workers. Because most of these local governments have limited understanding, knowledge, and capacities in formulating such policies, they require assistance including from migrant workers' advocates. As discussed further in Chapter 6, NGOs have been proactive in assisting the formulation of these local policies.

Local governments' initiatives to make policies which regulate labor migration from their area are largely a response to the economic pressure of gaining income and reducing unemployment in their area. This seems to be the reason

59 Cf. Eldridge 2005, p. 155.

why migrant workers' advocates see the need to ensure that there is a considerable attention toward the protection aspect of the policies.

4.3 Conclusion

This chapter has set out some of the government's policies and efforts to regulate and manage Indonesian labor migration and to improve the labor migration system and mechanisms. In order to describe the dynamics within the state, this chapter has outlined efforts made by some of the main state institutions involved. Particularly relevant to the issue of migrant workers, Law No. 39/2004 with its supporting regulations and the Presidential Instruction No. 6/2006 mandated reform of the placement and protection system for migrant workers. Nevertheless, the existing policies, system, and mechanisms are still deficient. The laws and regulations have loopholes. Implementation is slow and eroded by bad practices. Coordination among related ministries and other governmental institutions is still weak. Moreover, some newly-established institutions and sections under existing institutions are yet to demonstrate results and achievements. Although most of these policies and efforts can be criticized for being too little and too late, it has to be acknowledged that some concerned entities, for various reasons and with varying capacities, have made attempts at reform.

This chapter has shown that the Indonesian government's policies and actions on the issue of migrant workers tend to be responses to often contradictory pressures. Economic and unemployment pressures require the government to continue facilitating the sending of Indonesians to work abroad and expanding their market, while pressures from migrant workers‘ advocates have demanded that the government should increase its protection of migrant workers. This chapter has also shown that the responses of each state institution towards these pressures may vary, depending on their interests and political will. Thus, the main implication of this chapter is that for NGOs to successfully work with and influence a particular state institution, they need to have a good understanding of what type of pressure is likely to generate a response from the institution.

Finally, the situation described in this chapter shows that, due to various limitations, there are matters that cannot be handled by the government alone and urgently require assistance and cooperation from other stakeholders. This leads to the questions to be addressed in the next chapter: Where are NGOs positioned within the existing system and mechanisms, and how do they initiate and maintain their involvement?

5. Contextualizing Indonesian NGOs' Involvement in the Labor Migration System

This chapter aims to understand the context within which Indonesian NGOs conduct their activism on behalf of women migrant workers. It identifies the impacts of changes in the national and international political environment on the activism of NGOs, particularly those concerned with the issue of women migrant workers. It also investigates how the two NGOs researched, SP and Migrant CARE, began and maintain their engagement with the issue.

The chapter starts by briefly looking at the positions and activities of Indonesian NGOs before and after *Reformasi*. The fall of the New Order, which was partly due to the efforts of civil society, including NGOs, resulted in a shift of the political context in Indonesia. This shift and ongoing democratic reforms since 1998 have led to a more open political system that allows civil society to act openly and to be more involved in the policy process. Along with increasing national and international support for this trend, the political changes have resulted in an increase in the number and the level of activity of NGOs. Furthermore, the poor social and economic conditions after the economic crisis in 1997 required all stakeholders, including NGOs, to participate in national efforts to recover from the crisis. Increased legitimacy for NGOs' existence and involvement also comes from the requirements of international donor institutions. Their offers to assist Indonesia after the crisis were mostly linked to themes such as "good governance", "transparency", and "democratization", where participation of civil society, including NGOs, became indispensable.

The question remains as to how these changes have affected the activities of Indonesian NGOs, particularly those involved with the issue of migrant workers. Thus, the second section of this chapter focuses on NGO activism on the issue of women migrant workers. It starts by describing how the issue of women migrant workers initially caught the attention of Indonesian NGOs. This chapter shows how initiatives at the regional and international levels have brought more opportunities and support for such NGO activities. It then continues to examine briefly the management of labor migration in the Philippines, which is commonly considered as best practice. Besides showing how labor activism in Indonesia had a rather late start and comparing what has been done in these two countries, this section is most importantly aimed at identifying what can be learned from the Philippines' experience. Finally, the last section introduces the two NGOs researched, SP and Migrant CARE, by examining their key organizational features, how they initiated their involvement in the issue of women migrant workers and how they frame this issue.

5.1 Indonesian NGOs before and after *Reformasi*

5.1.1 NGOs in New Order Indonesia

Non-governmental organizations have existed as a significant part of Indonesia's civil society for many decades. As in many other places in the world, the initiators of these organizations were "concerned middle-class" people such as ex-student activists, lawyers, academics, researchers, and religious leaders.[1] This characteristic has been viewed both as a strength of NGOs – having the more educated elements of the society running organizations – and as a weakness, as compared to trade unions or in the case of this research, migrant workers' organizations, for being run by those who have not experienced the actual problem, thus making it difficult for the activists to fully understand and address the problems faced by those they are supporting. Moreover, unlike trade unions, NGOs are not accountable to members who encounter daily the working conditions they seek to improve. According to Ford, service delivery NGOs in Indonesia could be traced back to the 1950s.[2] This type of NGO concentrates more on activities like relief and delivering goods and services, rather than on activities such as policy advocacy and political movements. By the 1970s, the role of NGOs gained recognition although this was often instrumental, limited to complementing and assisting government in providing services and conducting programs in communities which could not be reached by the government.[3]

NGOs' limited room for movement continued during the New Order Era with their activities being closely monitored and controlled by the government within an authoritarian and centralized political context. The closed political system did not allow civil society participation in governance. Dissident opinions and stances were discouraged and critics of the government were silenced. Responding to this condition, in order to maintain their existence, NGOs in Indonesia tried hard to appear more "cooperative" to the government. Their organizations were often established in the form of foundations (*yayasan*), which were considered less threatening due to their lack of a mass membership. Also, this form allowed them to evade the tight control stipulated by laws and regulations such as the law on mass organizations, *UU Organisasi Kemasyarakatan* No. 8/1985, under

1 Cf. Hadiwinata 2003, p. 91.
2 Cf. Ford 2004, p. 106.
3 Cf. Antlöv et al. 2006, p. 148.

which mass organizations that conducted activities considered subversive or threatening to national security and order could be dissolved.[4] NGOs also made great efforts to appear non-political by focusing on development issues and conducting small scale programs. As noted by Eldridge, even when NGOs were supporting the formation of independent groups, they made sure that the activities appeared developmental rather than political.[5] Therefore, Indonesian NGOs during the New Order Era were commonly associated with charitable, humanitarian, or local small-scale works,[6] focusing on the social and economic aspects of development. Nevertheless, even with the limited space for civil society activism during the New Order, NGOs were still able to develop their activism, which, according to Eldridge, in due course enabled them to improve their networking capacities so that they could engage in policy dialogue with relevant authorities.[7] They also used public advocacy to reach out to wider constituencies and place issues such as the environment, public health, consumer rights, the status of women, and human rights on the public agenda.

Although in many instances Indonesian NGOs needed to work with the government to access services and resources for the people, they also tried hard not to be identified with the government, a delicate relationship which Eldridge described as "critical collaboration" or "loyal opposition".[8] The contests between government efforts to maintain control over civil society and NGOs' efforts to maintain independence while preserving their existence are reflected in the changing terminology used for NGOs in Indonesia. As noted by Eldridge, at the beginning of the 1980s there was an initiative to use the term "self-reliant community institutions" or *Lembaga Swadaya Masyarakat* (LSM) which was considered a less confronting term as compared to *Organisasi Non-Pemerintah* (*Ornop*), a direct translation of non-governmental organization.[9] At about the same time, although the New Order still considered the NGOs' role as instrumental, it had opened up to NGO participation in development. The NGOs' focus on community development gave a degree of assurance to the government that they would not take on grassroots political activities.[10]

According to Ford, economic liberalization, the end of the Cold War, and the period of political openness (*keterbukaan*) in Indonesia toward the end of the 1980s contributed to the raised expectations that NGOs would take more direct

4 Cf. Nyman 2006, p. 51.
5 Cf. Eldridge 1995, p. 28.
6 Cf. ibid., p. 5.
7 Cf. Eldridge 2005, p. 165.
8 Cf. Eldridge 1995, p. 11.
9 Cf. ibid., pp. 12 and 14. Nevertheless, the usage of the English term NGO could still be found in the international context and, to a limited extent, in Indonesia.
10 Cf. Hadiwinata 2003, p. 91.

and confrontational approach.[11] Changes started to surface from the mid-1980s and into the 1990s when students and informally organized networks began to confront the government openly, and NGOs working on issues like labor, legal rights, and the environment started to develop their movements by adopting an advocacy approach and monitoring state agencies.[12] By the 1990s, more NGOs established advocacy divisions within their organizations.[13] Hadiwinata considers this development in the early 1990s, which he identified as a "move toward empowerment approach", driven by several forces including the radicalization of students' movements, the return of graduates from overseas to work as academics and researchers and the increasing repression, exploitation and marginalization of the lower class.[14]

Besides the NGOs' ability to provide various services within the context of development, another factor that enabled them to prevail within the stringently controlled political context was support from the international community.[15] As argued by Antlöv et al., one of the factors that contributed to the growth of NGOs in Indonesia was the fact that more donors realized how important it was to have a close cooperation with NGOs to achieving their social goals.[16] International organizations perceived NGOs as potential actors in achieving "sustainable democratization" and "sustainable development" and used financial sanctions to put pressure on the government to allow NGO involvement.[17] One of the international institutions that demanded greater NGO involvement was the World Bank, which claimed to obtain quicker and more accurate feedback on the impact of policy at grassroots level from NGOs, rather than depending on the government bureaucracy.[18]

In 1998, the New Order Era ended and was replaced by the *Reformasi* Era, which was commonly claimed, or at least expected, to be an era of change toward a more democratic Indonesia. Literature on this reform movement in Indonesia generally acknowledges the role of NGOs in pushing for the change to happen.[19] Nevertheless, years after the *Reformasi* Era began Indonesia was still to recover from problems such as unequal social and economic condition and ethnic and religious tensions. The condition is worsened by weak leadership, competition among regions which have gained more power due to decentraliza-

11 Cf. Ford 2004, p. 106.
12 Cf. Eldridge 1995, pp. 2 and 5.
13 Cf. Antlöv et al. 2006, p. 150.
14 Cf. Hadiwinata 2003, pp. 110-12.
15 Cf. Eldridge 1995, p. 29, Antlöv et al. 2006, p. 149.
16 Cf. Antlöv et al. 2006, p. 149.
17 Cf. Eldridge 1995, pp. 20 and 29.
18 Cf. ibid., p. 30.
19 Cf. Gumay 2002, Nyman 2006.

tion policies and uncertain direction of the transformation and reform. In this context, the next section attempts to answer the questions: What changes have really occurred and what opportunities are available for NGO activism?

5.1.2 Post-New Order, NGOs in *Reformasi* Indonesia

The economic crisis that hit Asian countries, including Indonesia, in 1997 triggered the fall of Soeharto's regime. Nevertheless, as argued by authors like Nyman, indications of the decline in regime control had started to show in 1996 when demands for democracy, justice, media freedom, equality and elimination of corruption, collusion and nepotism intensified.[20] Rather than discussing how Indonesian NGOs became one of the agents of reform that played a significant role in bringing the New Order to an end, this section is focused more on how the *Reformasi* Era affects Indonesian NGO activism.

The *Reformasi* Era is associated with greater freedoms of expression, assembly and the media, which have allowed more room for civil society to grow. Particularly during the early years of *Reformasi* Era, there was rapid growth in civil society organizations; Antlöv described it as "the rising era of civil society in Indonesia".[21] According to Hadiwinata, the increased number, now estimated to be in the tens of thousands, is partly due to the removal of regulations that controlled organizational activities.[22] After the financial crisis in 1997, more NGOs were established, mostly for distributing loans and grants from international development agencies such as the World Bank, the IMF, and USAID, and to facilitate the democratic transition.[23] Involvement of civil society organizations like NGOs was one of the conditionalities for international development aid, funding, and projects, particularly for monitoring and evaluating the implementation. Much of the international aid was channeled through projects such as poverty alleviation and social safety nets. Donor institutions like the IMF and the World Bank continue to pressure the government to consult with civil society representatives.[24] This was a period when establishing NGOs was lucrative and since establishing one was not as difficult as before, there were those whom Hadiwinata called "overnight operators",[25] deriving personal benefit from development

20 Cf. Nyman 2006, p. 50.
21 Cf. Antlöv 2006, p. 147.
22 Cf. Hadiwinata 2003, p. 113.
23 Cf. ibid.
24 Cf. Nyman 2006, p. 201.
25 Cf. Hadiwinata 2003, p. 114.

funds.[26] This leads to the issue of NGOs' accountability. Along with the growth of the NGO sector came an increasing call for accountability within it. Civil society organizations' internal governance and external performance have become subject to greater public scrutiny, including in the media. As argued by Antlöv et al., like the government, NGOs may be corrupt and lose focus without a code of ethics, accountability mechanisms, and transparent control.[27] One of the critiques of the rapid growth of civil society is related to what Antlöv et al. define as quantity versus quality.[28] The balance between the increased number of NGOs and the quality of their activities and services is still debatable.

A shift in how Indonesian NGOs perceived and conducted their activities was shown in the way they identified their organizations. Nyman's interviews showed an increasing preference to use the term *Organisasi Non Pemerintah*, instead of the "softer" and more "cooperative" term, *Lembaga Swadaya Masyarakat*.[29] This indicates a change in NGO circles toward a more political stance, which entails more open expressions of their agenda. Nevertheless, it does not necessarily translate to a total shift from the development focus. As observed by Hadiwinata, a few years into the *Reformasi* Era the existence of both development and movement-oriented NGOs was still relevant for at least two reasons.[30] For the development NGOs, the reason lay in the growing poverty due to the failure of structural adjustment policies and social security system, and decreased government subsidies. At the same time, continuous conflicts and chaos throughout Indonesia decreased faith in the democratization process, particularly among those from the middle-class who longed for the return of order and stability even if it entailed control over political activities. Thus, the presence and activism of movement NGOs were needed to keep the democratization process going. The main themes of the Indonesian democratization process – good governance, accountability, and transparency – have also encouraged the growth of watchdog organizations which monitor state and political institutions.[31]

Changes have also occurred in the way the government perceives and interacts with civil society, including NGOs. Nyman noted attempts to allow greater in-

26 This phenomenon of establishing NGOs to gain personal benefit is not entirely new in Indonesia. During the New Order Era there were "Plat Merah" NGOs, which were established by or with the assistance from government officials to conduct governmental projects. Like the NGOs described by Hadiwinata, their aim was to gain personal economic benefit from those projects. The difference is the source of funding, which was the government budget during the New Order Era and funding from international donor institutions during the Reform Era.
27 Cf. Antlöv et al. 2006, p. 154.
28 Cf. ibid., p. 157.
29 Cf. Nyman 2006, p. 51.
30 Cf. Hadiwinata 2003, p. 114.
31 Cf. Antlöv et al. 2006, p. 150.

volvement of civil society in the form of formalized input through commissions and committees.[32] However, she argues that government officials' attitudes toward civil society remained highly varied, ranging from completely rejecting it as a nuisance to sympathetically welcoming and accommodating civil society participation. Changes in government perceptions of NGOs were also observed by Antlöv et al., who documented the diminution of direct government intervention in NGO activities, except for some vocal NGOs working on human rights and environmental issues.[33] The roles of NGOs are increasingly appreciated, particularly in the post-tsunami disaster and relief operations in Aceh.

Despite movement towards a more open political context for greater civil society involvement, both the NGOs and the government face challenges in adjusting to the new environment. They are still adapting to the idea of accepting each other, let alone cooperating with each other. Each side also faces the issue of internal consolidation to change the way they operate within a political context where power is more dispersed, accountability and transparency are demanded, and cooperation between various stakeholders is both needed and required. For various elements in the government, developing effective partnerships with NGOs has not been easy. Antlöv et al. argued that this is due to the absence of an umbrella organization to represent the interests of the NGOs, making it difficult for the government to obtain widely supported input or develop accord from the growing number of NGOs with varied backgrounds, characteristics, interests, and demands.[34] Antlöv et al. also considered the reluctance of some state actors to conform to NGOs' demands of limiting state power as a factor that made partnerships difficult.

Many Indonesian NGO activists realize that to strengthen its capacity, there is a need for the NGO community to consolidate among itself, mainly to avoid overlaps in conducting their activities. Indonesian NGOs have started to build coalitions in conducting their advocacy activities, but, as argued by Antlöv et al., they have not been able to build a nationwide coalition.[35] Coalitions may be useful in coordinating efforts in conducting programs, but there are various examples that show even coalitions have failed to coordinate NGOs' efforts and were not able to achieve the agreed goals. Chapters 7 and 9 illustrate this through discussions on the NGOs' networking efforts at the national, regional, and international levels.

32 Cf. Nyman 2006, p. 201.
33 Cf. Antlöv et al. 2006, p. 153.
34 Cf. ibid.
35 Cf. ibid., p. 151.

The *Reformasi* Era may be more accommodative to NGO activism, but as explained by Antlöv et al., it is at the same time more complex.[36] During the New Order the power structure was simpler because it was centralized at the national level; consequently NGO activism was more or less aimed at one target, the central government. Since the *Reformasi* Era, with the ongoing democratization process, power is more dispersed among government entities – namely parliament, political parties, judicial institutions, and also local governments and parliaments. Moreover, additional stakeholders have entered the arena. As an example, the monitoring role is also taken by media, academia, and other civil society organizations. Consequently, Antlöv et al. argue for a reformulation of NGO positions vis-a-vis the state (government) and other sectors in society. They also suggest a shift from protest politics to strategies of engagement through the process of lobbying and negotiations.[37] These conditions also apply for Indonesian NGOs working on the issue of migrant workers.

This discussion has identified some of the main political changes that have occurred in Indonesia during the *Reformasi* Era in relation to the activism of NGOs. As much as the more democratic environment has allowed more space for NGO activism, it has also created challenges for all stakeholders, including NGOs and the government, in adjusting to the new political context. In short, for NGOs to benefit fully from changes in the political environment, various adjustments also need to be made within the NGO community. The next section will introduce the two NGOs researched. Besides describing how the two NGOs initially established themselves in different political eras, New Order Era and *Reformasi* Era, it also aims to show how they adjust to the new environment and how they frame their activism within it.

5.2 Indonesian NGOs and the Issue of Women Migrant Workers

5.2.1 Taking up the Issue and Organizing Themselves

In Indonesia, NGOs began to adopt the subject of labor migration only toward the end of the New Order Era. According to Ford, while NGO activism on labor issues had started in the early 1980s with the establishment of labor NGOs, Indonesian migrant workers caught the attention of middle-class NGOs activists a decade later.[38] Similarly, Susilo states that although the initiative of migrant workers' advocates to reveal the problems faced by migrant workers began earli-

36 Cf. ibid., p. 161.
37 Cf. ibid., p. 162.
38 Cf. Ford 2004, p. 107, 2005, p. 18.

er in the 1980s, along with the rise of NGO activism and supported by media exposures, only in the 1990s did a number of NGOs, particularly women's NGOs, begin to show their concern on the issue of migrant workers.[39] According to Ford, the emergence and growth of NGOs concerned with the issue of migrant workers are very much due to the rapid increase in the numbers of Indonesians, particularly women, working overseas and in the mounting cases of abuse of female domestic workers.[40] Susilo also sees the abuse of women migrant workers as the main concern of migrant labor activism during the 1990s.[41] Significantly, the first NGO to take up this issue as one of its concerns was SP, a women's NGO.

The growth of migrant worker activism in Indonesia lagged behind that of the Philippines. According to Susilo, by the 1990s, there was already a consolidation in the migrant labor movement both by NGOs and trade unions in the Philippines.[42] Yamanaka and Piper have also confirmed how the work of the Philippine NGOs is far ahead of other labor sending countries, including Indonesia.[43] In fact, as stated by Tati Krisnawaty, one of the founders of SP, an event held by a Philippine NGO and attended by one of SP's activists at the end of 1980s had inspired them to take up the issue and begin their research and programs on it.[44]

With the minimum attention from other civil society organizations, including trade unions, NGOs have continued to take the major role in the migrant labor movement in Indonesia. Ford cited a survey conducted by The Consortium for the Defense of Indonesian Migrant Workers or *Konsorsium Pembela Buruh Migran Indonesia* (*Kopbumi*) showing that by 2005 there were more than 100 NGOs dealing with migrant workers' issues.[45] However, the survey also shows that migrant workers were the primary concern of only 16 percent of these NGOs, while for the others their involvement was more case-based.

As they grew in numbers, Indonesian NGOs concerned with the issue of migrant labor made attempts to coordinate their activism through networks. In early 1997, responding to the draft of Manpower Law No. 25/1997, which excluded migrant workers, around 100 NGOs established *Kopbumi*, which covered twelve provinces in Indonesia.[46] It conducted activities such as advocating policy, giving legal assistance, conducting training, gathering data, and campaigning for a national law on the protection of migrant workers and the ratification of the 1990

39 Cf. Susilo 2005.
40 Cf. Ford 2004, p. 107, 2005, p. 18.
41 Cf. Susilo 2005.
42 Cf. ibid.
43 Cf. Yamanaka and Piper 2005.
44 Interview with Krisnawaty, Tati on November 7, 2008.
45 Cf. Ford 2005, pp. 18-19.
46 Cf. ibid., p. 20.

International Convention on the Protection of the Rights of Migrant Workers and Members of their Families.[47] Until at least shortly after Law No. 39/2004 was passed, *Kopbumi* was at the forefront of national campaigns for the protection of Indonesian migrant workers and their families. It was the leading civil society network working on Indonesian migrant workers for that period, had a high media profile, handled a significant number of cases, and was referred to in most research on Indonesian migrant workers. However, as further explained by Ford, by the early 2000s, *Kopbumi*'s high profile had greatly declined.[48] There are various opinions on what actually caused this. Ford argued that it was the departure of *Kopbumi*'s main activists.[49] Meanwhile, Tati Krisnawaty, a senior Indonesian migrant workers' advocate, argued that it was closely related to the fact that *Kopbumi* started to act like an NGO, seeking funding and widening its activities, rather than just focusing on campaigning for a law on migrant workers, which was its mandate.[50] Another opinion came from Salma Safitri, who related *Kopbumi*'s declining profile to the completion of its original task as a network.[51] *Kopbumi* was established with the aim of pushing for a law on migrant workers, and since a law was finally passed in 2004, it could be considered that the aim of *Kopbumi* had been achieved. This is an example of how the lifespan of NGO networks in Indonesia is usually short, which will be discussed further in Chapter 7.

Since the establishment of *Kopbumi* in 1997, as documented by Ford, Indonesian NGOs concerned with the issue of migrant workers have attempted to organize themselves in a number of networks.[52] These groupings are based on the similar characteristics of the organizations involved or the common issue that they are focusing on. In 2000, 19 women's organizations including SP, *Komnas Perempuan*, LBH APIK, and a number of religion-based organizations, such as *Fatayat* and *Muslimat NU*, the women's wings of *Nahdlatul Ulama,* and the Organization of Indonesian Catholic Women (*Wanita Katolik Republik Indonesia*), established GPPBM. It employs what Ford calls a "dual strategy", which involves "advocating policy and legal change while working with government departments and agencies to improve the services they offer to migrant workers". In mid-2004, eleven organizations including *Kapal Perempuan*, *Kopbumi*, Mi-

47 Cf. Indonesian Peacebuilding Directory 2007.

48 Cf. Ford 2005, p. 20.

49 Wahyu Susilo was one of *Kopbumi*'s key activists that left. He then established Migrant CARE, with four others: Mulyadi, Yohanes Wibawa, Ali Muchsin, and Anis Hidayah. Interview with Hidayah, Anis on May 26, 2007.

50 Interview with Krisnawaty, Tati on November 7, 2008.

51 Interview with Safitri, Salma on August 2, 2007.

52 Cf. Ford 2005, pp. 20-21.

grant CARE, *Gema Perempuan*, *Ecosoc*,[53] and the Indonesian Migrant Workers Union or *Serikat Buruh Migran Indonesia* (SBMI)/the Federation of Migrant Workers' Organizations or *Federasi Organisasi Buruh Migran Indonesia* (FOBMI), established The Forum for Justice for Migrant Domestic Workers or *Forum Kerja untuk Keadilan Pekerja Rumah Tangga Migran* (*Foker*), focusing particularly on the issues faced by Indonesian women domestic workers in Singapore. Ford describes this as a loose network of five working groups with each group taking either advocacy, campaigns, capacity building, organizing, or research as its focus. The membership of *Foker* shows the complex structure of NGO networks in Indonesia, where a network like *Kopbumi* can also become a member of another network like *Foker*.

The NGOs' attempts to work together and coordinate their efforts are most apparent when they occasionally react to urgent and highly publicized cases.[54] As an example, in 2002, despite the absence of a law to regulate the issue of migrant workers, a group of Indonesian NGOs filed a citizen lawsuit against the government for its failure in handling the mass deportation of migrant workers from Malaysia that created a humanitarian crisis in Nunukan. According to Susilo, a significant result of this effort was the acceptance of a citizen lawsuit as a form of public law-suit (*gugatan publik*) in Indonesia.[55] He sees this as a contribution by the migrant workers' advocacy movement to reforming Indonesian law.

While increased freedom in the *Reformasi* Era has allowed more room for advocacy and organizing work, as argued by Ford, it has created fragmentation in the migrant labor NGO community.[56] With the increased demand for and the establishment of migrant labor organizations, Ford foresees the risk of overlapping actions, competition, and even friction between migrant labor NGOs and migrant labor organizations.[57] As discussed further in Chapter 7 of this book, although

53 Ecosoc is an NGO based in Jakarta which focuses on the issues of migrant workers, the urban poor, and malnutrition and hunger.

54 This tendency to create instant and temporary coalitions to react to a particular issue or campaign for certain policy continues to the present. Both NGOs researched have been involved in a number of *koalisi* (coalition) of civil society organizations, which frequently dissolve when their objectives are achieved or there is no promising result after a certain period.

55 Cf. Susilo 2005.

56 Cf. Ford 2005, p. 25.

57 A simplified differentiation of these two types of organization is that migrant labor NGOs consist of middle-class activists who work on the issue of migrant workers, while migrant worker organizations usually consist of ex-migrant workers and their families who organized themselves in Indonesia and migrant workers who are still working in receiving countries like Hong Kong. However, in practice, this differentiation is not rigid, since many NGOs claim that there are ex-migrant workers on their staff and point out that the members of some migrant worker organizations do not purely consist of ex-migrant

the NGOs claim that they have assisted the establishment of some migrant workers' organizations, a degree of competition remains, particularly at the national level and when it concerns matters such as funding, projects, and reputation.

5.2.2 Learning from the Philippines

When giving examples of relatively better managed labor migration on the sending country side, most studies will immediately refer to the Philippines, another major sending country. Obviously, the Philippines started earlier. By the beginning of the 1970s, when Indonesian individuals had just started going to work in the Middle East without any recognition from or involvement of the government, the Philippine government had already recognized the economic importance of labor migration to the state.[58] By 1982, it has established the well-known Philippine Overseas Employment Administration (POEA), which is often cited as a model for an institution to manage labor migration. As discussed earlier in this book, the Indonesian government only started to recognize the importance of labor migration for the national income in the 1980s, and only established the BNP2TKI in 2007. The Philippine government is known for its active efforts to protect its people working abroad. As pointed out by Yamanaka and Piper, although the implementation may be debatable, in 1995, the Philippines ratified the ICRMW and became the first country among the signatories of the ICMRW to pass a law to implement the convention, the Migrant Workers and Overseas Filipino Act (RA 8042).[59] As for Indonesia, it only became a signatory in 2004 and ratified the convention in 2012.

Yamanaka and Piper also highlighted how Filipino women have also pioneered activism in receiving countries by organizing themselves to address the problems they face.[60] The Asian Migrant Centre, which was formed in 1989 in Hong Kong, is one example. This organization has conducted activities like service provision, organizing grassroots migrant groups, lobbying for better working conditions, assisting migrant women in developing their skills and providing them with funds to start a business when they get home. The Filipino migrant organizations not only grew well, but were also able to consolidate in an alliance, known as United Filipinos in Hong Kong (UNIFIL-HK). Moreover, these Filipino organizations do not limit their work and service to their compatriots. They

workers and their families. This debate on the status of the organizations' members and staff usually surfaces in the context of arguing for their legitimacy in conducting activism on behalf of migrant workers.

58 Cf. Yamanaka and Piper 2005, p. 4.

59 Cf. ibid., p. 30.

60 Cf. ibid., p. 28.

have helped migrant workers from other countries and they have even assisted other nationalities, including Indonesians, to establish their own domestic worker unions.

There are various factors that contribute to the success of the Philippine NGOs dealing with the issue of migrant workers. One of them is the ability to build activism both domestically and internationally, connect them and make them support each other, as reflected in the statement of a Filipino activist quoted by Yamanaka and Piper: "The key to successful campaigning abroad is a strong movement 'at home'".[61] Another contributing factor is that the Philippines are "experienced" in grassroots civil activism and citizens' political engagement.[62] By the end of the 1990s, as stated by Clarke, the Philippine NGO community was among the largest in the developing world.[63] He argues that the growth of NGOs in the Philippines was due to the American colonial policy which encouraged the development of civic associations, while in Indonesia, a struggle for independence was followed by a strong state, which significantly controlled civil society, limiting the growth of NGOs. Yamanaka and Piper also argue that NGOs in the Philippines have benefited from an accommodative environment with an open political system, and from access to elites within the government brought about by the 1986 revolution.[64] The Philippine migrant worker activism emerged from its already strong grassroots democracy movement. Consequently, the Philippine NGOs have been involved in public policy debates and campaigns since the government began its efforts to promote labor export in 1974.

Although somewhat later than the Philippines, Indonesia has begun its democratization process. As already argued earlier in this chapter, Indonesian NGOs need to adapt to the political context after the fall of the New Order. Thus, the next section will introduce the two NGOs researched and give a general description of how they operate within Indonesia's changing context.

5.2.3 Introduction to Solidaritas Perempuan and Migrant CARE

Solidaritas Perempuan

Solidaritas Perempuan (SP) is a women's organization which has made the issue of women migrant workers one of its main foci. Although SP is well-known as the first Indonesian NGO to deal with the issue of women migrant workers, this

61 Ibid., p. 29.
62 Ibid.
63 Cf. Clarke 1998, p. 193.
64 Cf. Yamanaka and Piper 2005, p. 29.

issue was not one of their initial primary concerns. As described on SP's website, cases of evictions of Indonesian farmers from their land in the 1980s became the basis for the emergence of solidarity groups which had simple, temporary, and voluntary characteristics.[65] One of these solidarity groups was the Working Group for Women's Solidarity or *Kelompok Kerja Solidaritas Perempuan*, which aimed to strengthen people's struggle to get their land back. According to Tati Krisnawaty, one of SP's founders, their activities, mainly in the form of compiling data from the field and conducting protests, were attached to the student movement and funded by contributions from individuals.[66] Eventually they decided to concentrate on building solidarity among the group, specifically women, who were, and to a certain degree continue to be, threatened by the "greedy and authoritarian" system.

As an organization, SP was officially established on December 10, 1990 in the form of a foundation (*yayasan*).[67] On April 1, 1993, its organizational form was changed into an association (*perserikatan*) with individual membership.[68] As stated by Salma Safitri, the Chair of SP's National Executive Body for 2004-2007, since its establishment, SP has been active on various women-related issues, such as reproduction rights, land rights, globalization, and women's political participation.[69]

Safitri explained that SP's engagement with the issue of women migrant workers started when in 1992 and 1993 SP's activists traveled abroad and discovered cases of trafficking, unpaid salary, and abuses of Indonesian women migrant workers.[70] Compared to the cases concerning Philippine migrant workers, Indonesian women migrant workers did not receive adequate support because no Indonesians worked on the issue at that time. Thus, without any previous experience SP became the first Indonesian NGO to campaign on the cases by contacting relevant government departments such as the Department of Manpower and the Department of Foreign Affairs. As an illustration of how unique SP was in taking up the issue at that time, Safitri recounted how, when her organization contacted the Legal Aid Institution in Jakarta to get legal assistance, this institution did not see the abuse of women migrant workers as a violation of human

65 Cf. SP 2007b.
66 Interview with Krisnawaty, Tati on November 7, 2008.
67 Cf. SP 2007b.
68 Ford 2005, p. 17, argued that, by changing its form into an association which has an open membership structure, SP can no longer be qualified as an NGO, which commonly has a closed membership structure. However, she admits that, in practice, the national office of SP still operates like an NGO and funding from NGO donor sources continues to be SP's main source, although the members are now paying dues.
69 Interview with Safitri, Salma on June 6, 2007.
70 Ibid.

rights. However, SP saw it as a woman-specific case where women conducted what is considered as traditional women's work. The fact that most stakeholders did not see it as a problem was a problem for SP.[71] Since then the issue of women migrant workers has remained part of SP's platform and SP became one of the key players in the migrant labor movement.

SP's activities included providing legal advice, conducting training programs for migrant workers and their communities, running a shelter for abused women migrant workers, collecting data, and advocating policies at the national and international levels.[72] As the first organization to take up the issue of women migrant workers, SP enjoys a considerable reputation among both migrant worker advocates and the government. According to Asma'ul Khusnaeny, SP's Head of Legal Aid Division for 2004-2007, within the migrant workers' movement, SP is considered as one of the driving forces, which has made significant contributions to work on the issue and is regarded as the "mother" or "*ibunda*" by younger organizations.[73]

As an organization, SP is well-established. Thaufiek Zulbahary, SP's Head of Policy Advocacy Division for 2004-2007, explained that it is a membership-based organization with a National Secretariat located in Jakarta and branches consisting of members in 13 cities across Indonesia, which they call *komunitas* or "communities".[74] Every three years, the National Congress of SP members choose people to run the National Executive Body, which forms the National Secretariat as shown in Figure 5.1. There are around 25 staff in the national secretariat. The National Executive Body conducts SP's main programs, which are decided by and mandated to them by the members' National Congress. The National Executive Body is then held accountable for the implementation of these mandates at the next National Congress.

71 In the early 1990s, activism of human rights advocates were more directed toward the rights of the poor who were evicted from their lands, marginalized, or terminated from their employment. This was the period when there was a high number of cases of evictions (*penggusuran*) and forced termination of employment (*pemutusan hubungan kerja*) in Indonesia. Moreover, it is highly possible that during that period migrant workers were considered more fortunate compared to laborers in the country merely for having a job and getting paid with foreign currency.

72 Cf. Ford 2004, p. 108, 2005, p. 19.

73 Interview with Khusnaeny, Asma'ul on September 24, 2007.

74 Interview with Zulbahary, Thaufiek on May 16, 2007.

Figure 5.1: Structure of the National Secretariat of SP (2004-2007)

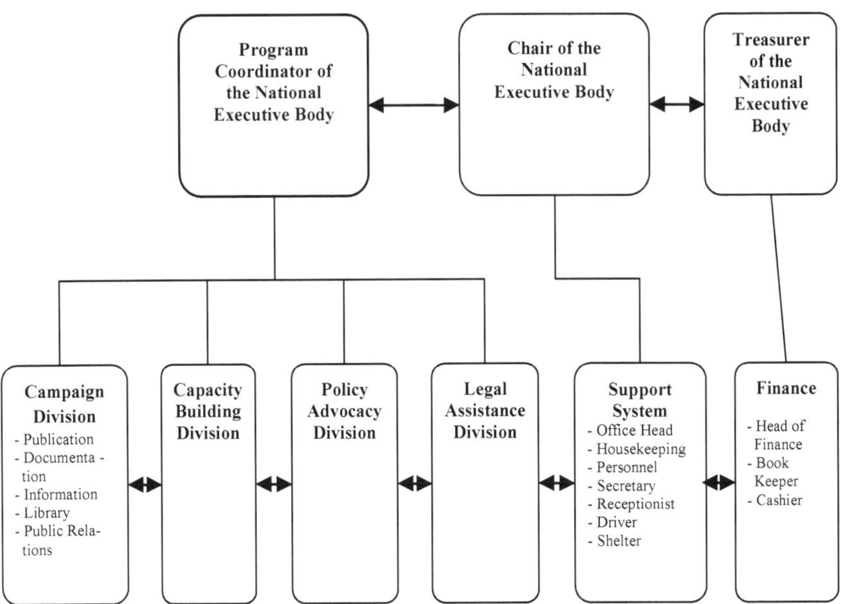

Source: Translated by author from SP's website[75]

SP also has partnerships with four migrant worker solidarity organizations. SP assisted the establishment of these organizations, but, as stated by Zulbahary, SP prefers not to refer to the organizations as *dampingan* (assisted) and to SP as *pendamping* (assistant),[76] terms commonly used in Indonesia to describe a national NGO and the local NGO it helps establish. SP prefers to call the migrant worker organizations SP's partners or *mitra*, which implies a more equal relationship and describe their relationship as "they grow together with SP".

Zulbahary explained that not all of those involved in SP's organization are members.[77] There are several requirements for becoming an SP member, such as administrative requirements, recommendation, and undergoing feminist training. After fulfilling these requirements, the membership status will be legalized in a community forum (*musyawarah komunitas*). Figures 5.2 and 5.3 show SP's decision-making mechanism at the national and community level.

75 SP 2007b.
76 Interview with Zulbahary, Thaufiek on May 16, 2007.
77 Ibid.

Figure 5.2: SP's Decision-making Mechanism at the National Level (2004-2007)

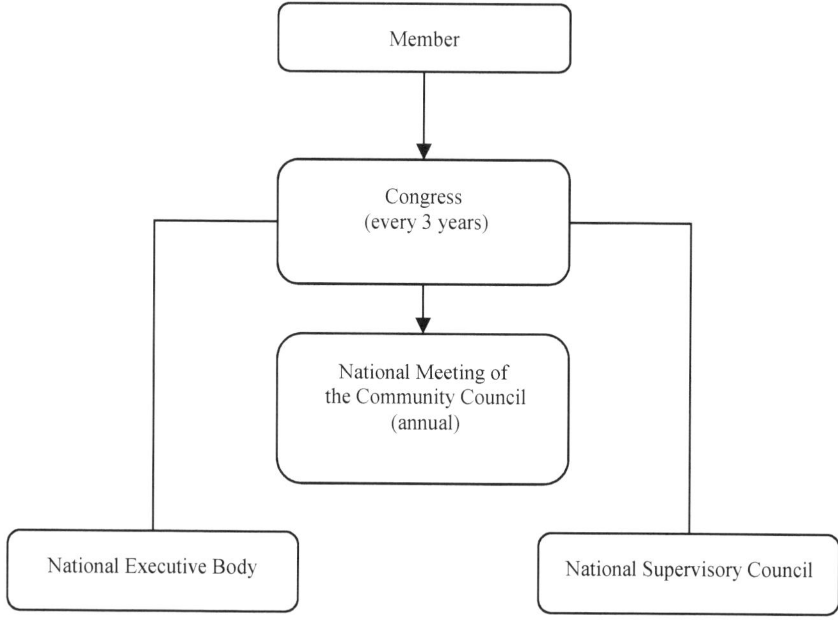

Source: Translated by author from SP's website[78]

78 SP 2007b.

Figure 5.3: SP's Decision-making Mechanism at the Community Level (2004-2007)

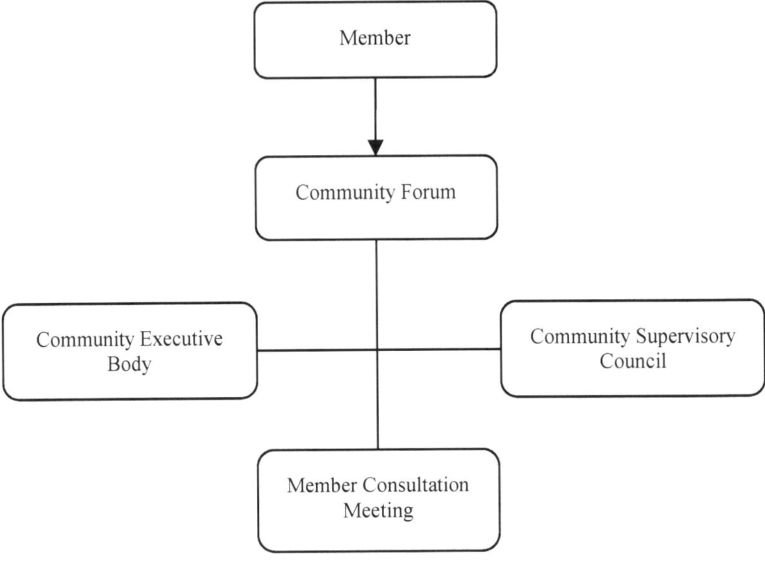

Source: Translated from SP's website[79]

In terms of accountability, Safitri explained that SP has two types of reporting mechanism, external and internal.[80] The external reports are made based on needs, whether it is for issue advocacy, programs, or activities. They are sent to related institutions at national and international levels. As an example, a report on the vulnerability of migrant workers against HIV/AIDS was sent to the MoMT, the BNP2TKI, the Ministry of Health, etc. Internal reporting is made for the purposes of internal program monitoring and evaluation.

79 Ibid.

80 Email from Safitri, Salma on February 11, 2008. Initially it was not easy for me to access SP's reports. However, at my second visit in 2008, which was made after SP's 5th Congress in Jakarta, I was given the Accountability Report of the 2004-2007 National Executive Body, which was a public document. I had a similar experience with Migrant CARE. At the first visit I could obtain annual reports which described the organization's main activities. Documents on budget and source of funding could only be obtained at my second visit in 2008. It seems that while some information is made public, other is kept for internal reports. I also sensed that the NGOs' staff was quite cautious in making some information public, particularly those related to budget and funding sources, which require them to first trust the receiver and what the information is going to be used for.

SP changed its organizational structure at its 4th Congress in Makassar.[81] Before the congress, the organization was structured based on sectors with three divisions: migrants, politics, and associations (*perserikatan*). After the congress, for the 2004-2007 period, the organization was structured based on types of activities with four divisions: policy advocacy, capacity building, campaigning, and legal assistance.[82] These divisions also constitute SP's main activities, along with research, training, workshops, and seminars.

The lists of activities of each division show that SP attempts to conduct a quite comprehensive range of activities.[83] A strong emphasis is put on the empowerment of migrant workers, which Zulbahary claimed as one of SP's strengths.[84] As an example, SP has made efforts to empower people at the origin areas through discussion of cases and regulations. Also, when the legal assistance division handles a case, it involves the migrant worker so that she understands the process. According to Zulbahary, by doing this SP aims to empower the "victim" so that she can help other women migrant workers with similar cases in the future. Risma Umar, who was the Program Coordinator of SP's National Executive Body for 2004-2007,[85] believed that the connectivity of the work of all divisions which made their work comprehensive was one of SP's strengths.[86] Other factors that she considered as SP's strengths included its commitment as an organization to handle the issue of women migrant workers, its accountability mechanism where the work of the national secretariat was monitored by the public, the staff and the members, and the way they interacted with the government – a combination of criticizing and providing information and data – which allowed SP to maintain its position as a source of information and advice to the government.

81 Email from Zulbahary, Thaufiek on March 11, 2008.

82 Cf. SP 2007b.

83 The main activities of the policy advocacy division include monitoring and policy analysis, responding to economic and political situations, lobbying decision-makers, and strengthening and building alliances with other organizations in promoting policy changes. The capacity-building division concentrates on strengthening the organizational capacities of SP's communities and partners through training and workshops, conducting issue strengthening and base organizing for SP's communities and partners, keeping the member database, facilitating member recruitment, and establishing new communities. The campaign division focuses on conducting campaigns, preparing campaign materials, organizing SP's library, data, and information, and providing data for SP members, national secretariat staff, communities, and partners. As for the legal assistance division, their activities include providing legal assistance and service, campaigning on strategic cases, discussing cases with SP's communities and partners, documenting cases, giving actual responses to cases, facilitating SP's communities and partners in handling cases and providing shelters for women migrant workers who are seeking redress of their problems.

84 Interview with Zulbahary, Thaufiek on May 16, 2007.

85 In 2008, Risma Umar became the Chair of SP's National Executive Body.

86 Interview with Umar, Risma on August 8, 2007.

As for funding, SP has two kinds of sources. The first is dues from the members, who numbered 870 in June 2008.[87] However, these dues did not constitute a significant source of funds since, as stated by Zulbahary, the amount was only around 1 USD per person per month.[88] It was mostly used by the branches as their operational fund while for SP's activities at the national level, significant funding came from institutional donors. As explained in the Accountability Report of the 2004-2007 National Executive Body, some of the funding institutions, such as NOVIB, acted as core funder, which means they provided funds for the operational needs of the organization and for all its programs.[89] Other funding institutions chose the programs they wish to support. As an example, funding for migration, trafficking, and HIV/AIDS came from institutions such as the ILO, Coordination of Action Research on AIDS and Mobility (CARAM Asia), NOVIB, Stop Aids Now, and UNIFEM. The summary of the funding that SP received 2005 to 2009 is shown in Table 5.1, comparing the funding for programs on migration, health and trafficking to the total funding received by the organization.

Table 5.1: Funding Received by SP 2005-2009 (approximately in USD)

Year	For the whole organization	For programs on migration, health, and trafficking
2005	157,000	0
2006	59,000	22,000
2007	478,000	123,000
2008	588,000	68,000
2009	464,000	49,000

Source: Accountability Report of SP's National Executive Body 2004-2007[90]

The table shows that the amount fluctuates considerably, particularly from 2005 to 2007. This was closely related to the number of committing funding institutions and the amount of funding that SP managed to secure for those particular years. As an illustration, in 2005, SP received funds from five funding institutions, and this number dropped to two in 2006 and went up to nine in 2007. Also in 2007, SP managed to secure funding for some middle term programs, which had three year-timespans and long term funding for organizational capacity

87 Cf. Badan Eksekutif Nasional Solidaritas Perempuan 2008.
88 Interview with Zulbahary, Thaufiek on November 19, 2008.
89 Cf. Badan Eksekutif Nasional Solidaritas Perempuan 2008, p. 130.
90 Cf. ibid., p. 132

building. This explains the rather steady amount from 2007 to 2009. Although it is apparent that SP depends heavily on foreign funding, Umar argued that SP does not want its work to be dictated by funding trends.[91] Umar's statement is supported by the accountability report of SP's 2004-2007 National Executive Body, which stated that the search for funding has to be based on the issues mandated by SP's Congress and the situation in the communities.[92]

According to Safitri, priorities for each period are based on SP's experience, existing cases and the mapping of Indonesian migrant workers' movements.[93] Information on who is doing what and which area is not yet covered is combined with SP's identified capacity, which will then determine the focus of SP's work for a certain period. As an example, in 2007, when I conducted my fieldwork, for the issue of migration, SP was focusing on health and trafficking aspects. SP's program for the period of 2004-2007 includes four main areas:[94] migration, particularly migrant workers' vulnerability to HIV/AIDS, and trafficking;[95] women and natural resources conflicts; women and food security; and empowering members and building organizational capacity. According to Zulbahary, allocation of funding among these areas fluctuates, depending on the donor.[96] Thus, the fact that the funding for migration programs has declined – from above 60 percent of the overall funding – can be considered as an indication of the declining interest in the issue by donors.

As more NGOs took an interest in the issue of migrant workers, and SP started to diversify its program in 1998,[97] SP's public profile on the issue of migrant workers became less dominant. Nevertheless, as shown in their agenda and at-

91 Interview with Umar, Risma on August 8, 2007.
92 Cf. Badan Eksekutif Nasional Solidaritas Perempuan 2008.
93 Interview with Safitri, Salma on June 6, 2007.
94 Cf. SP 2007b.
95 The migration programme involves: (1) promoting changes in policies to protect migrant workers and their families at local, national, regional, and international levels; (2) promoting changes in specific policies on the protection of migrant workers, which are related to their specific health rights, reproductive health and their vulnerability to HIV/AIDS at the local, national, regional, and international levels; (3) promoting changes in specific policies on the protection of migrant workers who are victims of trafficking at the local, national, regional, and international levels; (4) promoting change in the attitudes of the government, business sector, and society toward migrant workers and their families from treating them as commodities to human beings entitled to human rights; (5) promoting change in the recruitment system toward a safer one and upholding, protecting, and fulfilling the rights of migrant workers; (6) strengthening Indonesia's bargaining power with receiving countries; (7) promoting changes in policies to protect labor rights, including the policies of government, multinational institutions (financial and trade), and multinational companies.
96 Interview with Zulbahary, Thaufiek on November 19, 2008.
97 Cf. Ford 2004, p. 107.

tested by Salma Safitri,[98] migrant workers continue to be one of SP's main concerns and foci. According to Safitri, SP's decision to maintain this focus is due to a number of factors.[99] Firstly, as an organization, it is not possible to just abandon an issue which they have handled for years and in which they have invested significant resources. Safitri further argued that the more they build knowledge on the issue, the closer they get to the core of the problems which prevents them from stopping their work. Safitri argued that, as long as there is poverty and uneven economic development, migration will continue to exist, exacerbated by low education levels and the destruction of the environment. To address the problems of migration these kinds of problems need to be addressed also. The growing interest within SP's membership on the issue of migrant workers is another factor. Safitri claimed that all 13 SP communities acknowledged the significance of this issue and demanded support from the Jakarta office to conduct migrant worker capacity building in their areas. Since SP is a member-based organization, which means the programs implemented within a particular period are those mandated by the members' National Congress, and as long as the issue of women migrant workers surface in the congress, it will continue to feature on SP's national agenda.[100]

SP focuses on women migrant workers, particularly domestic workers, not solely because it is a women's organization. As stated by Zulbahary and Safitri, this is rather due to the fact that more than 70 percent of Indonesians going overseas to work are women, 90 percent of whom work as domestic workers.[101] By setting this focus, SP aims to advocate on behalf of the majority of Indonesian migrant workers. Zulbahary also argued that the more important matter is that SP uses women's perspectives in looking at the issue of women migrant workers and the various injustices they are experiencing, which include discrimination, violence, double burden, subordination, and marginalization.[102] Safitri explained further that, for SP, the issue of women migrant workers has layers.[103] Women migrant workers can be seen as human beings in general, as women, and as people who work overseas. Thus, they are entitled to their rights as women, as workers and as foreign workers in the country where they work. However, according to Safitri, as the problems grow bigger and more complex, SP has to set priorities because it is not able to advocate all the rights involved and address all aspects of the problems. After all, she said, it is the duty of the government, not the NGOs, to address the problems. Thus, as stated by Zulbahary, SP chooses a

98 Cf. Ford 2005, p. 19.
99 Interview with Safitri, Salma on June 6, 2007.
100 Interview with Zulbahary, Thaufiek on May 16, 2007.
101 Interview with Zulbahary, Thaufiek on May 16, 2007, and Safitri, Salma on June 6, 2007.
102 Interview with Zulbahary, Thaufiek on May 16, 2007.
103 Interview with Safitri, Salma on June 6, 2007.

specific part to campaign on, which is women migrant workers and the aim is to empower them.[104] Therefore, while other NGOs might look at the migrant workers' work and their economic, social, and cultural rights, SP concentrates more on exploring their experience as women.

Among the various problems faced by women migrant workers, SP's 2004-2007 programs focused on two issues – trafficking and health –, particularly on women migrant workers' vulnerability to HIV/AIDS.[105] Safitri explained that trafficking was chosen because of the high number of trafficking cases.[106] The weaknesses of the official sending mechanisms have created room for trafficking practices. Therefore, SP is campaigning for the protection of Indonesian women migrant workers from such practices. The focus on health is considered crucial because obviously a sick worker will not be able to work. Also, reproductive health is considered one of the most important aspects because the biggest exploitation of women migrant workers is sexual, which threatens their reproductive rights. Moreover, since most women migrant workers travel alone, they are vulnerable to unsafe sexual relationships, whether conducted by the women themselves or by their partners, who are left at home. According to Safitri, choosing these foci does not mean that SP does not handle other cases, but they are not SP's priority.

SP's networking effort is quite extensive, as shown in its involvement in various national, regional and international networks. At the national level, SP is a member of the Indonesian Forum for the Environment or *Wahana Lingkungan Hidup* (WALHI), the Consortium for Agrarian Reform or *Konsorsium Pembaharuan Agraria* (KPA), and INFID. Moreover, SP was one of the initiators of the Anti-debt Coalition or *Koalisi Anti Utang* (KAU), GPPBM, *Kopbumi*, and the Convention on the Elimination of All Forms of Discrimination against Women (CEDAW) Preparation Committee. At the regional and international level, SP is a member of theAsia-Pacific Forum on Women, Law and Development (APWLD), CARAM Asia for Indonesia, the Global Alliance Against Traffic in Women (GAATW), and the Migrant Forum in Asia (MFA). SP has also cooperated with receiving countries' NGOs such as Tenaganita in Malaysia. These networking efforts will be discussed further in Chapters 7 and 9.

This section has introduced one of the NGOs researched, SP, a women's NGO, which was the first Indonesian NGO to take up the issue of migrant workers. Organizationally, SP is quite developed as can be seen in the structure of the organization and how it operates. As the organization grows and there are efforts

104 Interview with Zulbahary, Thaufiek on May 16, 2007.

105 The foci on migrant and trafficking and migrant and health were set at SP's 2004 national conference. Interview with Zulbahary, Thaufiek on November 19, 2008.

106 Interview with Safitri, Salma on June 6, 2007.

to improve its management, there is a risk of becoming more bureaucratic. However, the efforts are worth making since they contribute to the improvement of the organization's work and accountability. SP's budget may show that the issue of women migrant workers does not receive the biggest allocation. However, it is not true to claim that SP has abandoned the issue of women migrant workers. In fact, it continues to be a key player, acknowledged by other stakeholders, including the government. Moreover, the decision to focus on the aspects they are most resourceful at, health and trafficking, may show a degree of learning process, experience, and maturity as an organization. The next section will discuss a younger organization, Migrant CARE.

Migrant CARE

As an organization, *Perhimpunan Indonesia untuk Buruh Migran Berdaulat* or Indonesian Association for Migrant Workers' Sovereignty, usually known as Migrant CARE, can be considered quite young. After initial efforts in January 2004, it was officially established on June 22, 2004.[107] In a relatively short time this organization has managed to establish its reputation at the national and international level and has gained a high media profile. Some of its founders, like Wahyu Susilo and Anis Hidayah, were active in *Kopbumi*. The decision to establish Migrant CARE was based on the founders' consideration that although there were NGOs concerned with the issue of migrant workers at various levels, the efforts to promote these workers' rights still needed to be strengthened.[108] Migrant CARE has a board which consists of two people, Wahyu Susilo and Mulyadi, with Wahyu Susilo as the chair. Anis Hidayah is the executive director assisted by a financial manager, a program manager, and administrative staff. While SP's leadership periodically changes, based on the result of its members' congress, Migrant CARE's top positions have not been changed since its establishment.

Migrant CARE has four divisions: counseling and case handling, advocacy (national and international), research and documentation, and education and public campaigning. A unique feature of Migrant CARE is that it has a Country Representative Malaysia Coordinator position which is held by Alex Ong. This can be considered as Migrant CARE's strength in the way that it has someone in a receiving country who can monitor the situation, take immediate action when

107 Email from Hidayah, Anis on January 2, 2007.
108 Interview with Hidayah, Anis on May 26, 2007.

needed, and use his business and government connections to lobby.[109] Compared to SP, Migrant CARE has fewer staff. In 2008, Migrant CARE only had 12 staff in total.[110] Nevertheless, Hidayah stated that expansion is not a priority because they did not want Migrant CARE to turn into a big and bureaucratic organization, a form that they had been criticizing.[111] Hidayah argued that one of Migrant CARE's strengths was its speed in response and she believed that adopting a bigger organizational form with official and strict management might slow them down. To overcome the challenge of their absence at the grassroots level and in receiving countries, Migrant CARE preferred to work with its partners, whom Hidayah considered the best choice because, based on the lessons they learned from *Kopbumi*'s failure, organizations with many members at the grassroots level had to face challenges in management, coordination, and synergy.[112]

As stated in Migrant CARE's organizational profile in 2006, its mission is directed mainly toward promoting global justice for migrant workers, particularly at the regional level (South East Asia) through building networks, campaigning for regulations and policies and advocating cases faced by migrant workers.[113] In relation to this, Hidayah stated that one of Migrant CARE's initial objectives was pushing for the existence of a mechanism and a convention for the protection of migrant workers in ASEAN countries.[114]

Migrant CARE's activities are divided into three programs: developing discourse on global justice for migrant workers, strengthening networks and advocacy in the South East Asia Region, and institutional capacity building.[115] Some

109 Ong's position and the way he operates are rather unusual. Although Ong is part of Migrant CARE, there are differences in the way he works compared to the staff in Jakarta. As an example, Ong claimed to have been funding his activities using his own money. Interview with Ong, Alex on August 16, 2007.

110 Interview with Hidayah, Anis on November 18, 2008.

111 Interview with Hidayah, Anis on September 14, 2007.

112 Ibid. Hidayah referred to *Kopbumi* and SP in talking about organizations which had difficulties in maintaining their network. She claimed that Migrant CARE tried to learn from the failure of these organizations. Interview with Hidayah, Anis on November 18, 2008.

113 Cf. Migrant CARE 2006.

114 Interview with Hidayah, Anis on May 26, 2007.

115 According to Migrant CARE's profile (Migrant CARE 2006), programs to develop a discourse of global justice for migrant workers include: holding discussions, seminars, and workshops on the global justice for migrant workers; promoting global justice for migrant workers at local, national, regional, and international levels; documenting and publishing the issues of global justice in the reports and journals; and making reports on the condition of migrant workers in South East Asia. Programs to strengthen networks and advocacy in South East Asia Region include: conducting advocacy in cooperation with the ASEAN Secretariat to have its own agenda on migrant workers; holding regular meetings with migrant workers movements in South East Asia; collectively supporting migrant workers who are facing problems in South East Asia; and developing a national network on the issues of migrant workers in South East Asia. Institutional capacity building pro-

of Migrant CARE's activities are: advocating cases, developing modules and training, developing and publishing guide books for migrant workers, assisting the establishment of FOBMI, assisting the establishment of migrant workers' organizations in origin areas, conducting monitoring at Terminal III of Soekarno-Hatta International Airport and the Police Hospital. Furthermore, they are conducting research on migrant workers in Hong Kong with the Asian Migrant Centre and the Indonesian Migrant Workers Union (IMWU), conducting investigation at the shelter run by Indonesian Embassy in Kuala Lumpur, holding an audience with members of the Malaysian Parliament on the condition of Indonesian migrant workers in Malaysia, and frequently making statements and press releases concerning the issue of migrant workers. These are only some of the activities that Migrant CARE has conducted, but even this short list shows that it has covered quite a varied range of activities.

Migrant CARE also attempts to work at various levels. As explained by Hidayah, at the local level Migrant CARE provides capacity building and education so that women understand their rights before leaving to work overseas and the safe way of migrating.[116] Migrant CARE has also approached and lobbied governments in the origin areas of migrant workers who were facing death penalties so they can sense the urgency of the matter, and urged them to take an active role by passing local regulations. Migrant CARE also conducts routine case handling by receiving reports on cases and providing legal assistance. At the national policy level, Migrant CARE pushes the government to use a bottom-up approach in policy-making by involving the civil society. At the regional and international level, Migrant CARE lobbies to maximize the utilization of various regional and international instruments, including those of the UN, on behalf of migrant workers.

In terms of setting the organization's priorities, Hidayah stated that every issue became a priority, although current developments and trends in labor migration were still the main consideration.[117] She explained that Migrant CARE's programs were based on worldwide migration trends and on which case had a particularly high profile at a particular time period. As an example, in 2007, Migrant CARE focused on repatriation, particularly through the infamous Terminal III at Soekarno-Hatta International Airport. The aim was to establish a 24 hours-help desk at Terminal III which would enable Migrant CARE to monitor the operation of that terminal for bad practices such as corruption and gather infor-

grams include: developing the capability and ability of human resources; developing the institutional management of Migrant CARE; developing the organizational format; and fundraising.

116 Interview with Hidayah, Anis on May 26, 2007.

117 Ibid.

mation from migrant workers returning home with problems that could be used to inform recommendations to the government. The help desk was established, literally in the form of a desk, and operated by Migrant CARE's limited human resources. Through the help desk, they were able observe the situation and common practices inside the terminal and gather data on the problems faced by a number of returning migrant workers, which was compiled in a monitoring report.[118] However, like most of other data compiled by Migrant CARE, it was mostly used by Migrant CARE in their press releases or by other related institutions and researchers. It has not become a significant policy input for the government's policy. In fact, it can be argued that the more apparent result was Migrant CARE's assistance to the returning migrant workers by providing them with information on their rights and accompanying them to the health center and/or related authorities that might be able to further assist them.

It is rather difficult for outside observers to determine Migrant CARE's focus since the organization has been responding to various issues. However, Hidayah believed that the organization was best known for its opposition to the death penalty.[119] It has been campaigning on cases of death penalties passed on migrant workers and became a source of information on this type of case. Hidayah stated that, because the issue of migrant workers was quite large and as an organization Migrant CARE had its limitations, they had no choice but to focus on certain aspects of the issue because if they tried to operate at all levels, they would not be able to maximize their effort.

Although Migrant CARE does not explicitly state in their profile that they focus on women who migrate overseas as domestic workers, most of the cases handled by Migrant CARE involve this type of worker. Thus the organization uses the term migrant domestic workers (*pekerja rumah tangga migran*) instead of merely women migrant workers (*buruh migran perempuan*) based on the argument that the majority of women work in the domestic sector. This explains Migrant CARE's involvement in the establishment of *Foker* and in the campaign to push for the passing of a law on domestic workers in Indonesia.

In conducting its activism, Migrant CARE has been working with organizations like Tenaganita, INFID Jakarta, and HRW. It is also a part of regional and international networks such as CARAM Asia, MFA, Global Call to Action against Poverty, International NGO Platform on Migrant Workers Convention (IPMWC), and Solidarity for Asian People's Advocacy (SAPA).[120]

As an organization, Migrant CARE has developed quite fast. It started with two to three people in 2004, and an annual budget of around 300-400 million

118 Cf. Migrant CARE 2007.
119 Interview with Hidayah, Anis on May 26, 2007.
120 Cf. Migrant CARE 2006.

IDR. By 2008, as stated by Hidayah their annual budget had reached around 1 billion IDR.[121] Unlike SP, Migrant CARE does not have a membership base, thus it does not have members' dues and depends more on funding institutions. Hidayah claimed that Migrant CARE had received cooperation offers from a number of funders. However, she argued that her organization tried to be quite selective because their aim was not building an organization with strong finances but more on building trust.[122] Most of Migrant CARE's funding comes from institutions such as The Asia Foundation, the TIFA Foundation,[123] Friedrich-Ebert-Stiftung (FES),[124] the Ford Foundation, and the Catholic Organization for Relief and Development Aid (CORDAID).[125] In addition, this organization also receives funding from the Ministry of Women's Empowerment and Commission IX[126] of the parliament for advocating cases. Table 5.2 shows the funding received by Migrant CARE from 2004 to 2008.

Table 5.2: Funding Received by Migrant CARE 2004-2008 (approximately in USD)

Year	Amount
2004	67,000
2005	50,000
2006	132,000
2007	198,000
2008	46,000

Source: Migrant CARE's Summary of Funding Sources[127]

Susilo claimed that Migrant CARE was the only organization supported by permanent funding, which concentrated exclusively on the issue of migrant workers.[128] Susilo stated that he actually would like to have his organization funded by membership fees, which he believed would enable them to have a long term framework. For the time being he admitted that they had to negotiate with the

121 Interview with Hidayah, Anis on November 18, 2008.
122 In relation to this, they do not take funding from institutions such as the World Bank or the government. Ibid.
123 A grant making non-profit foundation. One of its main activities is to channel grants from international donors to its partners in Indonesia.
124 A German non-profit political foundation. Its activities in Indonesia are aimed at supporting the democratization process and social economic development of Indonesia. FES 2010. Funding NGO projects is among its activities.
125 A Dutch development organization with partners in Asia, Africa, and Latin America.
126 The DPR's commission responsible for the issue of migrant workers.
127 Cf. Migrant CARE 2008.
128 Interview with Susilo, Wahyu on November 7, 2008.

funders. Susilo argued that conducting their own profit-oriented activities as a source of funding was quite risky because they were advocating on behalf of migrant workers with problems, people who had the potential to get a lot of money from compensation. Susilo believed that there was an ethical question there which might place them in a similar position with the "*calo*" or middleman if they took economic advantage of the case handling.

In order to illustrate the relative funding capability of SP and Migrant CARE, I have made a comparative listing of the approximate amount of funding received by SP and Migrant CARE for the years 2005 to 2008 as presented in Table 5.3.

Table 5.3: Comparison of Funding Received by SP and Migrant CARE 2005-2008 (approximately in USD)

Year	SP		Migrant CARE
	For the whole organization	For programs on migration, health, and trafficking	
2005	157,000	0	50,000
2006	59,000	22,000	132,000
2007	478,000	123,000	198,000
2008	588,000	68,000	46,000
Total	1,282,000	213,000	426,000

Source: Compared by author based on the data in Table 5.1 and Table 5.2

Firstly, and most strikingly, it can be observed that the amount of funding is actually quite small to cover the operational cost of the organizations and fund their various activities. *Secondly*, the comparison shows that as an organization SP generally received more funds. However, it needs to be noted that it does not necessarily reflect the cost of SP's programs on migration, health and trafficking, which in 2005 did not receive any funding. *Thirdly*, the table shows a significant decrease in funding in 2008. Although more data and further analysis are needed to understand this trend fully, it probably reflects funding institutions' level of interest in supporting Indonesian NGO programs related to the issue of migrant workers. The amount of funding that donors provide really depends on their own priorities for a particular period. Consequently, it is difficult for the NGOs to plan and sustain long term programs. This is one of the reasons for the increasing calls for NGOs to break away from their dependency on funding institutions. Riana Puspasari, who had worked in a number of funding agencies, argued for the NGOs to conduct income generating activities so that they would be able to stick to a certain issue, rather than crowding to the "sexy" issues which attract temporary donor funding.[129]

Indra Piliang from CSIS claimed that NGOs' human resources, budget and network with government personnel determined their ability to work with the government.[130] In this light, he argued that at the beginning of the Reform Era, Migrant CARE was still considered a small organization, trying to establish itself and survive; it had not been able to work even with other NGOs. More recently he had seen some improvements with the help of media coverage on certain cases which he argued had brought Migrant CARE to the fore. Despite its relatively young age and limited human resources, Migrant CARE tends to take up most cases concerning migrant workers. Although its Executive Director, Hidayah, stated that they did attempt to set priorities for the organization,[131] Migrant CARE continues to get involved in most cases and instances concerning migrant workers, even if it is merely by making a public statement. This may have contributed to the organization's current high media profile. In the long run, however, it may turn out to be a factor that hampers Migrant CARE's ability to develop its organization and activism, considering it has limited human resources and that most of the time it is occupied with case handling.

5.3 Conclusion

This chapter has explained briefly the roles and positions of Indonesian NGOs before and after 1998, a historical transition point for Indonesia as a nation when the New Order Era ended and the Reform Era began. *Reformasi* may have allowed more space for civil society organizations, including NGOs, to exist, express themselves, and conduct their activities. However, acknowledgment, particularly from the government, of their involvement in the governance system, especially on the issue of migrant workers, is still debatable. This chapter has also explained how Indonesian NGOs began to take up the issue of migrant workers as one of their concerns. The last part of this chapter has introduced the two NGOs researched, SP and Migrant CARE.

Discussion of the history, structure, and organization of these two NGOs highlighted the differences between them. At this point, it can be said that SP as an older and more established organization has been able to set its priorities, argue for its agenda and programs, and structure its activism. The more than a decade-long experience has enabled SP to determine better strategies to achieve its

129 Interview with Puspasari, Riana on August 10, 2007.
130 Interview with Piliang, Indra on September 3, 2007.
131 Interview with Hidayah, Anis on May 26, 2007.

goals. In term of migrant workers issues, it has also managed to narrow its focus to two issues, trafficking, and health. Migrant CARE, on the other hand, as a younger organization, is still working to consolidate itself. Nevertheless, in a relatively short time, Migrant CARE has established quite a high profile at national, regional, and international levels, among NGOs, international organizations, and especially with the media.

It is still quite early to determine the roles of these two NGOs within the Indonesia's migration system. Thus, the examination will be continued in the next part, which is divided into two chapters that investigate the NGOs' domestic activism within the context of democratization in Indonesia. Chapter 6 examines the involvement of these NGOs in the making of a domestic policy concerning migrant workers and Chapter 7 examines the NGOs' other activities conducted domestically, which support their efforts to influence policies on migrant workers.

6. Influencing Domestic Policy

The previous chapter highlighted the need for Indonesian NGOs to adapt to the Reform Era in Indonesia. Democratization efforts made since the end of the New Order Era in 1998 have brought various changes to state governance, which include the empowerment of the parliament and local governments. Consequently, the relationships between stakeholders and the way they conduct their activities have been adjusted to respond to this new environment. In this context, chapters 6 and 8 both explain how the NGOs researched have responded to changes within the context of policy-making. The discussions in these chapters will establish whether there have been any changes since 1998 in the way the NGOs interact with state and why. Also, in examining whether the NGOs have been able to secure a significant role in Indonesia's policy process, these chapters assess the ability of NGOs to influence the formulation of Law No. 39/2004 on the Placement and Protection of Indonesian Workers Overseas and the 2006 MoU between the Government of Indonesia and Malaysia on the Recruitment and Placement of Indonesian Domestic Workers. Instruments of both domestic and foreign policy are chosen in an attempt to understand the similarities and differences between these two types of policies in terms of the process and the stakeholders involved, the space available for NGO involvement, and the efforts that NGOs have made to influence the process.

This chapter focuses on Indonesia's first law on migrant workers. The first section assesses the law-making process by describing how the issue of migrant workers was put on the policy agenda, the legislative process, and NGOs' involvement in the process. The second section examines the policy product by briefly discussing how Law No. 39/2004 is different from previous regulations of migrant workers, compares the various drafts and the law and identifies the NGOs' criticisms of the Law. The third section analyses the NGOs' activism immediately after the Law was passed to show how they responded to it.

The law which was signed by the then President, Megawati Soekarnoputri, on October 18, 2004, has sixteen chapters. Table 6.1 features the overview of the content.

Table 6.1: Overview of the Chapters of Law No. 39/2004

Chapter	Title	Overview of the Content
I	General stipulations	
II	Duties, responsibilities and obligations of the government	This chapter states that the government has the duty of regulating, developing, implementing, and monitoring the placement and protection of Indonesian workers overseas. It is also states that the government is responsible for increasing the efforts of protecting Indonesian workers overseas.
III	Rights and obligations of Indonesian workers overseas	Some of the rights stated are: to get the right information on the labor market and the placement procedure; to practice their religions; to get wages according to the standard in the destination countries; to get legal protection; to be guaranteed protection during their repatriation and to get the original contract document. Migrant workers' obligations include abiding to the regulations in the sending and receiving countries, conducting their jobs according to the contracts; paying the placement fees; and reporting to Indonesian representatives in the receiving countries.
IV	Placement operators of Indonesian workers overseas	It is stated that placement can be done by both government and private agencies.[1] It focuses more on stating the requirements for private agencies.
V	Placement procedure	This is a quite detailed chapter, regulating the activities at each stage of the labor migration process, from before placement until repatriation.
VI	Protection of Indonesian workers overseas	It is stated that protection is conducted before, during, and after placement. This chapter also states that private agencies have the responsibility to protect Indonesian workers in accordance with the contracts. According to this chapter, the government can stop placement to certain countries or jobs based on a number of considerations, including protecting Indonesian workers.
VII	Conflict redressing	Between workers and private placement operators.
VIII	Development	Development efforts by the government which are focused on information, human resources, and protection of Indonesian workers overseas.
IX	Monitoring	Conducted by central and local government institutions and Indonesian government representatives in the receiving countries.
X	National Agency for the Placement and Protection of Indonesian Workers Overseas	As mandated in this chapter, this agency is a non-department government agency with direct responsibility to the president. Its function is to implement policies on the placement and protection of Indone-

1 Placement by the government can be done if there is a written government to government agreement.

		sian workers overseas. Chapter XV which stipulates the transition process then mandated that this institution is established at the latest two years after the law goes into effect.[2]
XI, XII, XIII, XIV, XV, XVI	Administrative sanctions, investigation, criminal sanctions, other stipulations, transition stipulation, and closing stipulation.	

Source: Extracted by the author from Law No. 39/2004 as documented on the website of the Department of Manpower and Transmigration[3]

6.1 Making Indonesia's First Law on Migrant Workers

6.1.1 Putting the Issue of Migrant Workers on the Policy Agenda

Since SP was the first NGO in Indonesia that took up the issue of migrant workers, SP's earlier activities concerning the issue of women migrant workers can generally be considered as initial efforts to put the issue on the government's policy agenda. Salma Safitri, the Head of SP's National Executive Body for 2004-2007, explained that starting with handling cases, SP then began to look into government regulations on the sending of migrant workers.[4] According to Safitri, after years of studying the problems and the existing regulations, SP realized that the issue of migrant workers could not be solved by regulations at the ministerial level because it involves various departments. Consequently, SP argued that the issue of migrant workers should be regulated by a specific law which has power over the related ministries and departments.

Furthermore, as argued by Wahyu Susilo, Migrant CARE's board member and policy analyst, Law No. 25/1997 on Labor which was initiated by the DPR in 1996 and finally passed in 1997 did not cover the issue of migrant workers.[5] The absence of a law that specifically addressed the issue of migrant workers was one of the factors that brought together a number of Indonesian NGOs, including SP, to set up *Kopbumi* with the main task of lobbying for a law on the protection of migrant workers.[6] Since its establishment in 1997, *Kopbumi* started

2 The law went into effect on October 18, 2004, but the BNP2TKI was not established until 2007.

3 Cf. Presiden Republik Indonesia, October 18, 2004.

4 Interview with Safitri, Salma on June 6, 2007.

5 Email from Susilo, Wahyu on May 26, 2008.

6 According to Susilo, who was still an SP activist at that time and became the executive secretary of *Kopbumi*, the NGOs alliance building effort began in 1996. Cf. Susilo 2005.

to campaign for the law by conducting research, making legal drafts, and conducting dialogues. According to Susilo, *Kopbumi* began to make a draft for the proposed law in 1997, and their drafts, which underwent various changes, were submitted to the DPR during Soeharto's, Habibie's, Abdurrahman Wahid's, and Megawati's presidencies.[7] By 2004, there were three proposed drafts before the parliament, one by *Kopbumi*, one from Brawijaya University, and another one by the parliament itself.[8]

As for the two NGOs researched, particularly SP, their involvement at this agenda setting stage was mainly through *Kopbumi*. As one of the founders and members, SP was involved in the Consortium's activities related to the campaign for the law on protection of migrant workers and their families. Since Migrant CARE was established in 2004, the same year as the law was formulated, it was not, as an organization, involved in the initial campaigns for the law. However, Migrant CARE's main activists such as Anis Hidayah and Wahyu Susilo were members of *Kopbumi* before they left the consortium and established Migrant CARE.

With the various events that occurred between 1997 and 2004 such as the increased number of migrants after the economic crisis, the start of the reform era in 1998, and the Nunukan tragedy in 2002, the need for a law on the protection of migrant workers gained in urgency. In August-September 2002, when tens of thousands Indonesian workers were deported from Malaysia to Nunukan in Kalimantan, *Kopbumi* was quite vocal in exposing the conditions at the camps there and criticizing the government's slow response on the matter. *Kopbumi* also lobbied the then vice-chairman of the DPR, Muhaimin Iskandar, who then called for

7 Email from Susilo, Wahyu on May 26, 2008.

8 Cf. Komnas Perempuan and SP 2003, p. 40.The documentation compiled by the DPR's Centre for Data and Information Analysis and Processing does not record the drafts from *Kopbumi* and Brawijaya University. As shown in the documentation, only two versions were compared and deliberated in the legislative process, the DPR's draft and the government's draft. The staff of the Centre explained that the "academic drafts" from universities or NGOs are usually submitted to the commission dealing with that particular bill. In the case of the bill on migrant workers, it was Commission VII. The commission uses the academic drafts as inputs to formulate the DPR's draft. A definition of academic draft or academic script (*draft akademis/naskah akademis*) can be found on the website of Hukumpedia, which refers to a research which is used as a basis in the drafting of a bill, providing background, important issues and solutions, broad regulatory framework, and/or the content of the proposed bill. Cf. Hukumpedia 2010. It is a preliminary document consisting of regulatory ideas and material for the bill. According to Hukumpedia, it is not compulsory to make an academic draft and even if it is produced, it often becomes merely a justification basis for the bill and does not explain the content. The task of making of an academic draft is usually given to universities or other third parties which are considered to have the expertise. Cf. Parlemen.net 2010. This explains why, as shown in table 6.3, the DPR seems to adopt more from the Brawijaya University's academic draft than from *Kopbumi*'s draft.

the government to pay more attention to addressing migrant workers' problems, which he considered had reached a critical point.[9] Moreover, the media had exposed the relentless saga of the abuse of Indonesian women migrant workers. This would have also been strong evidence of the need to pass a law to protect Indonesian migrant workers.

Furthermore, on various occasions before 2004, the Indonesian government and parliament had promised to work on such a law. Muhaimin Iskandar, the deputy speaker for the DPR, after meeting *Kopbumi* in 2002, mentioned the possibility of the DPR forming a special committee on Indonesian migrant workers.[10] He also mentioned a DPR plan to take the initiative in proposing a law to protect migrant workers.[11] As for the government, the commitment to improve the protection of Indonesian migrant workers had been stated in a number of state documents such as the Principal Outlines for State Policy 1999-2004. Also in the first National Plan of Action on Human Rights (*Rencana Aksi Nasional Hak-Hak Asasi Manusia Indonesia*) 1998-2003, the Habibie government made ratification of the 1990 ICRMW one of its priorities. In her annual address to the People's Assembly in 2002, the then president, Megawati Soekarnoputri, in her recommendations on the protection of migrant workers and their families, had also recognized the need to speed up the passing of the law and increase efforts to establish bilateral agreements with receiving countries.[12] Moreover, as pointed out by Wahyu Susilo, who was then the Executive Secretary of *Kopbumi*, Jacob Nuwa Wea, the Minister of Manpower and Transmigration for 1999-2004, had on five different occasions made promises to finish the draft of the bill on the protection of migrant workers.[13] Nevertheless, the initiative to begin the legislation process of deliberating and formulating the law was taken only in 2004 and the process was rushed toward September that year, when the DPR and the government were approaching the end of their term of office.

There is no official explanation on why the issue of migrant workers was not one of the policy priorities of Indonesian governments after Soeharto. However, it can be assumed that the Habibie and Abdurrahman Wahid governments were more occupied with issues like economic recovery, political transition, and state

9 Cf. Pikiran Rakyat 2002.

10 Cf. ibid.

11 Cf. Kompas, August 15, 2002.

12 Cf. Komnas Perempuan and SP 2003, p. 39.

13 Kompas, June 5, 2004. *Firstly*, when he was the head of the labor and transmigration sub commission in the DPR at the beginning of 2001; *secondly*, when he was elected as Minister of Manpower and Transmigration, deliberation of the bill was listed as part of his first 100 days program; *thirdly*, when the Nunukan case escalated in 2002; *fourthly*, when there was repatriation of migrant workers with problems from Kuwait; and in 2004, he again promised that the bill would be passed before the election that year.

reform, which put other issues, including the issue of migrant workers, low down on their agendas. Their presidencies were also relatively short; leaving them limited time to work on the issue. Moreover, since law-making involves both the government and the parliament, it requires a reasonably cooperative relationship between them, which was lacking during the early periods of *Reformasi* Era, particularly during the Abdurrahman Wahid presidency. As for Megawati Soekarnoputri, she was highly criticized, particularly by migrant worker advocates, for her responses to problems faced by migrant workers, particularly during the Nunukan tragedy.[14] Nevertheless, the bill on the placement and protection of migrant workers was deliberated during her office and eventually endorsed as a law toward the end of her presidency. The next section will look into the legislative process of this law.

6.1.2 Legislative Process

In Indonesia's legislative system, law-making involves the DPR as the legislative branch and the government as the executive branch. The following is a brief explanation of the official law-making process inside the parliament.[15] Every bill is deliberated by the DPR and the president to get joint approval. The bill can come from the DPR, the president or a local parliament. If there are two bills proposed in one session, the bill deliberated will be the one from the DPR and the bill from the president will be used for comparison. The initiative for the law on Indonesian workers overseas came from the parliament. A bill will then go through two levels of deliberation. The first deliberation is conducted in a commission meeting (*Rapat Komisi*), a legislative body meeting (*Rapat Badan Legislasi*), a budget committee meeting (*Rapat Panitia Anggaran*), or in a special committee meeting (*Rapat Panitia Khusus*), which was where the bill on migrant workers was first discussed. The deliberation involves views and opinions from the DPR, responses from the president, and then deliberation by the DPR and the president based on a problems inventory list. The decision is then made by a vote at the second deliberation of the bill in the general meeting of the DPR. For the whole process, the president usually appoints a minister to represent him/her in dealing

14 When the Nunukan tragedy occurred, Megawati went to Johannesburg for the Earth Summit, and from there she made a statement saying that the media had blown up the issue out of proportion. Her statement was highly criticized by the NGOs and the media. She was also compared by the media and migrant worker advocates to the Philippines' President, Gloria Macapagal Arroyo, who canceled her trip to Johannesburg to visit the Philippine migrant workers who were deported from Malaysia.

15 Cf. DPR 2008.

with the issue. For the bill on Indonesian workers overseas, the government was represented by the Minister of Manpower and Transmigration.

Within seven days of both the DPR and the president agreeing to accept the bill, the head of the DPR will send the bill to the president to be endorsed as a law. After 15 days, if the president has not endorsed the law, the chair of the DPR will send a letter to the president to ask for explanation. If the agreed bill is still not endorsed by the president within 30 days after the agreement, the bill officially becomes a law and has to be endorsed. The bill on the placement and protection of Indonesian workers overseas was immediately sent to the president after it was accepted by the DPR's General Meeting on September 29, 2004, and was signed by the then President, Megawati Soekarnoputri, in less than 30 days.

It is important to also take into account the context in which the bill was deliberated and passed. Law No. 39/2004 was passed by a reformed Indonesian parliament, which was in the process of adjusting to a democratic transition. A study conducted by Ziegenhain analyzed the changes and continuities in Indonesia's parliament during the transition period 1997-2004.[16] During this period, all elements of the state had to adjust to the new political context and their new role and functions within the more democratized system. As for the members of parliament, the adjustment process includes familiarizing themselves with their new composition and power and rebuilding their relationship with the government.[17] These tasks have preoccupied the parliament, contributing to its low productivity in deliberating, passing and drafting new legislation, which Ziegenhain believes earned it the nickname of "talking shop".[18] As a result, within the five year term, which ended in October 2004, the parliament had low productivity both in quantity and quality of legislation.[19]

Law No. 39/2004 was one of those drafted, deliberated, and passed in a transitional period by a parliament that consisted of new members, who mostly had low levels of experience, who were still adjusting to its new form, mechanisms,

16 See Ziegenhain 2008.

17 During Abdurrahman Wahid's presidency, the relationship between the legislative and executive branches of the state became sour, ending in the impeachment of Wahid. Consequently, during Megawati Soekarnoputri's presidency, the legislative and executive had to rebuild their relationship. Cf. ibid., p. 177.

18 Cf. ibid., p. 164. Ziegenhain suggests that several factors contributed to this low productivity including: the new members of parliament's lack of experience; the adoption of new mechanisms and legislative procedures; the ample time consumed for repositioning the legislature in the government system and conducting its supervisory functions. Cf. ibid., pp. 165-66. The members' low skills, expertise, and lack of professionalism also contributed to the low quality of their output. Cf. ibid., p. 196. An example of the low professionalism is the low attendance in the parliament's sessions, which frequently delayed the sessions due to lack of a quorum.

19 Cf. ibid., pp. 167 and 169.

procedures and increased authority, and who were still in the process of redefining the parliament's position within the state system and its relation with other state branches, particularly the executive. According to Ziegenhain, as an attempt to be remembered as an effective legislature, toward the end of its term, the 1999-2004 DPR rushed the passage of a number of bills without holding adequate public hearings.[20] Law No. 39/2004 was one of the bills passed during the last two weeks of the term. The fact that quite a number of bills were being deliberated in a short period of time, divided the attention of civil society. As explained by Safitri, instead of supporting the action for the law on migrant workers, most women's NGOs concentrated on another bill on the elimination of domestic violence.[21]

In line with Ziegenhain's argument, in the case of Law No. 39/2004, Safitri argued that both the DPR and Megawati's government, particularly the MoMT, wanted to be remembered as having passed a law on migrant workers before they finish their terms.[22] She described how, during the two weeks of deliberation, the then minister, Jacob Nuwa Wea, closely monitored the process in the DPR. In fact, Nuwa Wea stated that he intentionally allocated his time to work on this law and his statements in the deliberation meetings show his strong intention to have the law passed before his office ended.[23] Safitri called the law "*undang-undang sulapan satu malam*" (a law magically made in one night), and "*undang-undang kejar setoran*" (a law made to fulfill the quota).[24] Her strong criticism of the short deliberation period of the bill is shared by most migrant worker advocates, most of who highlighted that the process in the DPR only took around two weeks toward the end of its term. This is the basis for their argument that the law-makers did not allow enough time to deliberate on the issues that needed to be addressed in the law. On the other hand, the law-makers, particularly the government, tended to argue that the process had begun long before the parliamentary process started. The government claimed that the issue had been discussed in the State Secretariat even before the DPR conveyed its initiative to the government.[25]

To provide a general description of the legislative process for this law, I summarize the stages from the documentation made by the Centre for Data and Information Analysis and Processing of the DPR.

20 Cf. ibid., p. 169.
21 Interview with Safitri, Salma on August 2, 2007.
22 Ibid.
23 Cf. Pusat Pengkajian Pengolahan Data dan Informasi 2008.
24 Interview with Safitri, Salma on August 2, 2007.
25 Cf. Depnakertrans 2004a.

Table 6.2: Summary of the Legislative Process of Law No. 39/2004

Date	Event
September 2002	The DPR's legislation body[26] submitted the proposed Bill on the Protection of Indonesian Workers Overseas to the Head of the DPR.
November 18, 2002	All fractions in the general meeting of the DPR agreed to adopt the Bill proposed by the Legislation Body as a bill proposed by the DPR to be sent to the government.
May 27, 2003	The DPR sent the proposed Bill on the Protection of Indonesian Migrant Workers Overseas to the President and asked the President to appoint a minister to represent the government in the deliberation.
June 21, 2004	The President sent to the DPR the government's version of a Bill on the Placement and Protection of Indonesian Workers Overseas and assigned the Minister of Manpower and Transmigration to represent the government.
August 30,31, 2004; September 1,2,3,6,7,8, 2004	The special committee met with the Minister of Manpower and Transmigration, deliberating the bill.
September 9 and 14, 2004	The working committee met with the Minister of Manpower and Transmigration, deliberating parts of the bill which could not be decided in the special committee meetings.
September 29, 2004	The head of the special committee reported the result of their deliberation to the general meeting. All fractions accepted the bill.
September 29, 2004	The head of the DPR sent the Bill on the Placement and the Protection of Indonesian Workers Overseas accepted by the General Meeting to the President to be passed as a law.

Source: Documentation compiled by the Centre for Data and Information Analysis and Processing of the Archives and Documentation Section of the Secretariat General of the DPR[27]

There are some points that need to be made on this legislative process based on documentation by the DPR's Centre for Data and Information Analysis and Processing.[28] *Firstly*, the above stages only represent the official legislative process in the parliament. Both the government and DPR members claimed that they sought advice from various stakeholders, and some NGO staff acknowledged that they had meetings with members of parliament in the form of audiences and public hearings. However, the documentation does not record these input gather-

26 For bills proposed by the DPR, the inside initiative can come from the legislation body (*badan legislasi*), a commission (*komisi*), joint commissions (*gabungan komisi*), or 17 members who propose the initial draft of a bill to the head of the DPR. Cf. Parlemen.net 2010. The draft will then be brought to the general meeting (*Rapat Paripurna*) to be adopted as a bill proposed by the DPR.

27 Cf. Pusat Pengkajian Pengolahan Data dan Informasi 2008.

28 Cf. ibid.

ing meetings and the drafting process. Consequently, it cannot provide further confirmation on what happened in the advisory meetings and whether the inputs were actually consulted during the drafting process.[29]

Secondly, the government's response was only given around 13 months after they received the bill proposed by the DPR. In his speech to the DPR's General Meeting on September 29, 2004, the then Minister of Manpower and Transmigration, Jacob Nuwa Wea, stated that since the issue of placement and protection of Indonesian workers required careful and meticulous treatment, and that they needed to accommodate various aspirations of the public, the government could only finish their response draft by June 21, 2004.[30] He claimed that the government had taken advice from various stakeholders such as labor agencies, workers' organizations, NGOs, observers, the ILO, and others. On August 30, 2004, there was finally a meeting between the special committee of Commission VII[31] and the Minister of Manpower and Transmigration. The series of meeting from August 30, 2004 to September 8, 2004 focused on comparing the drafts from the government and the DPR. Because these meetings were open to public, they were monitored by NGOs. However some points that could not be agreed on in the special committee meeting were referred to working committee meetings on September 9 and 14, 2004, which were closed to the public. One of the significant points referred to the working committee, which obviously could not be monitored by NGO activists, was whether to use only "protection" or "placement and protection" in the title of the bill.

Thirdly, the statements of Jacob Nuwa Wea, during the deliberation meetings confirmed that there were intentions to rush the passing of the law. On a number of occasions he made statements which showed his eagerness to have the law passed immediately.[32] Nuwa Wea even stated that he wanted the law to be a leg-

29 A possible way to check whether or not the NGOs' inputs were accommodated is to compare the NGOs draft to the DPR's and the government's draft, which will be done later in this chapter.

30 Cf. Nuwa Wea, September 29, 2004.

31 In conducting their tasks, all members of the parliament, except for the leaders, are assigned to various commissions that have different tasks and working partners, i.e. departments or ministries, in the government. For example, within the 2004-2009 DPR, manpower and transmigration fell under Commission IX together with population and health. Within the 1999-2004 DPR, the issue of migrant workers, which is part of manpower and transmigration, was put under Commission VII on health and population, which partnered, among others, with the office of the State Ministry of Women's Empowerment, the Department of Health and the Department of Manpower and Transmigration.

32 Cf. Pusat Pengkajian Pengolahan Data dan Informasi 2008. In the first special committee meeting he already stated his expectation that the deliberation of the bill could be finished before his and the DPR members' time in their offices ended. In relation to this, he even suggested to change the quorum from being based on the number of members present to

acy for subsequent generations and that people would remember that Commission VII of the DPR and the Minister of Manpower and Transmigration of that particular period passed a law on migrant workers. NGO activists such as Salma Safitri noted critically that the law was rushed through for reasons of personal achievement.[33]

The main debate between the government and the NGOs concerned the time allocated to work on the bill and whether it accommodated the NGOs' inputs. The government claimed that, since receiving the DPR's proposed bill, about a year before the deliberation, they had prepared their version of the draft which incorporated the interests of various related elements of the society, including NGOs. However, most NGOs argued that that they were not adequately involved in this process and their advice was not heeded. For the purposes of this study, i.e. in considering the impact of democratization on NGOs involvement in policy-making, it needs to be determined whether the legislative process actually allowed inputs from civil society, and if so, through what mechanisms. The next section attempts to answer these questions by examining NGOs' involvement in the law-making process.

6.1.3 Involvement of NGOs in the Law-Making Process

As mentioned earlier in this chapter, since the Soeharto era *Kopbumi* had made several drafts for a law on the protection of migrant workers and submitted them to the DPR. Also, both the DPR and the government claimed that they had consulted other stakeholders, including NGOs, to obtain recommendations for their drafts. Jacob Nuwa Wea, the then Minister of Manpower and Transmigration, even stated that 70 percent of the draft from the government had undergone adaptation and changes to accommodate aspirations from the community, particularly labor agencies and migrant worker NGOs.[34] However, there is no evidence on whether this accommodation and adaptation actually occurred and the NGOs argue that the bill which was then endorsed as a law did not accommodate their inputs.

Tina Suprihatin, an activist from *Kopbumi*, stated that, before the deliberation process, the coalition had conducted a seminar involving members of parliament to provide advice on the needs of Indonesian migrant workers that should be ac-

being based on the number of fractions, so that the meetings would not be postponed for lack of a quorum. He reminded DPR members of his intention to pass the law on time every time there was a dead-lock or a lengthy deliberation.

33 Interview with Safitri, Salma on August 2, 2007.

34 Cf. Kompas, September 1, 2004.

commodated in the bill.[35] However, based on the monitoring conducted by the coalition during the deliberation process, Suprihatin argued that NGOs' ideas were ignored. Salma Safitri gave a similar report.[36] These statements from Suprihatin and Safitri show that a change has occurred in the legislative process in Indonesia. During the New Order, law-making was exclusive to the government with the DPR as the rubber stamp. Since 1998, both the government and the DPR, which has regained its legislative authority, have started to involve other stakeholders in the initial process to obtain inputs for laws. However, the statements also mirror the NGOs' views that the advice-gathering does not necessarily result in the NGOs' recommendations being reflected in the law.

It is the opinion of Thaufiek Zulbahary, from SP, that although SP has access to the policy process, the impact was negligible because their advice tended to get lost in the process.[37] To illustrate this, he explained that in workshops conducted by the government, the participants were usually divided into small groups, consisting of a mixture of government and civil society representatives, who were expected to formulate group reports. He argued that the small groups were frequently dominated by government representatives and the NGOs never received any follow-up news from them. He also pointed out that when they were invited to meetings of the working group they were involved in, unlike the government representatives, they were not supported with funding for transportation. Furthermore, he claimed that often the agenda and decisions for some meetings had been set from the start. As a result, SP had withdrawn from a working group by sending a letter and a book based on research conducted by a number of organizations and networks, including SP.[38] In the letter, SP expressed its thanks for the invitation to participate but explained that SP saw the involvement merely as a way for the government to claim the legitimacy of having NGO participation. Because SP was not involved in determining the content of the bill and thus could not benefit migrant workers, the organization withdrew. Zulbahary saw this move as a good one since it would be recorded in the report that the NGO withdrew.[39] This can be considered as the NGO's effort to make a strong statement criticizing the way the input gathering was conducted, which it considered not to be in a properly democratic fashion.

Zulbahary's explanation of SP's involvement and their following withdrawal from the working group confirms that, although NGOs were involved in a number of forums prior to the official policy-making process, they were frequently

35 Cf. Tempo Interaktif, September 14, 2004.

36 Interview with and email from Safitri, Salma on August 2, 2007 and on May 14, 2008.

37 Interview with Zulbahary, Thaufiek on November 19, 2008.

38 Cf. Komnas Perempuan et al. 2006a.

39 Interview with Zulbahary, Thaufiek on November 19, 2008.

not accommodative toward NGOs' inputs. Thus, my argument remains that the issue was not whether NGOs were able to get involved,[40] but rather whether their inputs are taken into account and included in the policy product. It seems that at the time when Law No. 39/2004 was formulated, involving stakeholders in the policy-making process was still interpreted and executed as merely providing events where the stakeholders, including the NGOs, could express their views.[41]

Zulbahary's statement that they were not financially supported to come to meetings of the working groups brings back the long standing question of NGO independence, particularly in the financial area. In the present Indonesian political context, which has allowed more involvement of NGOs, it has become more important for NGOs to be able to finance their participation in the policy process. Besides allowing the NGOs to preserve their independence during such involvement, adequate financial capability would also assist them in expanding their activities. However, to date, the NGOs continue to depend on funding from foreign donor institutions and occasionally state institutions.

NGO efforts to influence the deliberation process in the DPR were made both outside and inside the DPR. They released statements and made press conferences to express their views during the two weeks of parliamentary deliberation and almost every day NGO activists and women ex-migrant workers conducted demonstrations in front of the parliament building, demanding the DPR to postpone the passing of the bill.[42] According to them, it was better to postpone endorsement of the bill than to pass it without adequate deliberation. By September 27, 2004, closer to the passing of the law, demonstrations were also conducted in

40 As stated by Zulbahary, even if SP was not involved initially, SP could demand to be involved in the next meeting. Interview with Zulbahary, Thaufiek on November 19, 2008.

41 Nursyahbani Katjasungkana, a member of the DPR for 2004-2009 and one of the founders of SP, argued that there should be no more complaints about the lack of access to the law-making process. Interview with Katjasungkana, Nursyahbani on July 6, 2007. She refers to Law No. 10/2004 on the Making of Laws and Regulations, which stipulates in one of its clauses that the public has the right to give verbal or written inputs in the preparation or deliberation of laws and local regulations. Thus, Katjasungkana argued that migrant workers' advocates need to be more proactive and more willing to work with state institutions. According to her, although *Kopbumi* had created a draft law, they did not proactively lobby the decision makers. Although I agree with Katjasungkana that the NGOs need to actively lobby the law makers and closely monitor the process, it is important to note that the law that gives legal guarantee for public participation in law- and regulation-making process was only passed in June 2004, a few months before the deliberation process for a law on migrant workers. Thus, given Indonesia's notorious reputation in postponing the implementation of policies, there was a possibility that it had not been properly implemented by the time the bill on migrant workers was deliberated.

42 Cf. Tempo Interaktif, September 14, 2004 and September 16, 2004.

various cities in Indonesia.[43] In Jakarta, more people joined the demonstration which involved a long march, orations, street theatre performance in front of the parliament building to show the abuses experienced by migrant workers, and carrying posters which contained their criticisms of the bill.[44] The NGOs' actions outside the DPR building received attention and support from some members of parliament who came out to talk to them.[45] This indicates that there were parliament members who shared the opinion of the NGOs and supported their cause.

Inside the building, the NGOs closely monitored the debates. According to Safitri, activists from organizations such as SP, *Komnas Perempuan*, *Kopbumi*, GPPBM, and Migrant Workers Solidarity Cianjur[46] monitored the process from the balcony of the meeting room.[47] Safitri claimed that they were present in the balcony for the whole two weeks, twelve hours a day, bringing office equipment like laptops, printers, paper, etc. to support their lobbying efforts. They even called themselves the "balcony faction". Safitri explained that their lobbying efforts involved providing short written submissions or articles to members of parliament and the government during their lunch and break times. They also sent text messages during the deliberation meetings to members of parliament if they appeared to be unable to counter the government's arguments on certain clauses. According to her, these efforts were needed because many DPR members did not know the real problems faced by migrant workers in the field.

Safitri admitted that just as in cases of any other deliberation for a law, the role of NGOs was limited to lobbying individual members of the parliament.[48] NGOs' limited involvement and reliance on personal lobbying are confirmed by Wahyu Susilo's explanation of their activities.[49] Susilo stated that NGOs were

43 Demonstrations were held in Lampung, Jambi, Semarang, Yogyakarta, Surabaya, Kupang, Mataram, Makassar, Pontianak, Palembang, Medan, Cirebon, and Blitar. Cf. Bambang S, September 27, 2004.

44 Some of the protests written on the posters were "Stop Legitimacy of Slavery through Law", "Protect Women Migrant Workers from Laws that Disadvantage Them", "Migrant Workers are not Commodities", "Bill on Migrant Workers is Bill for the Oppression and Exploitation of Indonesian Workers Overseas", "Don't Burden Migrant Workers With Placement Fee", "Bill on Migrant Workers Does Not Have the Intention to Protect But to Exploit". Ibid. The escalation in the number of people demonstrating on September 27, 2004, according to Tina Suprihatin, happened because the working committee was scheduled to report to the special committee, which was expected to be followed by the endorsement of the bill by Commission VII of the DPR. Cf. Ibid. She said that the coalition of NGOs was demanding that the endorsement should be postponed because what they wanted was a law on protection, not a law that exploited migrant workers. However, Commission VII continued with its deliberation.

45 Ibid.

46 A migrant worker organization affiliated with SP.

47 Email from Safitri, Salma on May 14, 2008.

48 Interview with Safitri, Salma on August 2, 2007.

49 Email from Susilo, Wahyu on May 26, 2008.

only involved in the public hearing meetings after the DPR's special committee for this bill was established. Beyond that, they had to rely on personal lobbying. According to him, they were able to lobby the members of the special committee but their relationship with the government, particularly with the Department of Manpower and Transmigration, remained tense. Susilo mentioned that the NGOs lobbied a number of key parliament members whom he considered personally close to Migrant CARE activists such as Muhaimin Iskandar,[50] the deputy speaker for the DPR and Pramono Anung, one of the leaders in *Partai Demokrasi Indonesia Perjuangan* (PDI-P). These explanations by Safitri and Susilo show that, in many circumstances, personal relationships between NGO activists and some key figures in the parliament, government, parties or other key national institutions play a significant role in their lobbying efforts. It illustrates how the NGOs built their strategies in channeling their agenda into the state system through key actors. Nevertheless, the experience during the making of Law No. 39/2004 also shows that these individual lobbies were not strong enough to put their agenda forward. The key actors lobbied by the NGOs still had to abide by the majority voice in their parties and in the DPR. Moreover, there is a possibility that the members of parliament lobbied by the NGOs were not actually involved in the deliberation meetings and there was no guarantee that those involved would be able to promote the NGOs' agenda. The minutes of the deliberation meetings show that the members of PKB, a party which the NGOs considered quite sympathetic, were not among the most vocal during the deliberation meetings.[51] The members of another supposedly friendly party, PDI-P, were more actively involved in the deliberation but in some occasions they differed among themselves. Moreover, at the end, like other fractions in the committee, they agreed to pass the law. Thus, it can be said that the NGO lobbying was not able to reach enough legislators to have significant impact.

On September 29, 2004, in a general meeting of the DPR, Law No. 39/2004 was endorsed, with unanimous approval from all factions of the DPR and the Minister of Manpower and Transmigration.[52] Immediately after the law was passed, the NGOs unfurled a banner at the balcony that said "The Endorsement of the Migrant Worker Protection Bill Means the Death of Conscience" and spread flower petals to commemorate this death.[53] This peaceful action became chaotic when the parliamentary security personnel forced them to furl the banner, although members of parliament actually did not complain. The security person-

50 Muhaimin Iskandar was the leader of *Partai Kebangkitan Bangsa* (PKB) and deputy speaker for the DPR for both the periods of 1999-2004 and 2004-2009.

51 Cf. Pusat Pengkajian Pengolahan Data dan Informasi 2008.

52 Cf. Suara Pembaruan, October 1, 2004.

53 Cf. Bambang S, September 29, 2004, The Jakarta Post, September 30, 2004.

nel also bashed and arrested the NGO activists who were considered to be creating unrest.[54] Several migrant worker organizations reacted strongly, condemning all harsh actions toward civil society and urging the government to investigate the action of the security personnel.[55] The NGOs also made statements demanding the cancelation of the law.[56]

The deliberation process shows that the NGOs lobbied members of the parliament, coordinated their efforts, and utilized various approaches to influence the law-making process. Nevertheless, these efforts did not bring satisfactory results from their perspective because, according to them, most of their suggestions were not incorporated in the law. Two parties, PDI-P and PKB, showed a degree of support for the NGOs' campaign. However, without a strong party platform on the issue of migrant workers, they could not be relied on to channel the NGOs' agenda into the legislative process. In short, the NGOs were left with limited options.

While the NGOs managed to build relationships with some members of the parliament, their relationship with the government, i.e. the MoMT, remained distant. Part of the reason was the ministry's unsympathetic view of NGOs. Although Jacob Nuwa Wea, the Minister, was from PDI-P, one of the parties lobbied by NGOs,[57] his responses to the NGO demands were quite negative, as reflected in his statements on various occasions. In an interview with the media during a break from the deliberation meetings, Nuwa Wea, made statements that showed his lack of appreciation and acknowledgement of the NGOs by questioning the status of those protesting outside the parliament building and the legitimacy for the demand of involving NGOs' in the law-making process.[58] After the

54 Cf. ibid. Miftah Farid from FOBMI was arrested, hit, and kicked by the security personnel. An activist from SP was hit and verbally abused when security personnel wanted to grab the banner while they were leaving the meeting room.

55 Cf. Bambang S September 29, 2004.

56 This is shown in a statement by Tina Suprihatin, who requested the next elected government in its first 100 days in the office to cancel the law and make a new law which protects migrant workers. Cf. Lim 2004.

57 Email from Susilo, Wahyu on May 26, 2008.

58 Cf. Bambang S September 28, 2004. He said that the NGOs who were protesting should not be heard. In his view, because the government had to be responsible for migrant workers from placement to repatriation, there was no need to involve NGOs. When asked about who could monitor the government, he answered that the government already had guidelines and a structure to monitor itself. He also stated that, even if the government wanted to involve the NGOs, there were still questions of how and as what. To him, NGOs were not part of the official system; thus their monitoring effort should not be stipulated by the law. When asked about the demand to postpone the law, he answered that the law-making process would continue and "just because one or two people said 'postpone', we [the government] cannot postpone". He even questioned the status of the ex-migrant workers who participated in the demonstration, stating that they were just creating problems, only talking without actually doing something.

law was passed, he again made similar statements.[59] Although Nuwa Wea claimed that the draft of the law had been discussed with stakeholders before it was deliberated, he also stated that the NGOs and labor activists opposed the bill because they did not understand the core problem and did not know the precise contents.[60] His statement sounds contradictory because if the government had actually discussed the draft with the stakeholders, including the NGOs, there should have been no problem for them in understanding the draft.

"Having a law despite its weaknesses is better than having no law at all" seemed to be the main view of the government, particularly the MoMT. During the deliberation process, an official from the ministry stated that it was most important to have a law as a legal umbrella for the placement and protection process and amendments could still be made after the law was passed to accommodate the interest of various stakeholders.[61] A similar statement came from the minister.[62] Nevertheless, two presidencies later, the amendments demanded by most migrant workers' advocates are yet to occur.

This section has shown how there have been changes in the way the NGOs interact with members of the parliament and the government. As shown in their actions and statements, it seems that NGOs could establish better relationships with members of the parliament than with the government, particularly the MoMT. It is commonly known that the relationship between migrant worker advocates and the ministry has always been distant, if not sour. This ministry has been the main target of migrant worker advocates for its failure to protect migrant workers and for exploiting them for economic reasons, including as a way to deal with the high unemployment rate. On the other side, the ministry has been quite defensive, maintaining minimal interactions with migrant worker advocates. Up to the present, most migrant worker advocates see the MoMT as the most uncooperative government institution.

The next section will examine Law No. 39/2004 in order to understand NGOs criticisms of its content.

59 Cf. Lim 2004. He again questioned the status of the protesters and claimed that not all of them had read the final draft of the bill, which he considered as one of the most advanced bills in the field of manpower. This statement reflects that he did not see that those who protested, including the NGOs, represented the voices of migrant workers.

60 Cf. The Jakarta Post, September 30, 2004. He did not explain further what he meant by "core problem" and "precise contents".

61 Cf. Kompas, September 24, 2004.

62 Cf. The Jakarta Post, September 30, 2004.

6.2 Law No. 39/2004

6.2.1 A Change in Indonesian Regulation of Labor Migration

Before Law No. 39/2004 on the Placement and Protection of Indonesian Workers Overseas was passed, regulation of migration of Indonesians working overseas was based on ministerial decisions and government regulations.[63] The main regulation on labor migration before Law No. 39/2004 was the Ministerial Decision No. KEP.104A/MEN/2002 on the Placement of Indonesian Migrant Workers Overseas. As reflected in the title, the ministerial decision only focused on regulating the placement of Indonesian migrant workers overseas while the law was intended to cover both the placement and protection aspects. As for the content, while the ministerial decision regulated the placement process in some detail,[64] the law – although it still covers the placement aspect in a rather detailed way – has other chapters which contains protective elements such as those on the protection of Indonesian workers overseas, duties, responsibilities and obligations of the government, and rights and obligations of the workers.

The endorsement of Law No. 39/2004 is a significant development in the management of Indonesia's labor migration because the parliament and the government finally passed a Law, which is considered as a stronger policy instrument compared to other types of regulations. In his statement after the law was passed, Jacob Nuwa Wea mentioned some of its strengths, including the mandate to establish a national institution to regulate the placement and protection of migrant workers overseas, its coverage of all Indonesians working overseas, not just those working in the informal sector, and the imposition of harsh sanctions on illegal migrant workers.[65] Nevertheless, most migrant workers' advocates have criticized and rejected the law, mainly because according to them, it does not provide adequate protection for migrant workers.

Given that migrant workers' advocates claimed that the content of the law did not benefit migrant workers, it may be assumed that the law would benefit labor agencies which have quite a strong lobby with the government. However, although for reasons different from those given by migrant workers' advocates, labor agencies associations also voiced objections to the law, as shown in the

63 These regulations concerning the placement of Indonesian workers overseas can be found on the website of the Department of Manpower and Transmigration.

64 The main clauses are requirements for the establishment of labor agencies, procedures for the placement of migrant workers, mostly relating to how the labor agencies must conduct their activities and their responsibilities from pre-placement to the post-working overseas period, reporting, evaluation, monitoring, and administrative sanctions for labor agencies, which are considered as an effort to protect migrant workers.

65 Cf. Lim 2004.

statement of Saleh Alwani, Head of the Monitoring Body of Indonesian Workers Service Companies' Association or *Asosiasi Perusahaan Jasa TKI* (*Apjati*).[66] His objection was directed toward the limitation of placement only to destination countries which have MoUs with Indonesia, as specified in the law, which according to him would restrict opportunities for formal migrant workers. He also said that the law should differentiate the placement programs for formal and informal migrant workers.[67] Furthermore, he insisted that the government remained a regulator rather than becoming involved as a placement operator so it could become a fair referee when a problem occurred. He questioned the ability of the government to sanction itself if it takes both roles. Aswani also argued that the government is taking over the market which was initially opened by the private sector.

In understanding the NGOs' rejection of the law, Table 6.3 contrasts the main features, particularly the title of the chapters, of the drafts made by *Kopbumi* and Brawijaya University, the bills from the DPR and the government, and Law No. 39/2004.[68] This general comparison aims at identifying the differences between the documents and determining which draft is accommodated more in the law.

66 Cf. Sinar Harapan 2004.

67 The law applies to labor migration in both the formal and informal sector. There are significant differences between these two sectors such as the process of migration, the requirements, the status of the workers under the receiving countries' law and the problems entailed. Thus, as argued by the labor agencies and also by a number of migrant worker advocates, the law is not adequately addressing the different characteristics of these two types of labor migration.

68 Detailed analyses of the law have been done by migrant workers' advocates, including NGOs, such as the legal analysis made by *Kopbumi*. Cf. Seknas Kopbumi 2005.

Table 6.3: Summary and Comparison of the Drafts and the Law on Indonesia Migrant Workers

Item	Draft proposed by *Kopbumi*	Draft proposed by Brawijaya University	The DPR's Bill	The Government's Bill	Law No. 39/2004
Title	Protection of Indonesian Migrant Workers and Members of Their Families	Protection of Indonesian Workers Overseas and Members of Their Families	Protection of Indonesian Workers Overseas	Placement and Protection of Indonesian Workers Overseas	Placement and Protection of Indonesian Workers Overseas
Considera-tion	– Emphasis on rights – Subjects: migrant workers (both documented and undocumented) and their families – Refers to national constitution, a number of laws and international conventions	– Emphasis on rights – Subjects: migrant workers (both documented and undocumented) and their families – Refers to national constitution, a number of laws and international conventions	– Subjects: migrant workers – Refers to national constitution and 2 laws	– Subjects: migrant workers – Refers to national constitution and 1 law	– Subjects: migrant workers – Refers to national constitution and 1 law

Chapter 1	General Stipulation (defining key terminologies)	General Stipulation (defining key terminologies)	General Stipulation (defining key terminologies)	General Stipulation (defining key terminologies)	General Stipulation (defining key terminologies, principles, objectives, and banning placement by individual)
Chapter 2	Basis, Principles, and Objectives	Principles and Objectives	Principles and Objectives	Duties and Responsibilities	Government's Duties, Responsibilities, and Obligations
Chapter 3	State's Responsibility	Rights of Indonesian Workers Overseas – Basic Rights – Freedom of association and the right organize themselves – The rights of undocumented migrant workers	Workers' Rights and Obligations	Rights and Obligations of Indonesian Workers	Rights and Obligations of Indonesian Workers

Chapter 4	Rights of Migrant Workers and Members of Their Families 1. Basic rights 2. Freedom of association and the right to organize themselves 3. The rights of undocumented migrant workers 4. Fulfillment of the rights of Indonesian migrant workers	Rights and Obligations of Operators	Operator and Operating Institution	Operator of the Placement of Indonesian Workers Overseas	Operator of the Placement of Indonesian Workers Overseas

<table>
<tr>
<td>Chapter 5</td>
<td>Placement Procedure
1. Operator
2. Information
3. Operator of the placement of Indonesian migrant workers
4. Recruitment
5. Education and training
6. Apprenticeship
7. Offshore jobs
8. Entertainment
9. Repatriation</td>
<td>Government's obligation</td>
<td>Government's obligation</td>
<td>Placement of Indonesian Workers
1. General
2. Pre-Placement of Indonesian Workers
a. Recruitment
b. Job training
c. Health check and psychological test
d. Document preparation
e. Departure
3. Placement period of Indonesian workers
4. Post-placement of Indonesian workers
5. Funding</td>
<td>Placement Procedure
1. General
2. Pre-Placement of Indonesian Workers
a. Mobilization license
b. Recruitment and selection
c. Education and job training
d. Health check and psy-cho-logical test
e. Document preparation
3. Work agreement
4. Waiting period at the shelter
5. Placement period
6. Post-placement
7. Funding</td>
</tr>
</table>

Chapter 6	Work Relation	Placement Procedure – Placement operator – Recruitment – Education and training – Departure and repatriation – Protection while working	Placement Procedure – Placement management – Recruitment – Education and training – Departure and repatriation – Protection while working	Protection of Indonesian Workers	Protection of Indonesian Workers
Chapter 7	Conflict Redressing	Work Agreement	Work Agreement	Conflict Redressing	Conflict Redressing
Chapter 8	Legal Assistance	Conflict Redressing and Legal Assistance – Conflict redressing – Legal Assistance – Fund for the protection of Indonesian migrant workers overseas – Public monitoring	Conflict Redressing and Legal Assistance – Conflict redressing – Legal Assistance – Fund for the protection of Indonesian migrant workers overseas – Public monitoring	Coordinating Body for the Placement and Protection of Indonesian Workers	Development

Chapter 9	Fund for the Protection of Indonesian Migrant Workers	Stipulation for Administrative and Criminal Sanction	Stipulation for Administrative and Criminal Sanction	Development	Monitoring
Chapter 10	Monitoring	Transition Stipulation	Transition Stipulation	Monitoring	National Agency on the Placement and Protection of Indonesian Workers Overseas
Chapter 11	Monitoring by Public	Closing Stipulation	Closing Stipulation	Investigation	Administrative Sanction

Chapter 12	Sanctions Criminal Stipulation Compensation		Criminal Stipulation and Adminis-trative Sanction	Investigation
Chapter 13	Transition Stipulation		Other Stipulations	Criminal Stipulation
Chapter 14	Closing Stipulation		Transition Stipulation	Other Stipulations
Chapter 15			Closing Stipulation	Transition Stipulation
Chapter 16				Closing Stipulation

Source: Extracted and compared by author

The above comparison shows similarities between the draft made by Brawijaya University and the bill proposed by the DPR. The explanation is that, as stated on the cover of the Brawijaya's draft, there was cooperation on the legal drafting between the Law Faculty of Brawijaya University and the Secretariat General of the DPR. The government's bill is obviously very similar to the final law. Combined with the information from the minutes of the special committee and the working committee meetings,[69] the similarities show that more parts were taken from the government's bill than from the DPR's bill.

As for the draft made by *Kopbumi*, virtually none of its points emerged in the law. Only a slight similarity can be found in the clause on recruitment. The recruitment and education and training clauses in *Kopbumi's*, Brawijaya's, and the DPR's bill were actually quite similar. However, most of these clauses were changed or eliminated in the law. Other points, such as the inclusion of members of migrant workers' families and undocumented migrant workers, rights to organize themselves, legal assistance, funding for protection, and monitoring by public did not appear in the law. The absence of these points in the law may have been the basis of migrant workers' advocates' argument that the law has not provided adequate protection for migrant workers. Responding to this, the government argued that protection measures are included in other sections such as government responsibilities and the placement procedure.

In terms of specifically protecting women migrant workers, particularly domestic workers, *Kopbumi*'s draft had a number of clauses which specifically addressed problems faced by this group, such as rest day, working hours, reproduction rights, and maternity leave. Most of these specific clauses cannot be found in the law, including a clause under the education and training section, which stipulates that the placement operator must guarantee access to better education and training for women migrant workers. Although slightly altered, this clause still existed in the DPR's bill but not in the final law.

In short, a comparison of the drafts shows that *firstly*, *Kopbumi*'s draft strongly emphasized the protection and fulfillment of the rights of migrant workers. It also gave special attention to the conditions faced by women migrant workers. *Secondly*, although there were similarities between *Kopbumi*'s and Brawijaya's draft, it seems that the DPR adopted more from Brawijaya's draft, most probably due to their cooperation in the legal preparation. *Thirdly*, after the deliberation process where the DPR's and the government's bill were compared and combined to produce a final document for the law, more was taken from the government's draft, eliminating further some points which migrant workers' advocates considered important for the protection of migrant workers. This has been one of

69 Cf. Pusat Pengkajian Pengolahan Data dan Informasi 2008.

the main causes of the NGOs' disappointment and criticisms of the law, which will be discussed further in the next section.

6.2.2 NGOs' Criticisms of the Bill

Although Indonesian NGOs had been campaigning for a law on migrant workers, they wanted a law which focused more on the protection of migrant workers. This explains why, toward the end of the deliberation process in September 2004, they intensified their rejection of the bill for not providing the demanded protection for migrant workers. The naming of the bill itself had already raised NGO concern because it included the word "placement".[70] For the NGOs, this brought back bad memories of the policy instruments they had been criticizing, the Ministerial Decision No. 104A/2002 on the Placement of Indonesian Workers Overseas, which focused more on regulating placement rather than providing protection.[71]

The main debates between migrant worker advocates and the government revolved around whether protection for migrant workers was adequately addressed in the clauses of the law. According to migrant workers advocates, with only one chapter containing seven clauses on protection, the law was more about placement than protection. The government, on the other hand, argued that protection measures were not limited to the chapter on protection, but were also embedded in other chapters of the law.[72] The chapter on placement procedure does have several clauses which can be considered as a form of protection such as stipulating that migrant worker candidates are not allowed to be employed while they are in training. This clause may be useful in eliminating the practice of forcing prospective migrant workers to work without pay in local households while they

70 In the first meeting between the DPR's special committee and the Minister of Manpower and Transmigration on August 31, 2004, there were already different views between the government and the DPR on the title of the bill. The DPR suggested a Bill for the Protection of Indonesian Workers Overseas, while the government suggested calling it a Bill for the Placement and Protection of Indonesian Workers Overseas. Cf. ibid. This implies that the DPR was possibly more accommodative toward the ideas of migrant worker advocates. However, to avoid a deadlock, the deliberation of the title was referred to the working committee meeting where again there was a lengthy discussion. It is not quite clear when the title was decided, but the end result was that the title of the law contained both the words placement and protection.

71 Cf. Suara Pembaruan, October 1, 2004.

72 In responding to the NGOs' rejection of the word "placement", Hotma Pandjaitan, Head of Public Relations in the Department of Manpower and Transmigration, argued that using the word "placement" did not mean that the government ignored protection. Cf. Tempo Interaktif, September 17, 2004. He claimed that protection efforts exist throughout recruitment, selection, training, and departure as well as placement.

are in training. There is also a clause which forbids labor agencies to place migrant workers in a job which is different from that mentioned in the contract agreed and signed by the migrant workers. However, most of the clauses are quite general, allowing loose and varying interpretations. Moreover, there are clauses which still need other regulations to support their implementation which amount to six governmental, two presidential, and 23 ministerial decrees.[73] In practice, although urgently required to support the implementation of the law, the making of the regulations has taken quite some time.[74] Moreover, there is always a risk of overlap since coordination among government entities is still an issue. Regarding this, Tina Suprihatin said that Indonesia should take as a model the Philippines' law on the protection of migrant workers, which she considered quite comprehensive.[75]

The NGOs' criticisms of the content of the law can be observed in their statements in the media during the deliberation process and immediately after the law was passed, like those made by Suprihatin.[76] According to her, the protection clauses were more focused on protection during placement or the working period and she questioned the ability of Indonesian national law to regulate protection abroad. Indisputably, Indonesian national law is only effective within the country's jurisdiction and has no authority in receiving countries. It is limited to regulating how Indonesian representatives and labor attaches in the receiving countries protect their citizens through diplomatic measures, and to stipulating the

73 Cf. Kompas, October 30, 2004.

74 Regulations made after the endorsement of Law No. 39/2004 until 2007: Ministerial Regulation No. Per-04/MEN/II/2005 on the Organization of Final Training Before Departure for Indonesian Migrant Workers Overseas; Ministerial Regulation No. Per-05/MEN/III/2005 on the Determination of Administrative Sanctions and the Means through which those Sanctions are Imposed in the Conduct of the Placement and Protection of Indonesian Migrant Workers Overseas; Ministerial Decision No. KEP.14/MEN/I/2005 on the Team for the Prevention of Non-Procedural Departures and Return Services for Indonesian Migrant Workers; Ministerial Regulation No. Per-07/MEN/IV/2005 on the Standard of Holding Centres for Intending Indonesian Migrant Workers; Presidential Instruction No. 06/2006, on the Reform Policy on the Placement and Protection System of Indonesian Migrant Workers; Presidential Regulation No. 81, year 2006, on the National Agency for the Placement and Protection of Indonesia Overseas Workers; Ministerial Regulation No. PER-19/MEN/V/2006 on the Implementation of Placement and Protection of Indonesian Migrant Workers Overseas; Ministerial Decision No. KEP.258/MEN/VI/2007 on the Placement Fee and Protection of Indonesian Worker Candidates in Destination Country, Republic of Korea; Ministerial Regulation No. PER. 20/MEN/X/2007 on the Insurance for Indonesian Migrant Workers; and Ministerial Regulation No. PER.18/MEN/IX/2007 on the Implementation of Placement and Protection of Indonesian Migrant Workers Overseas.

75 Cf. Kompas, October 30, 2004.

76 Cf. Tempo Interaktif, September 14, 2004, Bambang S, September 29, 2004, Kompas, October 30, 2004.

government's authority to stop and/or ban placement in certain countries or certain jobs. The chapter on protection of migrant workers does mention that protection is implemented before, during, and after placement. However, the clauses are more focused of how protection is provided during the placement period, over which the law actually has limited authority. Protection of migrant workers while they are in Indonesia, during recruitment and when they re-enter Indonesia after their employment abroad, is not elaborated in this chapter. Also related to protection, Suprihatin pointed out that the bill ignored the special situations faced by women and undocumented migrant workers.

Suprihatin also criticized the bill for allowing the government to regulate, monitor and at the same time conduct the placement of migrant workers.[77] According to her, this showed the government's multiple interests which made her question its ability to be objective in monitoring and regulating when it had an economic interest in conducting the placement. On a similar note, Salma Safitri argued that the bill was unfair because in the case of violation of the law, while labor suppliers or individuals might be harshly penalized, the government was not liable to any sanctions.[78] In defending the government's multifunctional role, Jacob Nuwa Wea said that labor export fell under the government's jurisdiction and that the private sector was not ready to take over the sector of labor export.[79] This is a difficult statement to sustain given the fact that labor migration was started and has been conducted by private agencies since the 1970s and the government had only started to regulate this sector in the 1980s.

According to the law, there are several requirements that a labor agency has to fulfill to get a license, including financial ones. Labor agencies have to pay a certain amount of money to a government bank as a guarantee fund and they also have to have a certain amount of collateral. The collateral requirement was increased from around 30,000 USD to around 375,000 USD on the grounds that only big agencies can afford to hire lawyers if the migrant workers have problems. According to Safitri, this is not always the case: in fact, the smaller agencies often have better and problem-free placement systems.[80] Moreover, because of the increased financial requirements, there is a high possibility that labor agencies will increase recruitment fees which already created a financial burden for migrant workers. Safitri also highlighted the inconsistencies of some parts of the bills and the absence of clear standards.[81] As an example, there is a clause

77 Cf. Kompas, October 30, 2004. This issue of the government also acting as a placement operator was also questioned by some members of the DPR during the deliberation process. Cf. Pusat Pengkajian Pengolahan Data dan Informasi 2008.

78 Cf. The Jakarta Post, September 30, 2004.

79 Cf. ibid.

80 Cf. Tempo Interaktif, September 14, 2004.

81 Cf. Tempo Interaktif, September 16, 2004.

that stipulates that the government is obliged to post a labor attaché in a destination country "if considered necessary", but there is no further explanation on what situation is considered fulfilling this condition. The NGO coalition, however, had suggested that labor attachés should be posted in a country where there are at least 15 thousand Indonesian workers.

Migrant workers' advocates criticized almost all aspects of the bill and the statements made by Suprihatin and Safitri generally represent these criticisms. In brief, they did not see the bill (and therefore the law) as protecting migrant workers. More detailed discussions of the weaknesses of the law can be found in a number of analyses produced after the law was passed, such as the one made by *Kopbumi* in cooperation with the ILO in which they analyzed the substance of the law and recommended postponing its implementation because it did not provide a guarantee for the protection of Indonesian migrant workers.[82]

Despite all the criticisms of the law, a number of individuals interviewed during my fieldwork, like Lisa Noor Humaidah who was in *Komnas Perempuan* and Riana Puspasari, who worked for UNIFEM, acknowledged some positive aspects.[83] Humaidah argued that migrant worker activists needed to recognize that better systems and management of labor migration were also forms of protection.[84] It should also be noted that although NGOs like SP and Migrant CARE strongly criticized Law No. 39/2004, they admitted that there were clauses in the law that could still be used in addressing the problems faced by women migrant workers, particularly clauses that stipulated protection of migrant workers and sanctions for private agencies which conducted illegal placement or put migrant workers in a disadvantaged situation.

To this point this chapter has discussed NGOs' involvement in the law-making process and their criticisms of Law No. 39/2004. This leads to the question of what happened after the Law was passed. The next section will discuss what SP and Migrant CARE did after the endorsement of the law.[85]

82 Cf. Seknas Kopbumi 2005.

83 Interview with Humaidah, Lisa Noor on July 12, 2007, and with Puspasari, Riana on August 10, 2007.

84 In her analysis, Humaidah looks into the clauses of the law in more detail. Some of her notes include: higher emphasis on protection during placement period, absence of government commitment toward the families of migrant workers, conflicting roles of the government as the regulator and implementer and the government's lack of liability as implementer, absence of undocumented workers, and inadequate protection for women migrant workers.

85 From this point forward it is possible to discuss the two NGOs comparatively since they have both been in existence since the law was passed.

6.3 NGOs' Activism after the Law Was Passed

In the early days after Law No. 39/2004 was passed, some NGOs considered requesting a judicial review of the law by the Constitutional Court (*Mahkamah Konstitusi*).[86] However, they made no statement on the grounds for this judicial review. It can only be assumed that this discourse emerged from NGOs' dissatisfaction of the law-making process and its content. The absence of a clear ground and the different views among NGOs on how to response to the endorsement of the law have prevented the judicial review discourse from materializing. Interestingly, judicial reviews were actually requested by associations of labor agencies and individual migrant workers. In 2005, there were two cases of judicial review of some clauses in Law No. 39/2004 submitted by a number of labor agency associations, i.e. *Apjati*, the Indonesian Employment Association for Asia Pacific (*Ajaspac*), the Indonesian Workers Service Entrepreneurs' Association (*Himsataki*) and an NGO, Indonesia Manpower Watch.[87] Out of twelve petitions submitted, only the petition against the stipulation of junior high school as the minimum level of education for migrant workers was granted while other petitions were denied.[88] In 2007, two other cases of judicial review were submitted

86 Cf. Media Indonesia 2004.

87 A Jakarta-based NGO focusing on advocating migrant workers' cases.

88 Cf. Mahkamah Konstitusi Republik Indonesia 2005. Summary of the 2005 cases: Petitioners in Case 019/PUU-III/2005 were *Apjati*, the Indonesian Employment Association for Asia Pacific (*Ajaspac)*, and the Indonesian Workers Service Entrepreneurs' Association (*Himsataki*). Petitioner in Case No. 020/PUU-III/2005 was the Indonesia Manpower Watch (IMW) Foundation. The principal issues argued in the petitions were on the following articles of Law No. 39/2004: 1) Article 13 on the requirements for minimum capital and collateral, which was considered burdensome for some private agencies. 2) Article 14 on the requirements for the issuance and extension of permit (every five years) for private agencies, which was considered difficult to fulfill because it depends on various circumstances. 3) Article 18 on the authority of the Minister of Manpower and Transmigration to revoke private agencies' permits and the conditions for revoking, which was considered to be vulnerable to discriminatory likes and dislikes. 4) Article 20 on the requirement for PJTKI to have representatives in receiving countries, which was considered difficult to implement. 5) Article 46 that prohibits the migrant workers to be employed during their training, which, according to private agencies, should be allowed as long as it does not interfere with the training schedule. 6) Article 69 on the requirement for every migrant worker to join final training before departure (conducted by the government), which, according to private agencies, has added to the chain of bureaucracy and less useful expenses because the materials in this final training can be included in an integrated training. 7) Paragraphs in article 75 which contradict each other in stipulating who is responsible for arranging the return of migrant workers home: the government or the private agencies. 8) Article 82 on the obligation of private agencies to provide protection for migrant workers, which was considered as shifting the state's responsibility for protection to private agencies. 9) Article 103 on penalties for placement of migrant workers who have not met health requirements, which was considered difficult to implement

by prospective migrant workers. These cases were rejected.[89] As of 2010, the judicial reviews submitted to the Constitutional Court have not resulted in any significant changes to the law. Nevertheless, the effort made by labor agencies clearly shows that although the reasons behind their objections may not be similar to those of NGOs, they too opposed to some elements of the law.[90]

The judicial review also highlighted the complex nature of Indonesia's labor migration. The law set minimum age and level of education requirements for migrant workers, presumably to make sure that those departing to work overseas are mature and informed enough to take care of themselves. However, the reality is that there are many Indonesians, particularly women, who are eager to migrate but younger than 21 and/or only have a maximum of elementary education. This points back to what has been discussed earlier in Chapter 3 on how semi- or unskilled migration along with its problems will persist as long as poverty and unemployment continue to exist in Indonesia. It further highlights the need to accommodate various considerations in a law which is intended to regulate the placement and protection of Indonesian workers overseas and signifies inputs from various stakeholders, including NGOs as part of the civil society.

since health check results in sending and receiving countries are often different. 10) Article 103 on who will be penalized, individual or agencies, which created legal uncertainties. 11) Contradictions between article 107, which states a time frame for adjustments, and article 109, which states that the law shall come into effect from the date of its enactment. 12) Article 35 sub-article d on the minimum educational requirements of SLTP (junior high school) for prospective migrant workers, which was considered difficult to fulfill since most Indonesian workers are elementary level graduates. They also argued that most of the articles above contradicted Indonesia's 1945 Constitution, particularly Article 27 on the right of every citizen to work and Article 28 on economic rights. In a combined decision for these two cases, the Constitutional Court declared that Article 35 sub-article d of Law No. 39/2004 is contradictory to the 1945 Constitution and has no binding legal effect. Other petitions were denied.

89 Cf. Mahkamah Konstitusi Republik Indonesia 2007. Summary of the 2007 cases: Petitioners for Case No. 028/PUU-IV/2006 were five prospective migrant workers represented by IMW, and petitioners for Case No. 029/PUU-IV/2006 were four prospective migrant workers represented by lawyers from Sangap & Partners. The petitioners argued that Article 35 Sub-article a, which requires migrant workers recruited to work for individual users (which usually refers to those working as domestic workers in households) to be of the minimum age of 21, contradicted article 27 of the 1945 Constitution on the right of every citizen to work. The provision in this article prevented them from being sent to work abroad. This petition was rejected because, according to the Constitutional Court, the requirements are not "an elimination of the right to an occupation" but is instead "a justifiable requirement in the interest of fulfilling the duty of the state to protect its citizens".

90 According to Humaidah, in conversations during certain occasions, some labor agency people pointed out that they took a similar stand toward the law as did migrant worker advocates. Interview with Humaidah, Lisa Noor on July 12, 2007. Although the grounds for their objections are different, it seems that the labor agencies people wanted to highlight that they are on the same side as the NGOs in objecting the law.

Although virtually all migrant worker advocates consider that Law No. 39/2004 has not provided adequate protection for migrant workers, the NGOs were not able to come up with coordinated action to push for revision. According to Safitri, after the law was passed, the NGOs began to think of ways to continue expressing their criticisms.[91] However, they could not agree on whether to push for immediate revision and whether to pursue a judicial review or to go through other routes such as campaigning for ratification of the 1990 ICRMW. In October 2004, shortly after the President signed the Law, *Kopbumi*, and FES conducted a discussion on the Strategy and Advocacy post Law No. 39/2004 in Jakarta with the intention of coordinating opposition by civil society to the implementation of the Law.[92] However, as discussed further in Chapter 7, coordination has been one of the main challenges for Indonesian NGOs addressing the issue of migrant workers. Safitri stated, "I think NGOs' serious advocacy stopped when the Law was passed".[93] This is understandable if one considers that the coalition of NGOs, *Kopbumi*, was established in 1997 with the main aim of pushing for a law on migrant workers through coordinated NGO efforts. Thus, since the law was finally passed in 2004, as argued by Safitri, *Kopbumi* no longer had a mandate.

With the absence of coordinated action, each NGO has continued by taking its own path. Although SP's program for 2004-2007 did include the intention "to encourage change of policies that protect migrant workers and their families at the local, national, regional and international levels",[94] this has not been pursued by demanding from the parliament to revise Law No. 39/2004. Realizing that there was little possibility for the newly elected parliament to revise the law[95] and the effort that the NGOs needed to make in pushing for revision was enormous, as explained by Safitri, SP has been employing other advocacy means such as concentrating on campaigning for the ratification of the 1990 ICRMW.[96] For SP, this was a more realistic move because they expected that after ratification, all national laws will have to be adjusted to concur with the Convention. This campaign was also timely because the government included the ratification in its 2004-2009 National Plan of Action on Human Rights.

SP also participated in the preparation and submission of the 1998-2007 CEDAW shadow report in 2007, in which it focused on the lack of protection

91 Interview with Safitri, Salma on August 2, 2007.

92 Cf. Bambang S, October 28, 2004.

93 Interview with Safitri, Salma on August 2, 2007.

94 SP 2007a.

95 At the 2004 election, Indonesia began to implement the direct presidential election system. Thus, both the legislative and executive branches of the state were quite occupied with the adjustments to this new system.

96 Interview with Safitri, Salma on August 2, 2007.

and redress for the cases faced by Indonesian women migrant workers.[97] SP also participated in the campaign for and monitoring of Law No. 21/2007 on Elimination of Crimes of Human Trafficking which is considered to be a quite comprehensive law. Many migrant workers' advocates see this law as a potential means to address some of the problems faced by migrant workers for it provides definitions of various forms of human trafficking crimes, both out of and into the country, and states the penalties for these crimes. It also outlines prevention and case handling procedures and includes a chapter on international cooperation and society's participation. Document forgery, usually for age reasons, commonly occurs in Indonesian labor migration, which leads to illegal status for the migrant workers and makes them victims of trafficking. This law categorizes document forgery as a criminal act related to trafficking. Also, since this law stipulates protection of witnesses and victims of trafficking, it can be used as a basis to protect Indonesian migrant workers who are victims of trafficking.

Meanwhile, SP continues to respond to other government policies on migrant workers, including the Presidential Instruction No. 6/2006 on Policy for the Reform of the Placement and Protection System of Indonesian Workers Overseas.[98] *Komnas Perempuan*, GPPBM, the Human Rights Working Group (HRWG), *Kopbumi*, LBH Jakarta, SBMI, and SP, calling themselves the Civil Society Network for the Reform of Policies on Indonesian Migrant Workers, conducted an initial monitoring on the first 100 days of the implementation of this policy instrument in December 2006. In the general conclusion of their final report it was emphasized that the content of the Presidential Instruction does not reflect its title as a reform policy. They argued that the actions and improvements were only directed toward improving the efficiency of the administrative work rather than to perfecting the protection of migrant workers' rights. The changes made did not address the root causes of the problems faced by migrant workers such as the need for accurate and adequate information; social protection; having their own effective organizations; and access to service institutions. Other than this one activity, until 2007, when the fieldwork for the research was conducted, campaigning for ratification of the 1990 UN Convention had been the main strategy for SP in terms of policy advocacy.

97 Cf. Badan Eksekutif Nasional Solidaritas Perempuan 2008, p. 78.

98 This policy instructed several related ministries, the police force, governors, mayors and heads of districts to take the necessary steps for implementing a number of policies and programs. This includes policies on the placement of Indonesian workers overseas, the protection of Indonesian workers overseas, eradication of sponsors (*calo*), migrant workers placement agencies, and on support by banking institutions. The policies are divided into programs, each with the actions to be taken, the targeted outcomes, the time frames, and the responsible institutions.

As an organization which was just established in 2004, Migrant CARE was not very much involved in the campaigns during the deliberation process. However, Migrant CARE's standpoint is similar to that of other NGOs, rejecting the Law. Although Anis Hidayah, the Executive Director, stated that her organization was demanding amendment of the law, she emphasized that it did not totally reject it.[99] According to her, and supported by Wahyu Susilo,[100] a board member and policy analyst, a legal vacuum was worse than having a very bad law. Her concern was that if the law was repealed, it would take a long time to wait for a new law and the legal vacuum would influence NGOs' advocacy on migrant workers' cases. Thus, although Migrant CARE rejects the clauses which are more on the placement than the protection of migrant workers, she admitted that the law contains clauses which can be useful. As an example, Hidayah referred to clauses which stipulate that labor agencies are responsible for migrant workers who face problems like unpaid wages, and labor agencies which send workers overseas without proper documents can incur criminal sanctions. However, she also pointed out that those clauses still require operational regulations before they can actually be implemented and as of 2007, most such operational regulations were not in place.

Although Migrant CARE rejected Law No. 39/2004 and wanted it to be revised, like other NGOs, in the years after the law was passed, it did not conduct any activities directly demanding the parliament to revise the law. Most of Migrant CARE's activities, as shown in its 2004 and 2005 annual report were dominated by handling cases, lobbying local governments, conducting training, and campaigning through the media.[101] Similar to SP's point of view, Migrant CARE also considered that Law No. 21/2007 on Elimination of Crimes of Human Trafficking could be used to gradually address some of the problems faced by migrant workers. Migrant CARE was also involved in the campaign for the bill on the protection of domestic workers through the National Network for Domestic Workers Advocacy or *Jaringan Nasional Advokasi Pekeria Rumah Tangga* (Jala PRT). According to Lita Anggraini, the coordinator of the network, they drafted a bill in 2000 and tried to submit it to the DPR in 2000 and 2004.[102] But only in 2009, in its general meeting on November 30, 2009, did the DPR agree to include the bill in the priority list of the National Legislation Program or *Program Legislasi Nasional* (Prolegnas) for 2010. However, on June 2, 2010, in an internal meeting of Commission IX[103] of the DPR, the bill was removed from the pri-

99 Interview with Hidayah, Anis on May 26, 2007.

100 Interview with Susilo, Wahyu on June 14, 2007.

101 Cf. Migrant CARE 2004, 2005a.

102 Cf. Koran Tempo, May 10, 2010.

103 This commission oversees the issue of migrant workers for the 2009-2014 cabinet.

ority list and the deliberation was postponed to 2011, which immediately generated strong reactions from civil society organizations.

The involvement of migrant workers' NGOs in the advocacy for a national law on the protection of domestic workers is motivated by at least two reasons: *Firstly,* because domestic workers, whether they work in Indonesia or overseas, are facing similar problems such as long working hours, inadequate salary, no rest days, and abuses. *Secondly*, as stated by Hidayah, as long as Indonesia does not have its own law on domestic workers which stipulates matters such as minimum wage, it will always be difficult for its representatives to push for the inclusion of such a matter in the MoU with receiving countries.[104] In her statement to the media and in an audience with members of parliament from PKB, Hidayah repeatedly put emphasis on how difficult it is for Indonesia's delegation to negotiate protection for Indonesian migrant workers with representatives of receiving countries, particularly Malaysia, who usually question the fact that Indonesia itself does not have a law on domestic workers. Until this book was finished, the parliament and the government were still working on the bill to revise Law No. 39/2004. Thus, while continuing to monitor and influence the law revision process, the NGOs have tried to work on other available and applicable regulations, including the law on trafficking and law on domestic workers. This can be considered as a strategic move from the NGOs.

The absence of activities in favor of revision of Law No. 39/2004 until 2013 may also be partly due to the fact that the parliament and the government had shown little intention of revising it despite the fact that, in 2006, the president issued two instructions, No. 03/2006 on the Policy Package of Investment Climate Improvement and No. 06/2006 on the Reform Policy of the Placement and Protection System of Indonesian Workers Overseas, which contain mandates for revising Law No. 39/2004.[105] According to Susilo, the parliament started to conduct meetings to discuss the possibility of revision and, in 2007, he was invited to a consultation forum conducted by a working group in the DPR to discuss the revision of Law No. 39/2004.[106] Although the intention to revise the law was frequently suggested, the process only began in 2013.

104 Cf. Kompas, June 15, 2010.

105 Presidential Instruction No. 3/2006 was issued with the aim to improve the investment climate in order to increase Indonesian economic growth. One of the listed policies for the labor sector was protection and placement of Indonesian workers overseas. The program for this policy is to amend Law No. 39/2004, but it was not explained in which way this should be done. According to the time frame, the amendment draft should have been submitted to the DPR by October 2006 and the Minister of Manpower and Transmigration was supposed to be responsible for the implementation of this program.

106 Interview with Susilo, Wahyu on June 14, 2007.

Meanwhile, the government had slowly carried out the mandate of Law No. 39/2004 such as establishing the BNP2TKI. As part of the national war against corruption, Indonesian former officers in the embassy and consulates in Malaysia, including former the ambassadors Hadi A Wayarabi Alhadar and Rusdiharjo, were sentenced on corruption charges for scams on immigration document application fees. There are also reports of legal actions taken against human traffickers and private agencies which have violated the regulations.

6.4 Conclusion

During the early period of *Reformasi* immediately after 1998, both state and civil society elements were in the process of defining their position within the new system and finding a feasible strategy in building cooperation with the government and the parliament. This was the condition in which the law on migrant workers was campaigned for and drafted. Six years after the 1998 reform and seven years after *Kopbumi*, the coalition of NGOs, started to push for a law on migrant workers, a bill on migrant workers was eventually deliberated and passed as a law. The law may not have completely met their expectations, but most NGOs admit that it is better to have a law than no law at all, and there are clauses that can still be used in their efforts to improve protection of migrant workers.

This chapter has described the NGOs' involvement in a domestic law-making process. There are indications that NGOs are more involved in the policy-making process, particularly in providing policy advice through their participation in various input gathering activities and lobbying individual members of the parliament. Some activists may already have had experience from working on other issues or have learned from the policy advocacy work of NGOs in other fields. However, since Law No. 39/2004 is Indonesia's first law on migrant workers, all involved stakeholders, including the government, the parliament and the NGOs, had gone through a learning process of how to interact with each other within the new political system and environment and how to achieve their aims. This learning process involves negotiations and adjustments. After the law was finally passed, the learning process continued. The NGOs, particularly, have to redefine their strategies to adjust to the new condition where there is now a law on the placement and protection of migrant workers.

Despite the NGOs' disappointment on Law No. 39/2004, the interactions between NGOs and state entities throughout the law-making process show improvement in their relations. Before 1998, it was difficult for the NGOs even to communicate with the government, let alone provide advice and get involved in the policy-making process. The MoMT may remain "untouchable", but more accommodative attitudes are found in other state institutions. Thus, in seeking for alternative channels to be involved in the policy process, the NGOs lobbied members of parliament during the deliberation process of the law. However, besides their limited knowledge of the migrant worker issue, the members of parliament were also occupied with a number of tasks such as redefining their position and role within the democratic system and working on other bills which were waiting to be deliberated and passed in the short period of time before their office ended. Consequently, the deliberation process tended to be dominated by the government, i.e. the Minister of Manpower and Transmigration, reducing the chance for NGOs to influence the law.

Although the NGOs may have had a significant role in pushing the government and the DPR to formulate a law on migrant workers through their campaigns, as soon as the official policy-making process started, their role was very much limited to lobbying sympathetic members of parliament. The government and the DPR claimed that they had obtained policy recommendations from various stakeholders, including NGOs. However, the comparison between the NGOs' draft and the law shows that a claim that NGOs' inputs have been significantly accommodated in the law is hard to justify.

This chapter also shows how one major cause such as the campaign to pass a law on the protection of Indonesian migrant workers could bring a number of Indonesian NGOs with their varied characteristics and interests together to form *Kopbumi*. However, the collaboration was difficult to maintain and as soon as the initial mandate was achieved with the passing of the law, the consortium collapsed. The NGOs' inability to further coordinate their action after the law was passed is an example of the challenges which make it difficult for Indonesian NGOs to build and maintain cooperation and collaboration, a topic which will be discussed further in Chapter 7.

This chapter has examined NGOs' involvement in the making of a domestic policy instrument. Chapter 8 will investigate their involvement in the process of making a foreign policy instrument, the MoU between Indonesia and Malaysia, which was conducted in a slightly different context and involved other national and international actors. The next chapter will first look into the NGOs' efforts since the law was passed, putting it within the context of democratization in Indonesia.

7. Strengthening Influence on Policy: Working within the Context of Democratization in Indonesia

As discussed in the previous chapter, Indonesia finally adopted a law on the Placement and Protection of Indonesian Workers Overseas, Law No. 39/2004. We saw how NGOs made use of the opportunities offered by democratization to apply pressure on the government to enact that law, and attempted to influence the policy process. This chapter focuses more on the activities of SP and Migrant CARE after the law was passed, partly to see whether the fact that Indonesia now has a law on migrant workers has affected the NGOs' activism, while taking into account that they are not satisfied with the policy product. For that reason, this chapter aims to answer the following questions: How have the NGOs continued their work? And how do they reflect on what they have done to assist them in moving forward? These questions will help in answering the main question of this chapter: How do the NGOs strengthen their influence on existing policy? In other words: How are NGOs learning to operate more effectively in a more democratic environment?

This chapter is divided into four sections. The first three sections discuss three key activities that the NGOs researched have been conducting: building cooperation, working at the grassroots, and using the media. Piper and Uhlin pointed out that, in a more democratic regime, there is more space or more political opportunities for civil society activism.[1] In relation to this, the above activities are the NGOs' responses to changes brought by the reform and democratization in Indonesia, particularly in terms of the increased opportunity for civil society to operate, grow and expand their network, decentralization of power, and freer media. The fourth section then assesses whether there have been any self-evaluation and/or learning processes, which the NGOs need to further develop their activism.

7.1 Building Cooperation

Since NGOs have limitations in size, human resources, and funding, in order to conduct their activities they need to cooperate with other stakeholders within the labor migration system. Responding to the opportunities and challenges brought by changes since 1998, NGOs working on the issue of migrant workers have

1 Cf. Piper and Uhlin 2004a, p. 13.

made some adjustments to their methods. One way of understanding these adjustments is by looking at their cooperation with their partners. The assumption is that reform and democratization allow NGOs to work with more partners in a relatively wider space. Thus, the discussion in this section will investigate SP's and Migrant CARE's cooperation with their domestic partners by describing how the interactions occur, identifying the challenges that they are facing, and assessing whether they have benefited from the interactions in terms of supporting their efforts to influence policies on migrant workers.

7.1.1 Networking

Keck and Sikkink have identified the characteristics of a network, which according to them include "voluntary, reciprocal, and horizontal patterns of communication exchange" with information as its significant element.[2] They also suggest that networks, whether they are domestic or international, are built by "fluid and open relations among committed and knowledgeable actors working in specialized issue areas". On a similar note, Fisher defines networking as "a fluid web of relationships connecting NGO actions to numerous levels and fields".[3] Furthermore, Keck and Sikkink underline the central role of NGOs in advocacy networks in "initiating actions and pressuring powerful actors" for they "introduce new ideas, provide information, and lobby for policy changes".[4]

In line with the above way of defining "network", works on Indonesian NGOs such as those of Riker and Hadiwinata have noted the formation of networks between NGOs and other actors for reasons such as sharing experience, conducting collective actions, expressing concerns and interests, mainstreaming issues by bringing them to higher levels, and capacity building.[5] Nevertheless, efforts of developing countries' NGOs, including those in Indonesia, to cooperate within a network are usually hampered by factors such as internal tensions, rivalries, low commitment, lack of willingness to compromise, different perceptions on how to interact with the government, unwillingness to share certain information, unequal capacity, competition for international funding, and government reluctance to support NGO networks.[6] As later shown in this chapter and in Chapter 9, fluid and voluntary interactions characterize the networks joined by the NGOs researched and while these characteristics may be considered as strengths, they

2 Keck and Sikkink 1998, p. 8.
3 Fisher 1997, p. 450.
4 Keck and Sikkink 1998, p. 9.
5 Cf. Riker 1998, p. 292, Hadiwinata 2003, p. 40.
6 Cf. Eldridge 1995, p. 194, Abelson 2003, pp. 11-12, Hadiwinata 2003, pp. 40-41.

may also turn into weaknesses because of the lack of obligation and commitment among the members. Thus, although after 1998 there has been greater freedom of association in Indonesia, building a sustainable network of NGOs remains a difficult task.

As noted in Chapter 5, in 1997, around 100 NGOs established *Kopbumi*, which covers twelve provinces in Indonesia. *Kopbumi*'s declining profile is an example of how difficult it is to sustain a network which consists of a number of organizations with varied characteristics and interests. In 2000, 19 women's organizations established GPPBM. Through time, this network remains relatively active, although there were indications of dependency on one of its main members, *Komnas Perempuan*,[7] and questions about the members' commitments.[8] In 2004, eleven organizations established *Foker*. Less than five years after it was established, Anis Hidayah from Migrant CARE, one of the forum's key members, described it as stagnant and declining,[9] perhaps another example of a short-lived network of NGOs on the issue of migrant workers.

NGOs base their decision to form or join a network on whether it accommodates their organization's characteristics, vision, and the issues they are focusing on. As argued by Wahyu Susilo, the existence of smaller networks which are based on certain issues or similarities between members can strengthen work on the issue of migrant workers, as long as there is a synergy and there is no rivalry and sectoral ego among them.[10] At the same time, realizing that the issue of migrant workers is multifaceted, some NGOs have started to see as a weakness the fact that most NGO networks on the issue of migrant workers mainly consist of those which take the issue as their main concern. Hidayah, for example, sees the need to prevent the issue of migrant workers becoming exclusive by building networks involving NGOs with other concerns such as human rights and women.[11] This may also be the reason for SP, as a women's organization, to be involved in networks such as GPPBM, the CEDAW Working Group Initiative (CWGI), and the *Jaringan Kerja Prolegnas Pro Perempuan* (JKP3).[12] Migrant CARE, with its focus on domestic migrant workers, is involved in *Foker* and

7 Although Lisa Noor Humaidah, who worked on women migrant worker issues at *Komnas Perempuan*, did not explain this dependency in detail, it can be presumed that some of *Komnas Perempuan's* resources, including staff, were used to run GPPBM's office which was located in the building of *Komnas Perempuan*.

8 Interview with Humaidah, Lisa Noor on July 12, 2007.

9 Interview with Hidayah, Anis on November 18, 2008.

10 Interview with Susilo, Wahyu on November 7, 2008.

11 Interview with Hidayah, Anis on June 15, 2007.

12 Interview with Zulbahary on July 9, 2007. JKP3 is a network of NGOs which advocates bills on issues concerning women such as domestic violence, trafficking, nationality, and health.

works closely with INFID,[13] particularly in getting access to international institutions such as the UN, the World Bank, and the IMF.[14]

An effective and sustainable network requires role sharing among its members. The NGOs have attempted to define their roles within the networks, on the basis of a particular issue or activity. SP focuses on the trafficking issue within the CWGI,[15] and Migrant CARE focuses on the advocacy program within *Foker*.[16] Nevertheless, both Safitri and Hidayah consider that role-sharing remains one of the challenges they need to address.[17] Safitri sees funding institutions' interests as a factor that significantly influences NGOs' choice of activities as shown in the cases where NGOs adjust their activities in accordance with the available funding, which may lead to certain NGOs abandoning their initial commitment to the networks.

Competition for funding has also become one of the factors that prevent the development of collaboration between NGOs, whether inside or outside a network. In explaining how funding has created competition and lack of coordination between NGOs in Indonesia, Tati Krisnawaty recounted instances when instead of working together on one event, the NGOs tended to compete each other

13 Cf. INFID 2009. The profile page of INFID's website explains that INFID was established in June 1985 under the name of INGI (Inter-NGO Conference on IGGI Matters), based on the initiative of several Indonesian NGOs and their partners in the Netherlands. INFID is a network of NGOs from Indonesia and various member countries of the Consultative Group on Indonesia (CGI), international organizations and individuals with an interest in and commitment to Indonesia. Since 1985, INGI/INFID has given critical input and recommendations to the IGGI (Inter-Governmental Group on Indonesia) concerning development issues in Indonesia. The IGGI was a consortium of donor nations to Indonesia, which in 1992 was changed to become the CGI chaired by the World Bank. INFID aims at facilitating communication between NGOs inside and outside Indonesia in order to promote policies to alleviate structural poverty and to increase the capacity to improve conditions of the poor and the disadvantaged in Indonesia. More than 100 NGOs participate in INFID; around half of them are from Indonesia and the rest from 14 other countries.

14 Interview with Susilo, Wahyu on June 14, 2007.

15 Interview with Zulbahary, Thaufiek on July 9, 2007.

16 Interview with Hidayah, Anis on June 15, 2007. Hidayah explained how the members of *Foker* tried to divide the roles between them. Migrant CARE concentrates on policy advocacy, particularly at the local level. They approached local parliaments and governments of the origin areas of the migrant workers facing death penalties, encouraging them to become actively involved in advocating the death penalty cases and making local regulations which protect migrant workers. This policy advocacy activity is strengthened by the research conducted by other members of the network. Meanwhile, the information they obtain is used by members for campaigning. Those concentrating on capacity building conduct training for both members of the network and the migrant worker union in Singapore on topics such as leadership and advocacy.

17 Interview with Safitri, Salma on August 2, 2007, and with Hidayah, Anis on September 15, 2007.

by holding different events at the same time.[18] On a similar note, Susilo argued that coordinating programs between members of the networks is usually difficult to do partly because of their different funding resources.[19] He also considered that the failure of networks of NGOs is caused by what he called the lack of stamina, which seems to refer to the networks' lack of resources to sustain their existence and activities.[20]

Although the reform has allowed more freedom and space for NGOs to cooperate and the NGOs themselves have recognized the need to work together, the importance of maintaining their individuality and independency has prevented them from making any commitments which may put their existence, reputation, and accountability to their funders at risk. Concerns about NGOs' commitment within a quite fluid network is reflected in the statement of Lisa Noor Humaidah, who was with *Komnas Perempuan*:[21] She described the attitudes of most NGO representatives in GPPBM as "when they go back to their organizations they become themselves again, not bringing GPPBM into their organizations". This shows that, although the NGOs are willing to get involved in a network, their organizations' interests, aims, and principles are still their main priorities. Humaidah viewed this as a common problem in a coalition which has fluid characteristics and no binding authority. This tendency is confirmed by Krisnawaty, who maintained that some organizations still prioritize their independent existence and feel that, in an alliance or network, they cannot establish their own name.[22] In short, coordination and competition have become issues in NGOs'

18 Interview with Krisnawaty, Tati on November 7, 2008. Krisnawaty is a renowned migrant workers advocate who was one of the founders of SP and *Kopbumi*. According to her, when she became the convenor of an event to greet Jorge Bustamante, the then UN Special Rapporteur on the Human Rights of Migrants, in 2006, she invited Indonesian NGOs to meet Bustamante. However, at the same time, an NGO held a musical event to commemorate Migrant Day. Krisnawaty argued that this confused the journalists, who had difficulties in choosing which event to cover. She claimed that this was not the first time such a situation occurred. Her other example was when a group of NGOs planned to launch a "one day off campaign", demanding the right of migrant workers to get one day off in a week. Two days before the launch, one NGO withdrew and launched its own campaign.

19 Interview with Susilo, Wahyu on November 7, 2008.

20 Susilo considered the rivalry for support and funding between *Kopbumi* and some dominant members like SP as one of the factors that contributed to *Kopbumi*'s decline. In a slightly different way, Krisnawaty argues that *Kopbumi*'s decline at the end of the 1990s was due to changes in the network such as the shift toward an NGO forum, the adoption of other issues besides the campaigning for a law on migrant workers, and the decision to take funding from international donors. Interview with Krisnawaty, Tati on November 7, 2008.

21 Interview with Humaidah, Lisa Noor on July 12, 2007. Humaidah's position in *Komnas Perempuan* made her highly involved in GPPBM.

22 Interview with Krisnawaty, Tati on November 7, 2008.

network building which, as argued by Albert Yosua Bonasahat from the ILO, if not addressed, may weaken the advocacy process and be counter-productive for their activism in general.[23]

Despite the above challenges, significant cooperation between NGOs has occurred within or through the networks. Since factors like differences and rivalries have prevented direct cooperation between them, the NGOs seem to prefer interacting within a network while from time to time they can choose to cooperate with certain members of the network for particular issues.[24] As explained by Susilo, Migrant CARE's cooperation with SP has occurred through the international network MFA.[25] According to him, different rhythms and "sectors"[26] between them have prevented direct cooperation. In so doing, while a network can be seen as a place where differences, competition, and rivalries occur, it can also be considered as a forum where cooperation between NGOs, which are naturally competitors outside the networks, becomes more acceptable and possible.

The NGOs' experience in network building has shown how consensus, agreement, and common purposes and objectives are difficult to achieve, particularly when it involves a significant number of entities with different characteristics and interests. As observed by Antlöv et al., although there is a tendency for Indonesian NGOs to group themselves in coalitions to conduct advocacy to change, influence and draft laws, they have not been able to build a nationwide coalition.[27] Antlöv et al. suggested the establishment of an organization that monitors the NGOs or a professional NGOs' association. As ideal as it sounds, it is unlikely that this will materialize in the near future since even to build and maintain a national coalition of NGOs concerned with one issue of migrant workers has proven difficult. Differences and imbalances among the members have been the major factor that contributed to the failure of a number of such coalitions and networks.

7.1.2 Cooperation with State Institutions

In analyzing Indonesian NGOs in the 1990s, Eldridge had already predicted that although Indonesian NGOs insisted on maintaining their non-political identity,

23 Interview with Bonasahat, Albert Yosua on July 11, 2007.

24 Zulbahary noted that, in responding to certain issues, SP has worked with a few other members of the networks, which were also willing to respond. Interview with Zulbahary, Thaufiek on November 19, 2008. This situation is similar with Migrant CARE.

25 Interview with Susilo, Wahyu on November 7, 2008.

26 Most likely, he was referring to the women's organization status of SP and the migrant workers organization status of Migrant CARE.

27 Cf. Antlöv et al. 2006, p. 151.

they would realize the need to expand their coalition-building and get involved in the political process.[28] In his later work, Eldridge again emphasized that the NGOs cannot avoid being political, particularly in their engagement with the state.[29] In line with Eldridge's argument, I think that, although NGOs would like to maintain their distance from the government, if they seek a policy change, they cannot avoid involvement in the political arena and engagement with the actors within it. Thus, this section examines the interaction between NGOs and a number of state institutions in understanding the state-NGOs relationship within the context of democratizing Indonesia.

Safitri did not want to use the term "lobbying" to describe SP's interaction with the government before 1998 because, according to her, SP could not even talk to the government.[30] They could only do what she called "angry demonstration" (*demonstrasi marah-marah*).[31] Their actions were covered by mass media but the government at that time, including the Department of Manpower, would not agree to have dialogue. The letters that they sent did not get any replies and if they rang up, they would be transferred from one section to another, without getting any results. SP's advocacy at that time was limited to sending petitions, protests, and sending statements to journalists and other stakeholders. According to Safitri, this condition changed after Suharto stepped down with the door opening for dialogue. Their letters to the government started to get replies, and they can now request and get a hearing or an audience. This can be seen as an improvement in the interactions between NGOs and the government in the way that there are now forums through which the NGOs can channel their voices, and, more importantly, the initiation of these forums can come from the NGOs.

Cooperation between NGOs and state institutions is highly determined by their attitudes toward each other. Riker noted that working with supportive officials in central and local governments has been part of NGOs' strategy, the success of which is determined by the willingness of state institutions to support NGOs' activities.[32] Since 1998, a number of state institutions have become more accommodative toward NGOs, including the SMoWE, the MoFA, and the DPR. Hidayah also mentioned the Department of Social Services,[33] the office of the

28 Cf. Eldridge 1995, pp. 216 and 229.

29 Cf. Eldridge 2005, p. 149.

30 Interview with Safitri, Salma on June 6, 2007.

31 Safitri recalled one of their demonstrations, demanding that the State Minister of Women's Role should deal with the issue of women migrant workers. Because they were not admitted into the building, they could only shout on the terrace while making noises by banging pots.

32 Cf. Riker 1998, pp. 288-89.

33 Particularly the Directorate General of Social Assistance on Abused Victim and Migrant Workers (*Bantuan Sosial Korban Tindak Kekerasan dan Pekerja Migran*).

Coordinating Minister for Economic Affairs, the Coordinating Minister for Economy and Finance,[34] and the Coordinating Minister for People's Welfare as the more accommodative government institutions.[35]

As already noted in Chapter 6, the NGOs' relationship with the MoMT, the ministry responsible for the regulation of labor migration, has generally been sour. However, statements of the NGOs' staff indicate that there has been a degree of interaction and even cooperation between the NGOs and the MoMT. Susilo, for example, asserted that the Minister of Manpower and Transmigration for 2004-2009, Erman Suparno, usually accepted and listened to what he and Migrant CARE said.[36] He believed that this was very much influenced by Suparno's affiliations with *Partai Kebangkitan Bangsa* (PKB)[37] and Susilo's and Hidayah's close relationship with its former leader Abdurrahman Wahid. Hidayah, however, claimed that Migrant CARE had no cooperation with this ministry.[38] While Migrant CARE's staff had mixed views on their relationship with the MoMT, SP staff readily claimed to have worked with this ministry. As explained by Zulbahary, SP's legal assistance staff has arranged tripartite meetings[39] with the MoMT and labor agencies for cases faced by migrant workers.[40] Also when SP conducted research on the health status of migrant workers, they were able to arrange interviews and obtain data from the MoMT, and even get the ministry's recommendation to interview labor agencies. These different statements show that NGOs also have slightly varied perceptions and attitudes toward certain state institutions, which further determine the relationship that exists between them.

In most cases, cooperation between NGOs and a state institution is made possible due to changes within the institution. In May 2005, the SMoWE established the position of Deputy for Women's Protection with one of the Assistant Deputies focusing on women workers, covering those working both inside and outside Indonesia. Safruddin Setiabudi, the Assistant Deputy for Women Workers, stated that the ministry considers NGOs as working partners and they are involved in various activities.[41] As an example, Migrant CARE has worked with this ministry in handling cases[42] and establishing a help desk for returning migrant workers

34 Migrant CARE was involved in the working group on the Presidential Instruction No. 6/2006, which was handled by the office of the Coordinating Minister for Economy and Finance.

35 Interview with Hidayah, Anis on May 26, 2007, and on June 15, 2007.

36 Interview with Susilo, Wahyu on June 14, 2007.

37 As explained a bit later in this section, Erman Suparno was from PKB.

38 Interview with Hidayah, Anis on June 15, 2007.

39 A tripartite meeting usually involves migrant worker, labor agency, and the government.

40 Interview with Zulbahary, Thaufiek on July 9, 2007.

41 Interview with Setiabudi, Safruddin on June 19, 2007.

42 Hidayah described occasions when they tried to contact the MoMT and the President over cases of death penalty on migrant workers but did not get any responses. Interview with

in Terminal III, Soekarno-Hatta International Airport.[43] Hidayah realized the SMoWE's lack of authority in the regulation of labor migration, but she stated that at least the ministry can assist Migrant CARE in pushing the issue at a level where her organization has no influence. As for SP, although Zulbahary regretted the failure of the SMoWE to follow up some of its initiatives, he acknowledged SP's good relationship with this ministry, as shown through its support for SP's inclusion in the task force on trafficking and the working group on the protection aspect for the Presidential Instruction No. 6/2006.[44] The NGOs' cooperation with the SMoWE illustrates how given the relatively non-cooperative relationship with the MoMT, the NGOs have been engaging other state institutions to access the policy level.

As for the MoFA, one of the main changes is the increased commitment to protect Indonesian citizens abroad.[45] In 2002, the MoFA established a Directorate of Protection of Indonesian Citizens and Legal Entities.[46] According to Ferry Adamhar, who held the position of the director for three years, this directorate had what he called "two wings": one involved informal meetings with related directorate generals and another involved regular meetings with stakeholders, including NGOs.[47] He stated that they wanted information from the NGOs because they did not pretend that they knew everything.[48] The commitment to improve services and protection for citizens is also shown through the changes that occurred in the Indonesian Embassy in Kuala Lumpur. This is confirmed by Alex Ong, Migrant CARE's country representative in Kuala Lumpur, who stated that officials there were much more cooperative toward NGOs.[49] My interview with Tatang B. Razak, who was the Minister Councillor for the Consular Service

Hidayah, Anis on May 26, 2007. On the other hand, although it is not the main ministry responsible on this issue, SMoWE immediately responded by writing a letter to the president and the governors of the migrant workers' origin areas.

43 Interview with Hidayah, Anis on May 26, 2007, and with Setiabudi, Safruddin on June 19, 2007.

44 Interview with Zulbahary, Thaufiek on July 9, 2007, and on November 19, 2008. This policy instructed several related ministries, the police force, governors, mayors and heads of districts to take the necessary steps for implementing a number of policies and programs.

45 According to Ferry Adamhar, the ministry's attention and commitment to the protection of Indonesian citizens abroad increased after Hassan Wirajuda became Minister of Foreign Affairs in 2001. Interview with Adamhar, Ferry on July 6, 2007.

46 Cf. Menteri Luar Negeri Indonesia 2003.

47 Interview with Adamhar, Ferry on July 6, 2007.

48 In this light, Susilo believes that the closeness between the MoFA and NGOs is due to the fact that the staff of this ministry, particularly those in relevant embassies, has to be ready with answers to questions regarding the condition of Indonesian workers. Interview with Susilo, Wahyu on June 14, 2007. Susilo claims that the staff of the ministry admits that more objective and accurate answers come from the civil society.

49 Interview with Ong, Alex on August 13, 2007.

at the Indonesian Embassy in Kuala Lumpur and head of the Special Task Force for the Service and Protection of Indonesian Citizens, also confirmed the shift to a more welcoming attitude toward NGOs.[50] However, like most of the government staff I interviewed, Razak underlined the importance of a cooperative attitude from the NGOs. He also expected an understanding that both the government and the NGOs have their own rules and limits because, while the embassy has the mandate to secure the national interest, it also has to maintain good relations between the two countries, preventing them from being as blunt as NGOs.[51] Razak also pointed out that, in Malaysia, it is the embassy which has access and authority to take protection steps, including legal protection.[52] In describing the ideal relationship between NGOs and the government, Razak expected NGOs to give advice and information to support the government's work.

As previously described in Chapter 6, the NGOs have better relations with some supportive members of the parliament. In 2007, the intention to amend or revise Law No. 29/2004 started to surface both from the government and the parliament. However, according to Susilo, it was the parliament that took the initiative to involve civil society representatives by inviting him to the meeting of a working group on the revision of the law.[53] Moreover, Susilo expected that some members of parliament who supported the passing of the Law No. 21/2007 on Trafficking, such as Nursyahbani Katjasungkana, Eva Kusumah, and Tuti L. Soetrisno, were also pushing for the revision of Law No. 39/2004. In 2008, ac-

50 Interview with Razak, Tatang B. on August 14, 2007. Not all Indonesian NGOs have cooperation or even contacts with Indonesian representatives in receiving countries. SP, for example, was not familiar with the staff of the Indonesian embassy in Kuala Lumpur. Interview with Safitri, Salma on August 2, 2007.

51 In relation to this, Razak emphasized that the embassy is willing to cooperate and disclose information as long as the information is not used for publicity purposes. Interview with Razak, Tatang B. on August 14, 2007. He made this statement because, according to him, although there are NGOs which have their own ideals and conscience and are involved seriously from the beginning, certain NGOs only get involved in high profile cases at the end of the process but become really vocal about it. He also enunciated that there is the possibility that the victim, after being exploited by Malaysians, will be exploited further by other people for publicity. Razak was not willing to name the "good" and "bad" NGOs, but he categorized them into those which "have ideals, are strategic, tactical in working, and adequately intellectual" and those which "can only blame the embassy for not doing anything". Razak claimed that the embassy has often actually done much in addressing the problems faced by Indonesian migrant workers without publishing the achievements. On a similar note, Adamhar claimed that in many cases the government is better than the NGOs because they have clear commitment without any strings attached. Interview with Adamhar, Ferry on July 6, 2007.

52 In one of the interviews (June 5, 2007), Hidayah admitted that Migrant CARE may not be able to actively monitor all the cases abroad, and acknowledged the embassies' role in handling cases.

53 Interview with Susilo, Wahyu on June 14, 2007.

cording to Hidayah, Migrant CARE was working with those MPs who were concerned with the issues of human rights and migrant workers and who were planning to run again in the 2009 general election.[54] They were expected to support the amendment of Law No. 39/2004, ratification of the international convention on migrant workers, and the passing of a law on domestic workers. The above statements show how the NGOs continue to rely on their relationship with individual members of the parliament rather than approaching political parties for support. As argued by Susilo, in general there is no party in Indonesian politics that can be relied on to bring forward the issue of migrant workers, mainly because they do not have clear platforms.[55] Nevertheless, based on their responses, Susilo believed that there was hope from PDI-P, PKB, and partly from PAN, whose members had been voicing the need to ratify the ICRMW in the Commission IX of the parliament.

The NGOs have also attempted to cooperate with the BNP2TKI, a non-departmental government institution which was established as a mandate of Law No. 39/2004. Initially, there were expectations that this body, which reports directly to the president and was supposed to take over the operational roles formerly held by the MoMT, would improve the management of Indonesian labor migration. However, some migrant workers advocates took a cautious approach toward this institution. Hidayah, for example, stated that although the BNP2TKI is mandated to conduct reform, Migrant CARE was pessimistic because most of the personnel were from the MoMT.[56] Zulbahary mentioned that initially there were meetings between Jumhur Hidayat, the Head of the BNP2TKI, with organizations such as SBMI, Migrant CARE, *Komnas Perempuan* and SP, including some key migrant workers advocates such as Wahyu Susilo, Tati Krisnawaty, and Salma Safitri to discuss what the BNP2TKI should and should not do, who should and should not be in the institution, and set the agenda on what should be done in the near future.[57] However, since then, there has been no significant cooperative relationship between the BNP2TKI and most NGOs working on the issue of migrant workers.

Responding to Indonesia's decentralization of power to the local level since 2000, NGOs have engaged with local governments. Migrant CARE, for example, has conducted policy advocacy by approaching a number of local governments and encouraging them to pass regulations which protect migrant workers.[58] Furthermore, as argued by Risma Umar from SP, there was a lack of

54 Interview with Hidayah, Anis on November 18, 2008.
55 Interview with Susilo, Wahyu on November 7, 2008.
56 Interview with Hidayah, Anis on May 26, 2007.
57 Interview with Zulbahary, Thaufiek on July 9, 2007.
58 Interview with Hidayah, Anis on May 26, 2007.

knowledge at the local level where more influential regulations should come from within the decentralized governance system.[59] Thus, SP has also taken the initiative to educate members of local parliaments and in many cases even conducted the drafting of the local regulations because the decentralization of power, while part of the democratization process, has not been supported by adequate human resources. In terms of influencing policy, the NGOs seem to have more access and influence at district and provincial levels where, since decentralization, governments, and representative assemblies have increased authority but lack knowledge and expertise on issues such as migrant workers.

In understanding the relationship between the government and NGOs, mutual perceptions are important. Although the first decade of *Reformasi* has witnessed a shift in the way the state and civil society interact in Indonesia, relations are still not uniformly friendly and welcoming. A common NGO perception of the government is that it lacks political will to address the problems faced by migrant workers and has vested interest in the labor migration process. Umar, for example, stated that although SP has explained the problem and provided the data, when it comes to the stage where the NGOs and the government need to sit together to work on a concept, the process is stymied by lack of political will and the government's strong economic interest in encouraging labor migration.[60] She also pointed out the lack of knowledge and expertise in the institutions responsible for migrant workers.[61] She believes that the appointment of people in these institutions is highly influenced by political debt.[62] In many cases, such perceptions by NGOs may prevent the development of a more cooperative relationship with the government.

From the government side, the general perception of NGOs expressed in my interviews with government officers was that they are potential partners who can provide information and their involvement is welcomed, with certain conditions, despite their tendency to oppose government measures. Ade Adam Noch, the then Director of Preparation and Departure in the BNP2TKI,[63] stated that he had

59 Interview with Umar, Risma on August 8, 2007.

60 Ibid.

61 Susilo also pointed out the low quality of the parliament members and their debates by describing how the members of parliament prefers to get a maximum of one page input which they can read in the meetings immediately, rather than reading thick documents. Interview with Susilo, Wahyu on June 14, 2007. Although the preference to read an "executive summary" may not be exclusive to Indonesian members of parliament, it can be assumed that Susilo is trying to point out their lack of willingness to equip themselves with adequate information on the issue.

62 Political debt here most likely refers to the "debt" created by the support given during a general election, which is commonly paid by a strategic position in the government.

63 Before assigned to the BNP2TKI, Adam Noch was one of the directors in the Department of Manpower and Transmigration.

been positioning NGOs as partners (*mitra*) and pushed for cooperation.[64] He admitted that, because the government cannot solve all problems, public participation, which is organized through NGOs, is important. He welcomed NGOs' initiative to cooperate, as long as they were genuine, supportive, and not against the government.[65]

An emphasis on the need for NGOs to support the government's work also comes from Damos Dumoli Agusman, the Director for Economic and Socio-cultural Affairs of the MoFA, who argued that in the protection of Indonesian migrant workers, the government, and NGOs were actually compatible.[66] The difference was, according to him, that NGOs were too idealistic while the government was realistic. He also pointed out that, in conducting their work, unlike NGOs, MoFA personnel is required to go through diplomatic channels and there are international relations values that they have to respect. Agusman further argued that the NGOs were still using the old paradigm of "we should be in conflict with the government", could not work closely with the government, often did not realize that both the government and the NGOs had a "common enemy", had excessive expectations of what the government could do across borders, and lacked understanding of diplomatic and consular protection, which he expected them to learn more about to avoid being unrealistic.

The expectation that NGOs should support the government was also voiced by Ferry Adamhar, the Director of Directorate for Protection of Indonesian Citizens and Legal Entities of the MoFA.[67] He expected NGOs to share their knowledge with his office, channel information that needed to be passed to those planning to migrate, exchange information with the government, and support the government's mission and trust the government even though in some instances the government could not share all the information it had. A similar expectation came from Tuti L. Soetrisno, a member of Commission IX of the DPR, who highlighted NGOs' role in giving inputs to the parliament and monitoring the situation in the field.[68]

The discussion in this section has shown a degree of improvement in the way NGOs cooperate with state institutions. It is important to highlight the fact that the improvements were made possible by the changes brought by democratization, with NGOs' attempting to seize the opportunities to engage in a more open political system and the government institutions opening up to the involvement

64 Interview with Adam Noch, Ade on September 4, 2007.

65 However, when asked about the forms of their interaction, Adam Noch said that it was limited to what he called "intense communication" to discuss solutions for various problems, whether conducted in the BNP2TKI or in the forums held by the NGOs.

66 Interview with Agusman, Damos Dumoli on July 23, 2007.

67 Interview with Adamhar, Ferry on July 6, 2007.

68 Interview with Soetrisno, Tuti L. on July 17, 2007.

of civil society, including NGOs. Nevertheless, the main ministry responsible for the issue, the MoMT generally takes a distant approach toward NGOs.[69] Meanwhile, the government institutions which are more accommodative have limited authority in the policy-making process and their acceptance toward the NGOs is still varied and often conditional. As repeatedly emphasized by Keck and Sikkink, information has been the ultimate "currency" for NGOs, including in their relationship with the government, as reflected in the expectations for them to provide inputs for policy-making.[70] Nevertheless, while most government staff admitted that NGO advice is needed, they welcomed engagement with NGOs only as long as they were cooperative, abided by the rules, and supported the government's work. Thus, further improvements would require the NGOs and state institutions to develop more positive and accommodative attitudes toward each other which should involve the elimination of their resistance toward each other, which is to some extent the legacy of the New Order Era.

7.1.3 Working with Ex-NGO Members in Other Institutions

NGOs' efforts to strengthen their networks also benefit from the existence of their ex-members and migrant workers' advocates in related organizations and state institutions.[71] The NGOs particularly expect migrant workers' advocates who are currently in the government and parliament to help them in accessing the policy process. However, as argued by Susilo, there is a difference between migrant worker advocates who enter the parliament and those who join the bureaucracy.[72] According to him, in the government administration, those who were critical most probably would have to change, while in the parliament, they still had a degree of resistance and critical stance toward the government. Susilo believed that migrant worker advocates in the parliament such as Nursyahbani

69 Tuti L. Soetrisno mentioned, when being asked by the NGOs to talk to Erman Suparno, the Minister of Manpower and Transmigration, to have asked for a desk in Terminal III. Interview with Soetrisno, Tuti L. on July 17, 2007. This request was not granted because the answer was that "the NGOs will not solve the problem, they will only sell the cases [found in the terminal] for funding because, as long as there are problems, they will be supported by their sponsors". This again illustrates the varied perceptions toward NGOs among elements of the state.

70 Cf. Keck and Sikkink 1998.

71 Although a number of the earlier members and the founders of the NGOs, particularly SP, have moved on to other activities, many of them have continued to take various roles in migrant labor activism. They include Tati Krisnawaty, one of the founders of SP, who subsequently became active in *Komnas Perempuan* and GPPBM, Yanti Muchtar, who established *Kapal Perempuan*, which is also a part of *Foker*, and Wahyu Susilo, who became a key activist in *Kopbumi* and now Migrant CARE and INFID.

72 Interview with Susilo, Wahyu on June 14, 2007.

Katjasungkana, Eva Kusumah, Tuti L. Soetrisno, and Latifah Iskandar have shown a high degree of concern on the issue of migrant workers. He also considered that there were a few in the Department of Manpower and Transmigration who shared this concern but unfortunately they were not in decision-making positions. Hidayah also regarded the women parliament members who were NGO activists as key persons, who could help NGOs by providing them with an entry point for lobbying government institutions.[73] However, at the same time, she did not see them as doing something significant that could change the system because according to her they had become limited by the bureaucracy in the parliament. While stating that it is more appropriate for outsiders to judge their performance inside the parliament, Nursyahbani Katjasungkana, claimed that there were six women, including herself, who could be relied upon to bring the issue of migrant workers forward in the parliament.[74]

It is quite common for a migrant workers' advocate to bring along his/her concern about the issue of migrant workers into the new institution he/she is working in. Humaidah assumed that one of the factors influencing *Komnas Perempuan*'s decision to focus on the issue of migrant workers may have been the arrival of Tati Krisnawaty, one of the founders of SP, who has continued to give attention to the issue.[75] Some active members of the NGOs have also been using their position in and affiliation with other organizations to support their NGOs' activism. Migrant CARE, for example, has benefited from Wahyu Susilo's position in INFID.[76] Susilo acknowledged that since INFID has been conducting international advocacy work, his position in this organization had benefited Migrant CARE through access to international advocacy and mechanisms and could contribute to the migrant workers' movement in Indonesia so that it could respond to the transnational nature of the issue more by not only concentrating on domestic mechanisms.[77]

If employed strategically, the move of migrant worker advocates to other institutions, including the government and the parliament, offers potential for widening the NGOs' network. The challenge seems to be for the migrant workers' advocates, particularly those in the government, to sustain their activism while working inside the bureaucratic system.

73 Interview with Hidayah, Anis on June 15, 2007.

74 Interview with Katjasungkana, Nursyahbani on July 6, 2007. She also mentioned the existence of *Jaringan Kerja Prolegnas Pro Perempuan* (national network for pro-women national legislation program), which focused on 14 bills which affect women.

75 Interview with Humaidah, Lisa Noor on July 12, 2007.

76 Besides being one of the board members in Migrant CARE, in 2004, Susilo joined INFID as project officer for the Millennium Development Goals, and, in 2007, was head of the advocacy and networking division in INFID.

77 Interview with Susilo, Wahyu on June 14, 2007. See more on this point in chapter 9.

7.1.4 Working with Religious Organizations

The activism of Philippine NGOs, including those working on the issue of migrant workers, have benefited from the role of religious bodies like the Christian churches which besides providing reliefs, including for migrants, have also promoted an environment which allows views different from that of the state to grow.[78] In Indonesia, religious bodies have become more involved in public issues such as migrant workers. Consequently, more Indonesian NGOs working on the issue of migrant workers are approaching and working with religious organizations. This can be seen in the interactions between SP and Migrant CARE with *Fatayat* and *Muslimat*, the women's wings of *Nahdlatul Ulama* (NU), one of the main Moslem organizations in Indonesia and also in the involvement of organizations such as *Muslimat* and *Wanita Katolik Republik Indonesia* in GPPBM.

The move to collaborate with religious organizations was influenced by several factors. *Firstly*, religious organizations usually have a larger network, covering remote areas not covered even by local NGOs, which are usually located in the main towns at the provincial or district level. As explained by Hidayah in some cases, through *Fatayat* in Jakarta, which contacted its branches, Migrant CARE could immediately get the address of victimized women workers and identify the issues that need to be addressed.[79] *Secondly*, the leading persons of this organization such as Abdurrahman Wahid from NU have strong connections with some Moslem receiving countries like Malaysia and Middle East countries, which for NGOs like Migrant CARE have been helpful to them in handling cases.[80] *Thirdly*, for certain origin areas, many of those who migrate to work abroad are devoted members of NU. As illustrated by Humaidah, there was a case when one of the deported women migrant workers had no other documents except her *Fatayat* membership card.[81] Thus, approaching them through the organization, which has considerable influence in almost every aspect of their lives and which they trust, can be considered as a strategic choice for the NGOs.

The NGOs have also used the association of some bureaucrats with certain key religious institutions in their attempts to influence government policies. As explained by Susilo, Erman Suparno, the Minister of Manpower and Transmigration for 2005-2009, was from PKB, and Migrant CARE's staff was close to its leader, Abdurrahman Wahid.[82] Therefore, Susilo believed that Suparno's attention to Migrant CARE's demands and requests for meetings were not out of re-

78 Cf. Clarke 1998, p. 193, Yamanaka and Piper 2005, p. 29.
79 Interview with Hidayah, Anis on June 15, 2007.
80 Interview with Hidayah, Anis on May 26, 2007.
81 Interview with Humaidah, Lisa Noor on July 12, 2007.
82 Interview with Susilo, Wahyu on June 14, 2007.

spect toward NGOs but more because of Susilo's reputation and association with Wahid. Susilo admitted that this kind of favoritism based on personal relationship is not ideal. Also, Susilo admitted that he had used the fact that many of the migrant workers are members of NU to remind Suparno of his responsibility to them as his constituents.[83] However, it did not serve the NGOs' cause that well because as Susilo argued, Suparno was more influenced by his position than by his accountability to his constituents. This shows that while religious organizations may have assisted the NGOs in some of their activities such as case handling, their influence on the bureaucrats affiliated with the religious organizations and eventually their policies, is still debatable.

7.1.5 Non-Cooperative Relations with Labor Agencies and SBMI

Among the stakeholders of labor migration from Indonesia there are two significant entities with which the NGOs have minimum or no relations: labor agencies, usually known as PJTKI, and SBMI. Interactions between NGOs and PJTKI are dominated by their opposing positions, particularly during the process of redressing cases faced by migrant workers. This is greatly determined by NGOs' perception that PJTKIs' bad practice is one of the causes of the problems faced by migrant workers. According to Hidayah, most PJTKI are anti-NGO, because every time there is a case where the family of the victim is accompanied by NGOs, it is more likely to involve the media, and NGOs usually urge migrant workers to demand what PJTKIs are actually responsible for but reluctant to provide, such as unpaid salaries.[84]

The growth of migrant worker organizations has been another significant development in the past decade. Migrant workers have tried to organize themselves, whether in Indonesia or in the receiving countries, in some cases with the help of NGOs. They are called or registered or mentioned in the literature as migrant worker organizations or migrant worker unions.[85] In this book I am using the term migrant worker organization simply to differentiate them as organizations established and run mostly by current and ex-migrant workers, as compared to NGOs which are established and run by migrant workers' advocates.

While both SP and Migrant CARE have boasted of their roles in assisting the establishment of some migrant workers organizations as a part of their efforts to

83 Anis Hidayah has also been using this fact in lobbying members of parliament from PKB to support decisions and adopt policies which protect women migrant workers.

84 Interview with Hidayah, Anis on September 14, 2007.

85 A comprehensive discussion on the growth and development of this type of organization and their relationship with NGOs has been provided by Ford. See Ford 2004, 2006b, 2009.

empower migrant workers, there is minimal interaction, let alone cooperation, between the NGOs and SBMI, one of the leading migrant worker organizations centered in Jakarta.[86] Hidayah criticized SBMI for not being critical enough toward the government.[87] In 2007, SBMI made what they called *kontrak politik* (political contract)[88] with the BNP2TKI, a move which was criticized by a number of migrant workers advocates, including Hidayah who argued that political contracts should be made with parties, not with the government. This brings up the issue of how proximity to the government is perceived among civil society actors such as NGOs. There is also competition between SBMI and migrant worker NGOs, particularly on funding and projects. This can be sensed in Susilo's statement that Indonesian migrant worker unions in Indonesia or abroad could not yet be considered as unions because they still depended on foreign funding, not on members' contributions/dues (*iuran*) which he considered as a significant source of ownership, a significant principle for a union.[89] According to him, what was needed was a trade union of migrant workers which truly operated like a trade union, not like an NGO.

Despite their non-cooperating relationship with SBMI, NGOs do work with other organizations formed by migrant workers, particularly those they assisted in establishing such as the migrant worker solidarity organizations which are SP's partners and those they have been closely working with such as Migrant

86 I do not literally translate SBMI into English because the direct translation of SBMI would be "Indonesian Migrant Workers Union", which is another Indonesian migrant workers organization that operates in Hong Kong. As also noted by Ford there are various migrant workers' organizations which use the wording "*serikat buruh migran Indonesia*" in their naming, such as those associated with SP. Cf. Ford 2005. In this section I am referring to the SBMI established on February 23, 2003 in Solo with Miftah Farid as its chairman. In their blog, SBMI describes itself as an organization of Indonesian migrant workers, whether they are prospective, still working, or ex-migrant workers, their families or supporting organizations. Cf. SBMI, 2009. This organization has branches in some areas in Indonesia including: West Nusa Tenggara, East Java, Central Java, West Java, Jabodetabek (Jakarta Bogor, Depok, Tangerang, and Bekasi), Banten, Lampung, Jambi, and North Sumatra.

87 Interview with Hidayah, Anis on September 14, 2007.

88 The political contract refers to a memorandum of understanding which lists the actions both sides agreed on. This has become a quite common move in Indonesia recently, particularly during the 2009 presidential election campaign. There were many political contracts made between the candidates and civil society organizations, including those working on the issue of migrant workers. This political contract move can be considered as a new way to gain a degree of guarantee that the elected president will give attention to the protection of migrant workers.

89 Interview with Susilo, Wahyu on November 7, 2008. Ford also pointed out the criticism toward the not so "real unions" nature of migrant workers' associations or unions in origin countries, which, according to her, is based on the inclusion of ex-workers, migrant worker families, and prospective migrant workers who are not in an employment status as commonly required by trade unions membership. Cf. Ford 2006b, p. 306.

CARE's partner, the IMWU. Interaction between NGOs and migrant workers' organizations only dries up when they have different positions, particularly toward the government, and when they have to compete for funding.

7.2 Working at the Local/Grassroots Level

Both SP and Migrant CARE are Jakarta-based organizations. Nevertheless, realizing that many of the problems arise in the areas from which migrant workers come, thus requiring efforts to address the problems to be conducted there, both organizations have attempted to conduct activities in some origin areas. Hidayah claimed that Migrant CARE has done capacity building and education through training sessions for people at the grassroots level so that before they depart to work overseas they can understand their rights, safe mechanisms for working overseas, and the danger of forging documents.[90] As she further asserted, through these training sessions, which were held in origin areas like those in East Java, at least the prospective workers have a second source of information, other than the middlemen.[91] Hidayah also explained that, whenever they went to the "*daerah*" (origin areas), Migrant CARE coordinated and communicated with local NGOs, not limiting its interaction to NGOs which made the issue of migrant workers their main concern because this type of NGO might not exist in that particular area.[92] For this reason, they have worked with village, farmers, forest, environment, and religious organizations.[93]

Similarly, as explained by Asmaul Khusnaeny, from the legal assistance division of SP, SP had a pre-departure program where migrant worker candidates were given information on matters such as how to choose legal PJTKI endorsed by the Department of Manpower and Transmigration, what documents are needed, the acceptable amount of fee based on government regulations, access to the media, what is tested in medical check-ups and their rights to know the results.[94] According to Khusnaeny, this was usually done in regular discussions in villages, conducted by local SP communities. In the effort of expanding their coverage at the local level, while Migrant CARE had to rely on occasional cooperation with local NGOs with varied backgrounds and concerns, SP benefited from its 13 communities and four partners of migrant worker organizations.

90 Interview with Hidayah, Anis on May 26, 2007.

91 Interview with Hidayah, Anis on September 14, 2007.

92 Interview with Hidayah, Anis on June 15, 2007.

93 Hidayah believes that their willingness to get involved in the issue of migrant workers is influenced by the fact that the problems faced by migrant workers are also faced by the people of the villages in which these organizations operate. Ibid.

94 Interview with Khusnaeny, Asmaul on September 24, 2007.

Cooperation between Jakarta-based NGOs, which have better access to the central government and international networks, and local-based organizations, which have better access to the migrant workers at the origin and transit areas, is important for strengthening NGO activism. This argument is based on at least two reasons. *Firstly*, although with the decentralization policies, more power has been given to local governments, the division of authority between central and regional governments is still unclear. Therefore, the NGOs' response will be strongest if they maintain activism and influence policies at both levels. *Secondly*, origin and transit areas have gained more attention especially after the humanitarian crisis that happened in Nunukan in 2002.[95] Moreover, since the Jakarta-based NGOs have limited resources and coverage, partnership with local organizations – whether in the form of NGOs, migrant workers organizations or others – seems to be the more effective solution. An example of a good practice in bridging the gap between central and local NGOs, particularly in terms of funding allocation was explained by Puspasari who recalled an activity which SP conducted in the early 2000s.[96] With the support of the Asia Foundation, SP's National Secretariat conducted an event to which it invited a number of donors and their communities. Their communities were asked to explain their programs and write a proposal to be funded by the donors. Puspasari believes that this kind of activity is important because in that way, the central NGOs help grassroots organizations overcome the challenge of lack of access to networks and resources. Nevertheless, this is a rare instance since cooperation between the central and local NGOs is usually short lived, and most of the time there is a degree of competition, particularly for funding, between them.

7.3 Use of the Media to Influence Policy

One of the features of democratizing Indonesia is freedom of the press. The more open political atmosphere during the *Reformasi* Era has allowed the media to cover topics which were unlikely to make the headlines during the New Order era, such as human rights' related issues, including the rights of migrant workers. While the freer media has a thirst for alternative sources of information, NGOs also need the media to voice their demands and form public opinion in the effort

95 The work of Ford provides an analysis of the cause and conditions of the humanitarian crisis and Indonesian government's responses to the crisis, focusing on the relationship between central and regional governments in Indonesia. See Ford 2006a.

96 Interview with Puspasari, Riana on December 11, 2008.

to build pressure on the government. Also, as stated by Keck and Sikkink, the media is crucial in an effort to reach broader audience.[97]

Both SP and Migrant CARE have become sources of information for those interested on the issue of migrant workers, including the media, local, national, and international. Various national and international media have increasingly consulted Migrant CARE for data on migrant workers, particularly that of problems and abuses. According to Hidayah, the media's initiative to put Migrant CARE's data side by side with government data indicated that the government's documentation system for the sending of Indonesian workers overseas, including the number of those facing problems, was inadequate, and that the government was still not transparent in providing information to the public, particularly on problematic issues, and preferred to publish success stories.[98] Hidayah's opinion was confirmed by Ridwan Sijabat[99] from the Jakarta Post. Although Sijabat admitted that the NGOs might sometimes exaggerate their data, he considered their information more realistic than that of the government, which he considered "conservative" and not up-to-date.[100]

A unique form of NGO-media interaction is the one between Migrant CARE and *Deutsche Welle*, a German radio station. Hidayah explained that, besides regularly interviewing her, this radio had a program where Indonesian migrant workers could report their cases, which *Deutsche Welle* would pass on to Migrant CARE.[101] According to Hidayah, the program was developed after items on migrant workers broadcasted by this radio generated quite a number of phone calls from Indonesian migrant workers in Saudi Arabia who could receive their broadcast.

Migrant CARE's high media profile is also supported by the activities of its policy analyst and board member, Wahyu Susilo. Besides being frequently quoted in news on migrant workers and interviewed by radios and televisions, Susilo also frequently writes articles for newspapers and journals, nationally and internationally. He believes that using mass media is still an effective way to channel their voices because according to him the main reference of Indonesian executive and legislative members is the media.[102] He said that "the first thing they do when they wake up in the morning is read the newspaper, not an NGO position paper." This comment shows that the NGOs' decision to use the media may have

97 Cf. Keck and Sikkink 1998, p. 22.

98 Interview with Hidayah, Anis on September 14, 2007.

99 Sijabat is a senior journalist at the Jakarta Post who has been covering and writing articles on the issue of migrant workers. He frequently quotes NGO activists such as Wahyu Susilo, Anis Hidayah, and Salma Safitri in his works.

100 Interview with Sijabat, Ridwan on September 19, 2007.

101 Interview with Hidayah, Anis on June 15, 2007.

102 Interview with Susilo, Wahyu on June 14, 2007.

been a result of a learning process on what is the more effective way of gaining the bureaucrats' attention.

There are varied views from the government side on how NGOs have frequently gained attention by "blowing up cases" through the media. Ramiany Sinaga from the BNP2TKI argued that even without the publicity the government – Indonesian representatives overseas and particularly her office – would still handle the cases, because they were the government's responsibility.[103] Agusman from the MoFA on the other hand said that NGOs' publicity efforts could be useful in putting pressure on the Malaysian government.[104] He recalled refusing a request from a Malaysian representative to contain the Indonesian media by stating that the Indonesian media is now independent. However, Agusman also pointed out that it cannot be expected that blowing up a case in the media will immediately change the laws and policies. It takes time.

Both the media and the NGOs have benefited from their mutual engagement. With the lack of adequate and reliable official data, the NGOs have become alternative sources of information for the media. For the NGOs, the media is a strategic alternative channel to voice their demands, build public awareness and put pressure on the government. Although it may be difficult to actually measure the impact of the NGOs' media campaign on the policies, at least it can be considered as evidence of a democratization process occurring in Indonesia, with the two entities which tended to be silenced during the New Order era, the media and civil society organizations, working together to voice public demands.

7.4 Learning and Self-Evaluating

This research is concerned with how the NGOs determine or "measure" the success of their activism. One may argue that NGOs' success in terms of creating a significant impact or not is best judged by the recipient of their services or the group in the society they are fighting for, which in this study means the migrant workers themselves. However, it is also significant for the NGOs to be able to evaluate their performance in their own terms as a part of their learning process, which this study is more concerned about.

According to Zulbahary, for SP, a form of its self-assessment is the evaluation conducted during the national congress of its community board.[105] He explained that since SP is focused on strengthening the grassroots, a measurement of its success usually involved judging whether the migrant workers were empowered

103 Interview with Sinaga, Ramiany on August 31, 2007.
104 Interview with Agusman, Damos Dumoli on July 23, 2007.
105 Interview with Zulbahary, Thaufiek on September 24, 2007.

and whether they understood the existing policies and their rights. In other words, the evaluation was more about the impact of their work on migrant workers rather than on government policies. Susilo, meanwhile, recommended that a possible way of measuring NGOs' performance is by looking at the government's official documents, particularly speeches at international forums, to identify whether there is a shift in the government's policies.[106] Like Susilo, Ong suggested that a way to identify his achievement in Malaysia was to look at the change of the paradigm in the Malaysian parliament or quantitatively count the number of questions being asked in the parliament with regard to Indonesian workers and the number of exposures in the media.[107] Nevertheless, whichever ways are used to evaluate the NGOs' work, it remains still difficult to measure and claim their contribution to the changes in government policies. As argued by Hidayah, their success is hard to determine because it is difficult to choose indicators, the process is ongoing, and the approaches used by the government and migrant workers' advocates are different.[108] Based on her experience working in a number of funding agencies, Riana Puspasari, who worked for UNIFEM, stated that donors usually have indicators to measure the success of a project, including how NGOs' work.[109] According to her, most donor agencies would concentrate on policy changes and use quantitative measurements such as how many people are made aware of their rights, how much media exposure was received (which is usually counted through newspaper clippings), and how many people attended the seminars conducted. However, Puspasari suggested that NGOs and donors should favor qualitative rather than quantitative measurement and be more flexible with the timeframe so that more significant results and changes can be identified.

The two main activities of most organizations working on the issue of migrant workers are case handling and policy advocacy.[110] However, according to Safitri, SP did not make case handling a main pillar of its work in the sense of choosing

106 Interview with Susilo, Wahyu on November 7, 2008.

107 Interview with Ong, Alex on August 16, 2007.

108 Interview with Hidayah, Anis on May 26, 2007.

109 Interview with Puspasari, Riana on December 11, 2008.

110 In describing their activities, one of the terminologies frequently used by the NGO activists is *advokasi* or advocacy. This term is commonly defined as "an act to influence policy". Cf. Piper and Uhlin 2004a, p. 6. A broader way of understanding this term comes from Ibrahim et al., who proposed three types of advocacy: campaigning to strengthen the bargaining position of community organizations at the grassroots level toward authority so that they can influence policy, advocacy to give legal aid, and lobbying decision-makers and the public for alternative policy concepts. Cf. Ibrahim et al. 1996, p. 13. Ibrahim et al. maintained that the three types of advocacy are inseparable. During my research, I found that they are not only inseparable, but also used quite liberally by activists to describe almost all of their activities.

cases based on the consideration that they would help in recognizing the problems and identifying their causes.[111] Safitri argued that their aim was for the migrant workers to be aware of their rights to organize themselves and fight for their rights, for the government to change their exploitative policies, and for the public to support migrant workers' rights. As an illustration of Safitri's statement, Khusnaeny explained that when SP gave legal assistance to victims, the result was evaluated not according to whether the cases were solved, but according to whether the process had empowered the migrant workers.[112] Thus, SP staff did not work directly on behalf of the migrant workers, but involved them in the process with the expectation that they would then understand the process and its challenges, so that they would eventually be able to transfer that knowledge to other people. She claimed that this had occurred among SP's communities and partners, where many had become paralegals. By this means, as Khusnaeny maintained, not all cases needed to be referred to the center. This can be seen as SP's effort to empower the migrant workers and devolve some activities to the grassroots level.

Susilo argued that Indonesian NGOs have to focus more on monitoring policies, using as an example the World Bank's policy which, according to him, put more emphasis on increasing remittances rather than protecting migrant workers.[113] In a self-critical vein, Susilo observed that most NGOs working on migrant workers issue concentrated too much on handling cases, frequently overlooking the wider policy framework which might influence their work. Susilo admitted that his own organization, Migrant CARE, was still occasionally overwhelmed by case handling. One of the challenges for the NGOs is how to scale up their activities from providing services to a relatively more strategic activity of policy advocacy which is more directed toward preventing than addressing problems.

The discussion so far has illustrated changes in the relationship between state institutions and NGOs, with certain elements of the state becoming more open and accommodative toward NGO involvement. The question is, if there has also been a change in the NGOs' approach toward the state since a part of the learning process for NGOs is to identify, understand, and respond to the changes that occur around them, which may involve changing themselves.

Safitri stated that in interacting with the government, SP had moved from the "shouting on the street" approach toward a "let's talk" one.[114] Furthermore, as stated by Zulbahary, although protest or "*aksi*" was still used from time to time

111 Interview with Safitri, Salma on August 2, 2007.
112 Interview with Khusnaeny, Asmaul on September 24, 2007.
113 Interview with Susilo, Wahyu on June 14, 2007.
114 Interview with Safitri, Salma on June 6, 2007.

when lobbying does not work, it usually involved migrant workers who had been informed and empowered through training by SP's staff.[115] He believed that whether to use protest or a more cooperative approach was a tactical choice, which had to be made depending on the context. As for Migrant CARE, Hidayah maintained that protest through demonstrations was still considered to have a significant impact.[116] She believed that their action was one of the factors that accelerated government's efforts in handling cases and determined some changes in policies and the way matters were handled afterward.[117] Susilo perceived a change in the way the NGOs interacted with policy-makers where NGOs had shifted from being the government's enemy to cooperating with it.[118] However, Susilo believed that whether an NGO was involved in a policy-making process or not depended on whether it had the capacity to lobby and provide substantive inputs. According to him, on the issue of migrant workers, there were few NGOs which could see where they could be effective, and most NGOs did not understand state politics, the legislative process, or even what advocacy is.

Although in most cases the NGOs seem to oppose the government and frequently use "mobilization of shame" as their strategy, both NGOs researched have attempted to vary the methods they employ in conducting their activities. Occasionally, the NGOs show a cooperative attitude and even support government moves. For example, when in November 2008, Erman Suparno, the then Minister of Manpower and Transmigration lobbied Malaysia for amendment of the 2006 MoU, Hidayah reacted positively and made a statement in the media that "if the government is serious, we will support it".[119] She also claimed to have sent a text message to Suparno to the same effect. Susilo called Migrant CARE's approach a "critical collaboration", where they would support the government if it did something good and give hard criticism if it did not.[120] He claimed that although Migrant CARE tended to have a loud and hard voice, it was still invited to events held by the government. He believed that this was because they were still speaking within acceptable bounds, with a strong basis in verifiable evidence and that Migrant CARE would admit if they made a mistake,

115 Interview with Zulbahary, Thaufiek on November 19, 2008.

116 Interview with Hidayah, Anis on September 14, 2007.

117 Hidayah claimed, for example, the demonstration that they conducted in front of the Singapore Embassy and the State Palace in Jakarta on the death penalty of two Indonesian domestic workers in Singapore, contributed to the Singaporean High Court's decision to free those workers of the charges. Interview with Hidayah, Anis on May 26, 2007. She realized that Migrant CARE's demonstration was not the only factor, but she also believed that it had influenced the diplomatic process between the governments of Indonesia and Singapore.

118 Interview with Susilo, Wahyu on November 7, 2008.

119 Interview with Hidayah, Anis on November 18, 2008.

120 Interview with Susilo, Wahyu on November 7, 2008.

which according to him was not done by most NGOs working on the issue of migrant workers.

While statements by NGO activists indicate changes in the ways they operate, observers argue that they still have much work to do. A quite strong opinion comes from Tati Krisnawaty, one of SP's founders and presidium of GPPBM, who argued that NGOs needed to employ varied approaches to push for a policy change by doing more than creating bombastic news on TV and in newspapers and blaming the government for all the problems faced by migrant workers.[121] She was also concerned with the NGOs' practice of involving migrant workers who have problems in the case handling process and frequently exposing them in many forums and media, while stating that the intention is to empower them. Krisnawaty questioned whether this can be considered an act of empowerment rather than of exploitation. In terms of whether the NGOs should continue doing policy advocacy or concentrate more on service-providing activities, Krisnawaty preferred to see these activities as a continuum, on which NGOs could choose where to position themselves depending on their understanding of what the problems were and what needed to be done.

An opinion that NGOs still tend to focus more on blaming the government also came from Ade Adam Noch from the BNP2TKI, who said that, rather than bringing peace to the country, the reforms had tended to bring anger, which according to him, led to "*reformasi kebablasan, revolusi nggak nyampe*" or more than a reform but not enough to be a revolution.[122] To a certain degree, his statement can be considered to reflect the government's preference for a more benign approach from the NGOs.

Eldridge observed that although the political and constitutional reforms tended to lean toward more liberal democratic principles, there was still strong support for both conservative and radical discourses.[123] On the issue of migrant workers, the varied principles were reflected in the various means employed by the NGOs in channeling their voices to and building pressures on the government. Some had adopted more benign and cooperative ways, while others still maintained their oppositional stance. The means used also varied from consultation and public hearing to street demonstrations and hunger strikes. SP was more inclined toward low-key ways such as audiences and hearings, reasoning that if they wanted to influence the government, it should be done tactfully. On the other hand, Migrant CARE was more known for its media statements and street demonstrations, which they claimed had created significant impacts. However the distinction is not rigid. I agree with Eldridge, who found that in practice the elements

121 Interview with Krisnawaty, Tati on November 7, 2008.
122 Interview with Adam Noch, Ade on September 4, 2007.
123 Cf. Eldridge 2005, p. 154.

that form the ideal types of NGOs are combined according to the context and organizational needs.[124] SP, which showed a more cooperative attitude toward the government, claimed that it still conducted street demonstrations when needed and Migrant CARE, which is known for organizing street demonstration and hunger strikes, claimed that it has worked together with elements of the government in some instances. Furthermore, despite the tendency to utilize various methods in conducting their activities, "mass democracy" is not an option for the two NGOs researched, due to their lack of a mass base.

7.5 Conclusion

Facing the reality that their efforts to influence policy-making have not resulted in a law which provide adequate protection for women migrant workers, the NGOs have continued to seek and employ alternative ways to achieve their goal. This involves trying new approaches, engaging and working with more accommodative entities in the government and parliament, building cooperation to build pressure on the government, and using the media. Such efforts are based on the experience they gather during their activism, a form of self-evaluation, and a learning process.

In the course of the learning process, ways, which were initially considered potential alternatives, have proven to have their own weaknesses. As an example, networking was initially considered a way out for the limitations that the NGOs face. Eventually, the NGOs found that coordinating activities within a network and sustaining cooperation are not easy tasks, especially when there are factors such as different characteristics, visions, priorities, and resources involved. Furthermore, the networking experience has highlighted the absence of coordination and consolidation within the NGO communities which makes it difficult for them to speak with one voice. A sense of competition has also prevented the NGOs from developing collaboration among them. These are some of the challenges that the NGOs need to overcome if they plan to continue the effort of influencing the policies on migrant workers.

It is still too early to claim that there is a strategizing process going on. The activists may occasionally use the word "strategy", but it seems that they were using it to refer to a way or approach – another example of how terms are often used for various meanings, just like the word "advocacy". The learning process is more a matter of trial and error, conducted haphazardly by the NGO based on each effort made and program conducted. Thus, what comes out of the learning process is more like a remedy for a particular issue or case, rather than a com-

124 Cf. ibid., p. 155.

prehensive strategy. Even so, some of the steps taken, such as the initiative to engage accommodative state elements, religious bodies, and the media, can be considered as an indication that there is a potential for the development of a comprehensive strategy.

The next part, again divided into two chapters, will investigate the NGOs' regional and international activism in responding to globalization. Chapter 8 examines the involvement of these NGOs in the making of a foreign policy in the form of a MoU with Malaysia as a receiving country, and Chapter 9 examines the NGOs other activities conducted at the regional and international levels which are aimed at strengthening their influence on the policies on migrant workers.

8. Influencing Foreign Policy

Continuing the task of Chapter 6 of identifying the kind of relationship that exists between the NGOs and the government in the making of policies on migrant workers and assessing NGOs' ability to influence the policy-making process, this chapter will look into NGOs' involvement in the process of making a foreign policy instrument, the 2006 MoU between the Governments of Indonesia and Malaysia on the Recruitment and Placement of Indonesian Domestic Workers.[1] Besides establishing whether there have been any changes in the way the NGOs and the state interact and why, this chapter intends to investigate whether there was actually any space for NGOs' involvement in the process of making a foreign policy, using the MoU as a case study.

Involvement of civil society in a policy-making process, as a part of the democratization process and implementation of good governance, is usually discussed in reference to domestic policy-making process. As described in Chapter 6, in the process of making Law No. 39/2004, although civil society elements were not part of the official legislative process, they were allowed to make recommendations to policy-makers and to be present in the parliament to observe the process and advise members of parliament in informal ways. It has also become a common practice during the Reform Era in Indonesia for the government to arrange forums which allow civil society elements to give their views, although questions remain as to whether these forums have truly become a channel for the voices of civil society. The situation is very different in the making of foreign policies, particularly bilateral agreements, which involve other countries, such as a MoU: here decision-making is commonly limited to government representatives, with no room for the presence of outsiders, even to observe the process. Nevertheless, NGOs still attempted to influence the process and its result due to the transnational nature of the issue of migrant workers and their expectation that the MoU can become a source of protection for Indonesian workers. This is a case of a globalized labor issue, a real challenge for domestic NGOs to deal with.

1 Also known as the MoU on the informal sector or the MoU on domestic workers. This MoU was revised in 2011 when the governments of Indonesia and Malaysia signed the Protocol to Amend the 2006 MoU after three years of moratorium on the sending of Indonesian migrant workers to Malaysia. However, since this book is focused on the first decade of the Reform Era, the discussion will be about the process of making the 2006 MoU.

Identifying and examining NGOs' involvement in the process of formulating the MoU can be quite challenging because the process is mostly closed to the public and the involvement of stakeholders other than the government is minimal, if not non-existent. However, the extent to which NGOs have been able to push for their involvement is still worth assessing for the following reasons. *Firstly*, before 2006, the NGOs had been voicing a demand for MoUs between Indonesia and receiving countries like Malaysia for several years. This mirrors their great expectation that the MoU would provide protection for Indonesian women migrant workers. *Secondly*, the fact that some elements of the government of Indonesia interacted with NGOs to gather information before the official process and again met the NGOs after the MoU was signed shows that there were efforts to apply the practice of involving civil society in a policy-making process, similar to that applied in making a domestic policy. *Thirdly*, in campaigning for this MoU, Indonesian NGOs have worked with other regional and international actors to put pressure on both governments. Discussing their involvement in this process will therefore assist in understanding not only NGOs' interactions with the government, but also how they overcome their limitations, particularly in terms of authority and coverage.

This chapter is divided into two sections. The first section describes the background of the MoU, looks into the official negotiation and formulation process and investigates how NGOs were involved, or not, throughout the process. The second section documents NGOs' responses to the MoU and examines their activism since the MoU was signed.

Bilateral agreements are usually made in the form of a note of agreement or an exchange of notes which, in some cases, are then replaced by a MoU. As an example, with Malaysia, the 2004 MoU on formal workers replaced the 1998 exchange of notes on the Procedure of Recruiting Indonesian Workers to Work in Malaysia Other Than Maids and the 2006 MoU on informal workers replaced the 1996 note of agreement on the Guidelines on the Hiring of Indonesian Maids. Before signing the 2006 MoU on informal workers with Malaysia, the Government of Indonesia had signed various forms of bilateral agreements on formal migrant workers with a number of receiving countries such as:[2]

- the 1996 Note of Agreement on the Guidelines on the Hiring of Indonesian Maids between Indonesia and Malaysia;
- the 1998 MoU, which was then replaced by the 2004 MoU on Formal Workers between Indonesia and Malaysia;
- the 1996 MoU between Indonesia and Kuwait;

2 Cf. Wirajuda 2004, Menteri Luar Negeri Indonesia 2005, Agusman 2006, 2007.

- the 2001 MoU between Indonesia and Jordan;
- the 2004 MoU between Indonesia and South Korea.

The 2006 MoU with Malaysia on domestic workers was chosen as a case study for a number of reasons. The most obvious reason is the large number of Indonesian workers in Malaysia, the main destination country for Indonesian migrant workers in Asia, and the problems they are facing. The 2006 MoU is also chosen because it specifically concerns domestic workers, a group of migrant workers which is not regulated and protected by Malaysian or Indonesian labor law. Most importantly, this MoU has been the object of criticism by NGOs for not providing the protection much needed by Indonesian migrant workers while they are working in Malaysia.

Before discussing the NGOs involvement in the process of making the MoU, the following section will briefly discuss the main features of the MoU.[3] The MoU between the Governments of Indonesia and Malaysia on the Recruitment and Placement of Indonesian Domestic Workers was signed in Bali on May 13, 2006. The signatories were Erman Suparno, Minister of Manpower and Transmigration, on behalf of the Government of Indonesia and Dato' Seri Mohd. Radzi bin Sheikh Ahmad, Minister of Home Affairs, on behalf of the Government of Malaysia. It is stated that the objective of the MoU is "to develop the existing cooperation between the Parties (the governments of Indonesia and Malaysia) for the purpose of strengthening the mechanisms on the conveyance and recruitment of Domestic Workers from the Republic of Indonesia". Thus, this MoU focuses on the mechanism for recruitment and placement of Indonesian domestic workers. By signing this MoU, the Government of Malaysia "recognizes" that the employment of domestic workers shall be conducted in accordance with Malaysia's employment laws, rules, regulations, policies, and directives. As for the Government of Indonesia, it "agrees to ensure" that the domestic workers entering Malaysia meet certain conditions which include that they are aged minimum 21 and maximum 45 years, have sufficient knowledge of Malaysian laws, culture, and social practices, are able to communicate in Malay and/or English; satisfy Malaysian immigration procedures, are certified as fit and healthy, and do not have any criminal record. It is stated that the implementation of this MoU, in part or in whole, can be temporarily suspended by either government for reasons of "national security, national interest, public order or public health" after notification through diplomatic channels. The MoU has two appendices. Appendix A elaborates the responsibilities of the employer, Malaysian recruitment agencies, Indonesian recruitment agencies, and the domestic workers. Appendix B is a

3 Cf. Menteri Luar Negeri Indonesia 2005, The Government of Indonesia and The Government of Malaysia 2006.

template for the contract of employment, which specifies issues such as duration of the contract, the working address, duties and responsibilities of the domestic worker and the employer, the amount of the wages, allowance of adequate rest for the domestic worker, and conditions for termination of contract by the employer and the domestic worker.

A quick evaluation of the MoU immediately reveals its limited binding power and that the agreement requires more actions from the Indonesian government. As a bilateral agreement, a MoU does not legally bind the signatories, the states represented by their governments, let alone the subjects of the states. The implementation of the agreed points depends on the consent and willingness of each government. Naturally, a country agrees to sign a MoU to serve its interests while preserving its sovereignty. Thus, it is quite understandable if the government of a country is quite cautious not to sign a MoU which contradicts its national laws and policies. In the case of the 2006 MoU between Indonesia and Malaysia on domestic workers, there seems to be a different understanding between the government and the NGOs on the power, extension and coverage of the MoU. In fact, the question of what a MoU can and cannot do was the central debate among them. To gain a better understanding of the debate and NGOs' criticism toward the MoU, the following section will first look into the process of making this foreign policy instrument.

8.1 The Process of Making a MoU on Informal Workers with Malaysia

8.1.1 Background

Various works on Indonesian migrant workers, particularly those which specifically deal with the migration of Indonesians to work in Malaysia, such as those by Jones, Gurowitz, Sustikarini, and Tirtosudarmo,[4] have discussed the beginning of the migration flows out of Indonesia, the problems entailed, and the efforts made by both governments to address the problems. Until the mid-1980s, public, media, and government attention was still more focused on the waves of women labor migration to the Middle East,[5] because of their significant numbers as compared to those that went to Malaysia. However, as noted by Sustikarini, the relatively small number of Indonesian workers in Malaysia – around 12,000 by the end of the 1970s – quickly grew to 100,000 in 1981.[6] Combined with the

4 See Jones 2000, Gurowitz 2000, Sustikarini 2004, Tirtosudarmo 2007.
5 Cf. Jones 2000, p. 17, Tirtosudarmo 2007, p. 266.
6 Cf. Sustikarini 2004.

problems related to undocumented migrants and economic recession due to the oil crisis, the rapid growth led Malaysia to start making policies regarding migrant workers.[7]

Earlier agreements between the governments of Indonesia and Malaysia focused more on addressing the issue of undocumented migrant workers. As a response to the flow of Indonesian workers without proper official documents, in the early 1980s the government of Malaysia started to take some initiatives, including signing the Supply of Workers Agreement, also known as the Medan Agreement with the Government of Indonesia on May 12, 1984.[8] This agreement was intended to regulate the recruitment of Indonesian plantation and domestic workers through official channels by setting up a joint committee to deal with the sending, documenting and charging fees.[9] However, both the employers and workers did not respond positively to this official mechanism.[10] Since then, both governments have signed a number of agreements and engaged in joint efforts to address the issue of undocumented migrant workers.[11]

Malaysia's policies on migrant workers are reflections of its domestic political and economic situation. Chin has illustrated how acceptance toward migrant workers, including the undocumented ones, from Indonesia and the Philippines has shifted from time to time, depending on the political and economic dynamic within the country.[12] As an illustration, while the promotion of Malaysia's middle class under the New Economic Policy (1971-1990) allowed migrant workers

7 According to Sustikarini, objections from a number of groups in Malaysian society toward the presence of Indonesian workers in Malaysia related to the balance of races there became a political issue in this multi-racial country. Cf. Sustikarini 2004. Objection also came from trade unions because the undocumented workers were willing to accept low wages, which weakened the bargaining power of local trade unions.

8 Cf. Jones 2000, p. 16, Kaur 2004, p. 220, Tirtosudarmo 2007, p. 267.

9 Cf. Gurowitz 2000, p. 866, Jones 2000, p. 16.

10 Cf. Sustikarini 2004.

11 On July 1, 1988, another agreement between the governments of Indonesia and Malaysia came into effect stating that Malaysia would legalize the status of irregular workers on the condition that they first reported to the Indonesian embassy in Kuala Lumpur, and returned home to obtain a special travel document called *Surat Perjalanan Laksana Paspor* (SPLP, travel document in lieu of passport). Cf. Gurowitz 2000, p. 866, Jones 2000, p. 20. This mechanism did not work either. As explained by Sustikarini, between 1989 and 1991 only 19,984 out of around 500,000 undocumented Indonesian workers were "legalized". Cf. Sustikarini 2004. Based on this result, the Malaysian government conducted another legalization process through an amnesty program which technically only required Malaysian entrepreneurs who employed undocumented Indonesian workers to register them at the Indonesian Embassy. This policy was then followed by the *Ops Nyah I* ("Get Rid" Operation I) which was aimed at deporting the undocumented workers who had still not gone through the legalization process, and stopping the flow of undocumented workers.

12 Cf. Chin 1997, pp. 358-61.

to take on the plantation and domestic employment abandoned by Malaysians, many non-Malays then opposed the presence of large numbers of Indonesian workers, suspecting they represented a political move to increase the proportion of Malays in the population. In a work by Ford, it is also shown how Malaysian policies toward migrant workers, including the undocumented ones, are highly determined by the country's domestic economic situation.[13] Incoming flows will be limited and deportations will be higher during an economic downturn, and during better economic conditions the policy will be reversed. As an example, during the 1997-1998 financial crisis, to deal with a high unemployment rate, incoming flows of Indonesian workers were limited and deportation of undocumented workers was quite high, a situation which quickly changed in 1998 when the economy recovered.[14]

Agreements between the governments of Indonesia and Malaysia on migrant workers during the 1980s and 1990s have mainly concerned regulating the flow of Indonesian workers into Malaysia and were responses to the fact that a substantial number of them were working without proper documents. This situation persists despite the Malaysian government's efforts to deport "illegal workers" through a series of operations that started in 1992, the implementation of Malaysian Immigration Act No. 1154,[15] and the "Hire Indonesian Last" Policy launched by the then Prime Minister of Malaysia, Mahathir Mohamad, in 2002.

When another case of abused Indonesian migrant domestic workers in Malaysia is exposed in the media, many Indonesians think their country should have a strong bargaining position in relation to Malaysia because Malaysia's economy depends on Indonesian labor. However, it also needs to be considered that Indonesia depends on Malaysia to accommodate the surplus of its workforce. As for Malaysia, there has been no instance to prove the assumption that the Malaysian economy will significantly be affected by the absence of Indonesian workers. This is partly because there are always Indonesians who want to work in Malaysia and workers have also come from other countries such as India, Vietnam, Myanmar, and Bangladesh. Thus, Indonesian workers are not totally irreplaceable. For these reasons, threat cannot be used as an approach to push Malaysia to improve protection of Indonesian workers. Bilateral agreements such as a MoU represent a more feasible way to seek better protection for Indonesian workers while they are working in Malaysia.

Before the 2004 MoU on the formal sector and the 2006 MoU on the informal sector, the last agreements between the governments of Malaysia and Indonesia

13 Cf. Ford 2006a.

14 Cf. ibid., p. 236.

15 This law imposes penalties of caning, fines, and imprisonment for both undocumented employees and their employers. Cf. The Jakarta Post, September 14, 2002.

on migrant workers were the 1998 exchange of notes on the Procedure of Recruiting Indonesian Workers to Work in Malaysia Other Than Maids and the 1996 note of agreement on the Guidelines on the Hiring of Indonesian Maids. In a meeting between Indonesian and Malaysian representatives February 18-20, 2002 in Kuala Lumpur, it was agreed that the two agreements needed to be re-evaluated to accommodate changed conditions.[16] This intention was strengthened in the meeting between President Megawati Soekarnoputri and Prime Minister Mahathir Mohamad in Bali August 7-8, 2002. After the Bali meeting, representatives from the Directorate of Protection of Indonesian Citizens and Legal Entities and the Directorate of Economic and Sociocultural Affairs from the Department of Foreign Affairs together with the Department of Manpower and Transmigration met to discuss the possibility of revising the two agreements.[17] The result was a recommendation that there needed to be a MoU between the two countries which is considered as a stronger form of bilateral agreement as compared to a note of agreement.

The process of formulating the MoUs involved a series of Senior Official Meetings between representatives from Malaysia and Indonesia.[18] The plan was to simultaneously discuss MoUs on formal and informal workers. But due to what were claimed as "technical challenges" both governments decided to work on the MoU on the formal sector first.[19] The process took quite a long time due to factors such as difficulties for the two countries to agree on issues such as direct recruitment[20] and who should hold the migrant workers' passports.[21] Despite initial disagreements on the clauses, an agreement was finally achieved in the meeting between Mahathir Muhammad and Megawati Soekarnoputri in Kuching on August 28, 2003[22] and the MoU was finalized in a Senior Official Meeting in Semarang in December 2003.

17 months after the first meeting was held in Kuala Lumpur on December 23, 2002, the MoU on formal workers was finally signed in Jakarta on May 10, 2004

16 Cf. Irewati 2003, p. 41.

17 Cf. ibid., p. 42.

18 Senior Official Meeting I (SOM I) in Kuala Lumpur on December 23, 2002, SOM II in Kuala Lumpur on January 2-3, 2003 and SOM III in Semarang on December 19-20, 2003. Cf. Depnakertrans 2004b.

19 Cf. Depnakertrans 2004b

20 Direct recruitment was demanded by Malaysia, but rejected by Indonesia.

21 Cf. Irewati 2003, p. 53. Malaysia persisted in rejecting Indonesia's demand for migrant workers to hold their own passports, instead of them being held by their employers or agents. Malaysia tended to use security reasons for rejecting this demand, arguing that passports were needed as a guarantee that the migrant workers would not conduct criminal acts or just run away or move from one employer to another before their working period ended.

22 Cf. ibid.

by the Minister of Manpower and Transmigration, Jacob Nuwa Wea, from Indonesia and the Minister of Human Resources Datuk Wira Dr. Fong Chan, from Malaysia.[23] The MoU was instantly criticized by migrant workers' advocates. HRW listed a number of its weaknesses, including the exclusion of domestic workers, passports held by employers and agents, the lack of minimum standards for working conditions, the absence of remedy mechanism or sanctions for abusive employers and agents, and the absence of guarantees for workers' freedom of association.[24]

Since the 2004 MoU only covered those working in formal sector, *Komnas Perempuan* pushed the Department of Foreign Affairs and Department of Manpower and Transmigration to immediately work on the MoU on informal workers, particularly domestic workers, because of their vulnerabilities.[25] The next section will examine the process of making this MoU on informal workers, focusing on investigating the extent to which the NGOs were involved.

8.1.2 The Process of Making the MoU on Informal Workers: With or Without NGO Involvement?

Indonesia's Law No. 24/2000 on International Agreements stipulates the process of international agreements, including bilateral ones such as MoUs.[26] According to the law, the negotiation for an agreement is conducted by a delegation of the Republic of Indonesia, led by a minister or other officials, depending on the content and their authorities. Agreements are then signed by the president or a minister. Thus, the process for making a MoU requires coordination between the president, related ministries, and the Ministry of Foreign Affairs, which is often lacking.

As stated in the 2006 MoU between the governments of Indonesia and Malaysia on the Recruitment and Placement of Indonesian Domestic Workers, its formulation took into account the Agreed Minutes of the Seventh Meeting of the Joint Commission for Bilateral Cooperation between the two countries in Kuala Lumpur, February 18-20, 2002, and the Joint Statement of the Annual Consultation between the Prime Minister of Malaysia and the President of Indonesia at Bukittinggi on January 12-13, 2006. The first Senior Official Meeting (SOM) for this MoU was held in Penang, Malaysia, on February 6-7, 2006. This was followed by a technical committee meeting between officials of both countries in

23 Cf. Depnakertrans 2004b.
24 Cf. HRW 2004b.
25 Cf. Bambang S, May 25, 2004.
26 Cf. Presiden Republik Indonesia, October 23, 2000.

Yogyakarta, Indonesia, on March 3-4, 2006. As mandated by the First SOM, the technical committee meeting was aimed at discussing Appendix A and B of the MoU.[27] Matters that could not be agreed on were referred to the Second SOM, which was held in Bogor, Indonesia on April 17, 2006. The aim of this Second SOM was to continue the discussion on the draft of the MoU, focusing on the outstanding issues from previous meeting.[28] In this Second SOM the delegations finally agreed to adopt the draft of the MoU and its appendices.[29] On May 13, 2006, on the sidelines of the Developing Eight (D-8) Summit in Nusa Dua, Bali, Malaysian Internal Affairs Minister, Ahmad Mohd. Radzi, and Indonesian Manpower and Transmigration Minister, Erman Suparno, signed the MoU on the Recruitment and Placement of Indonesian Domestic Workers, also known as MoU on informal workers, witnessed by Indonesian President Susilo Bambang Yudhoyono and Malaysian Prime Minister Abdullah Ahmad Badawi.[30]

This section will not discuss in detail the process of the MoU formulation. Its emphasis is more on how both the government and the NGOs perceived the process leading to the signing of the MoU and the interactions that occurred between them. Due to the limited detailed official record available on the negotiation and formulation process, my analysis depends heavily on my interviews with respondents from the Indonesian government, particularly the Ministry of Foreign Affairs, and the NGOs researched, SP and Migrant CARE.

The Government's Point of View

Considering that the formulation process of a MoU as a foreign policy document is commonly handled by the MoFA and related ministries, I interviewed a number of officers in the MoFA whose directorates are related to the issue of migrant workers and who were involved in the formulation process of the 2006 MoU. Rather than obtaining a chronological description of the process, the aim was more to capture their views on the involvement of other stakeholders, including NGOs, in the process.

27 Cf. Governments of Indonesia and Malaysia 2006b. A number of officials from the State Ministry of Women's Empowerment and from the Directorate for Immigration Traffic of the Department of Legal and Human Rights were part of Indonesian delegation. However, the majority of the Indonesian delegation members were from the Department of Foreign Affairs and the Department of Manpower and Transmigration.

28 Cf. Governments of Indonesia and Malaysia 2006c.

29 According to the media, the two countries finally reached agreement on this MoU during the visit of the Indonesian Vice-President Jusuf Kalla to Malaysia in late March. Cf. The Jakarta Post, May 15, 2006. This indicates the high influence of the state leaders on the process.

30 Cf. ibid.

One of the main respondents in the MoFA was Damos Dumoli Agusman, the Director for Economic and Sociocultural Affairs of the Directorate General of Legal Affairs and International Treaties, who explained the process of formulating the MoU in which he was involved.[31] According to him, Indonesia's request for this MoU was conveyed through a common way of communicating between the two countries – through bilateral consultations which usually discuss various issues such as economy, trade, and politics. In these annual meetings, Indonesia suggested the need to address the problems faced by Indonesian workers by formulating a MoU.[32] Agusman's explanation indicates that the issue of migrant workers had been discussed together with other issues concerning the relationship between Indonesia and Malaysia until there was finally an agreement to work on a MoU which specifically addressed the issue.

According to Agusman, the 2006 MoU was an unexpected document for Malaysia because the making of this MoU was more in Indonesia's interest than in Malaysia's.[33] Therefore, he asserted that while Malaysia was very reluctant about the MoU, as shown during the ministerial level or senior official level meetings, Indonesian representatives persistently brought up this issue on most occasions including meetings between ambassadors of both countries. Ferry Adamhar, who was the Director of Directorate for Protection of Indonesian Citizens and Legal Entities of the MoFA, also admitted that the MoU process was not as easy as they expected and emphasized that diplomacy played a strong role in negotiating the 2006 MoU.[34] He pointed out that President Susilo Bambang Yudhoyono's first visit to Kuala Lumpur in 2005 was intended to provide a momentum, which resulted in agreed minutes, signed by Indonesia's Minister of Manpower and Transmigration and Malaysia's Minister of Domestic Affairs. The three points included in the agreed minutes were the establishment of one-stop (known as one-roof) immigration process centers at eleven entry points, the establishment of a team consisting of representatives from the two countries to work on the MoU, and discussion of the possibility of establishing the Mandatory Consular

31 Agusman led the technical committee meeting on the MoU in Yogyakarta. Cf. Governments of Indonesia and Malaysia 2006b. He explained that his directorate entered the process once the issue of migrant workers was going to be put into a legal instrument. Interview with Agusman, Damos Dumoli on July 23, 2007.

32 The results of these meetings, which were usually joined by representatives from related departments, were recorded in agreed minutes, which according to Agusman, are not categorized as public documents. Interview with Agusman, Damos Dumoli on November 6, 2008. Thus, I have not been able to consult the minutes of the meetings.

33 Ibid.

34 Interview with Adamhar, Ferry on July 6, 2007.

Notification.[35] The issue was then brought to the Annual Consultation between the Prime Minister of Malaysia and the President of Indonesia in Bukittinggi on January 12-13, 2006, where Malaysia finally agreed to work on this MoU. According to Adamhar, they started to work intensively after this annual consultation.[36]

Apparently the government preferred that NGOs should not be involved in the formulation process. Agusman stated that there was no need for NGOs to be involved because the government already knew what to do and their presence would not help the Indonesian delegation.[37] Agusman acknowledged receiving a request from migrant worker advocates to be involved in the negotiation process, which was refused on the grounds that it would result in breaking up the negotiation since their presence was rejected by the Malaysian representatives. He explained that the government was avoiding this possibility because even to get Malaysia to the negotiation table was already tough work. He pointed out that as a sovereign state, Malaysia could always refuse a MoU, as Singapore had done.

Although stating that he learnt nothing new from the NGOs, Agusman claimed that he took notes of the NGOs' requests from their meetings, such as demands for contracts and for religious sensitivity, which he claimed had been attained by the Indonesian delegation.[38] Some were included in the body of the MoU and others were included in Appendix B, the contract of employment, which specifically binds particular employers and employees, instead of the state. However, there were also NGO requests which the government did not take into account. One which Agusman considered to be hilarious was a request to include political rights (*hak berpolitik*) in the contract between the employer and the migrant workers.[39] He considered this a demand which would certainly

35 The Mandatory Consular Notification is an agreement between two countries which makes it mandatory for a country to immediately inform the other country if there is a citizen from the second country being arrested in the first country. Ibid.

36 It was Agusman's opinion that Malaysia operated like Indonesia during the New Order, using a top-down approach. Interview with Agusman, Damos Dumoli on November 6, 2008. This opinion most probably arose from the Indonesian representatives' perception that Malaysian representatives did not seem to do much until their Prime Minister finally came to an agreement with the Indonesian President on this particular issue.

37 Interview with Agusman, Damos Dumoli on July 23, 2007.

38 Ibid. Demand for religious sensitivity is a demand for the employer to respect the migrant workers' religious beliefs through acts such as allowing them to practice their religion and respecting Moslem workers' rejection to handle and/or eat non-halal food. Both Appendix A and Appendix B of the 2006 MoU contain a paragraph which says that "the Employer shall at all times respect and pay due regards to the sensitivity of religious belief of the Domestic Workers, including the right to perform prayers and to refuse to handle and consume non-Halal food". Cf. The Government of Indonesia and The Government of Malaysia 2006.

39 Interview with Agusman, Damos Dumoli on July 23, 2007, and on November 6, 2008.

be rejected because, as he explained, this right does not come from an employer but from the state through state law. Obviously, the government and migrant worker advocates had different views on what issues should be stipulated in the MoU or not and whether they should be included in the body of the MoU or in Appendix B (contract of employment).

Agusman questioned the NGOs' pressure on the Indonesian government by arguing that NGOs and the government actually had the same view and interest in putting pressure on the Malaysian government.[40] Thus, he criticized NGOs for protesting in front of the Indonesian National Palace in Jakarta instead of in front of Malaysia's Embassy. He pointed out that while Indonesia's government had to face both Malaysia's government and the NGOs, Malaysia's government did not get similar pressure from their NGOs.[41] Agusman also recalled that his response to the NGOs' demand that the Indonesian government push its Malaysian counterpart to agree to Indonesia's demands was "easy, make Malaysia into a province of Indonesia, case closed". This statement can be seen as his way of emphasizing that there are limits to what the Indonesian government can do, since Malaysia is obviously a sovereign country.

Despite his criticisms of the NGOs, Agusman acknowledged their role in giving inputs by emphasizing how he met with them to discuss the MoU with Malaysia in workshops conducted by the SMoWE before and after the MoU was signed.[42] It is significant to note that these workshops, where representatives of the government and the NGOs met, were not conducted by the two main ministries responsible for the formulation of this MoU, the MoMT and the MoFA. Significantly too, while Agusman came as a representative from the MoFA, no one from the MoMT attended.[43]

Agusman's statements on NGOs' involvement reflect most government officials' attitudes toward NGOs commonly found in Indonesia's Reform Era. NGO involvement is welcomed in certain parts of the policy process and in ways that suit the government's operating procedures. At this point, it is important to point out that Agusman is from the Department of Foreign Affairs, which most NGOs consider as one of the more accommodative ministries.

40 Interview with Agusman, Damos Dumoli on November 6, 2008.

41 This statement may derive from a general observation of Malaysia's political situation, which does not allow as much civil society participation as in Indonesia after *Reformasi,* and of the limited number of Malaysian NGOs working on the issue of migrant workers. Harun from Tenaganita, a major Malaysian NGO working on the issue of migrant workers, explained how difficult it is to establish an NGO in Malaysia, to get funding and to conduct their activism. Interview with Harun on August 16, 2007.

42 Interview with Agusman, Damos Dumoli on November 6, 2008.

43 Interview with Zulbahary, Thaufiek on May 16, 2007, and with Agusman on November 6, 2008.

As for the SMoWE, since the MoU was on domestic workers who are mainly women, this ministry submitted recommendations to the main negotiating team. However, because the main ministries representing the Indonesian government were the MoFA and the MoMT, and with the size of the SMoWE in terms of staff and budget and its status as a state ministry, its power to influence and apply pressure on the process and content of the MoU is questionable. Nevertheless, NGOs continued to work with this ministry due to its accommodative attitude towards them.[44]

This section has illustrated the government's view on NGOs' involvement in the MoU-making process. It can be summarized as "while NGOs' inputs are welcomed, their involvement in the formulation process is not required". NGOs' views on their position within the process of making the 2006 MoU will be discussed next.

The NGOs' Point of View

Despite the limited space for involvement of stakeholders other than government representatives, Indonesian NGOs still attempted to express their views during the formulation process of the 2006 MoU. As reported by The Jakarta Post, in April 2006, a number of Indonesian institutions, including NGOs, concerned with the issue of migrant workers, sent an open letter to the Indonesian President and Malaysian Prime Minister to express their concerns over the draft of the MoU.[45] They criticized the authority given to the Malaysian employers to hold Indonesian workers' passports and the prohibition of workers to form associations or unions and demanded stronger regulations governing recruitment and employment agencies, and demanded that Indonesian workers be equally protected under Malaysian labor laws, given a 24 hours rest period per week and fair minimum wage.

Without ignoring the efforts made by other migrant workers advocates, this section is mainly based on my interviews with the staff of SP and Migrant CARE. While some of their statements confirm the occurrence of particular events such as the workshop before the signing of the MoU, others show the difference in perceptions between the government and the NGOs, particularly when

44 Interview with Safitri, Salma on August 2, 2007, with Zulbahary, Thaufiek on July 9, 2007, and with Hidayah, Anis on September 14, 2007. As an example, when Migrant CARE failed in their attempt to lobby the Department of Manpower and Transmigration for the permit to open a help desk in Terminal III, they shifted their strategy by lobbying through the SMoWE.

45 Cf. The Jakarta Post, April 17, 2006.

they talked about how the interactions went and the results. The NGOs' narratives also illustrate their efforts to be involved in the process.

According to Thaufiek Zulbahary from SP, SP pushed for the MoU on domestic workers after the MoU on the formal sector was signed.[46] They worked together with the SMoWE, which at that time had a program that focused on making a draft of the MoU under its Division of Women's Protection. They conducted a workshop in January 2006 and invited various stakeholders.[47] This is an example of collaboration between an NGO which may have more information and experience of the issue and a government institution which has the authority to invite not only the public but also other government elements.[48] This event was aimed at giving updates of the latest situation of Indonesian domestic workers in Malaysia and formulating a framework for the MoU on the protection of Indonesian migrant domestic workers between Indonesia and Malaysia.[49] Zulbahary explained that the participants of the seminar-workshop formulated the elements that they thought should be included in an ideal MoU.[50] They were promised that this input would be presented to the negotiating team.[51] However, after the event, there were no updates on what happened to the inputs and the next thing they heard was that the MoU was already signed. Since the signed MoU was very different from the one proposed in the workshop, Zulbahary doubted the value of the workshop.[52]

46 Interview with Zulbahary, Thaufiek on November 19, 2008.

47 Based on the draft of the agreement on work/responsibility sharing between the SMoWE and SP, it seems that the ministry, which acted as the main host of this event, was more responsible for the operational aspects of the event and SP was responsible for the substance/content of the workshop. Cf. State Ministry of Women's Empowerment and SP 2006a.

48 As stated in the documentation of this event, it was actually called a *semiloka (seminar dan lokakarya)* or a seminar combined with a workshop. Cf. Organising Committee 2006. It began with a seminar on a number of topics related to the condition of Indonesian workers in Malaysia, followed by a sharing session on the previous MoU initiatives by GPPBM and Brawijaya University, and ended with a workshop which was aimed at making the draft of a MoU. The list of invitees included 16 NGOs in Jakarta, including SP and Migrant CARE, two representatives from the academic world, the Indonesian Institute of Science (LIPI) and the Faculty of Law at Brawijaya University, both the National Commission of Human Rights and National Commission of Women, and seven government officials from the Departments of Manpower and Transmigration, Foreign Affairs, Social Affairs, Health, Domestic Affairs, the Directorate General of Immigration of the Department of Law and Human Rights, and the State Ministry of Women's Empowerment. Unfortunately, as mentioned by Agusman and also by the NGOs, nobody from the MoMT came.

49 Cf. State Ministry of Women's Empowerment and SP 2006a.

50 Interview with Zulbahary, Thaufiek on November 19, 2008.

51 Interview with Safitri, Salma on August 2, 2007, and with Zulbahary, Thaufiek on May 16, 2007.

52 Interview with Zulbahary, Thaufiek on November 19, 2008.

Salma Safitri from SP even called the MoU an imposture (*jadi-jadian*) for its closed process and lack of transparency.[53] Similarly, Anis Hidayah from Migrant CARE said that "it has been a tradition in Indonesia that the emergence of a policy is like a ghost (*siluman*)".[54] They heard that the government was designing a MoU with Malaysia but there was no public consultation or the like to inform the public.[55] She claimed she was told informally by somebody from inside (*orang dalam*) the Department of Manpower and Transmigration that his department and the Department of Foreign Affairs were working with Malaysia to formulate a MoU. Since it was not possible for NGOs to be involved in the official process, Migrant CARE responded by making media releases, criticizing the content and the process of making this MoU. Hidayah also described how she "accidentally" knew about the signing of the MoU. In May 2006, Hidayah and Wahyu Susilo were attending a discussion in the Department of Foreign Affairs when they saw the teams from the Departments of Manpower and Transmigration and of Foreign Affairs discussing the plan to sign the MoU. She questioned them on why there was no consultation with the public. As a result, Hidayah and Susilo were invited to the signing ceremony but, as Hidayah recalled, on the day the document was already signed before they arrived. Thus, Hidayah argued that there was no transparency from the government.

The NGOs' views show that the initiative to gather inputs from civil society unfortunately did not come from the main ministries involved in the formulation of the MoU. While appreciating the forum organized by the SMoWE, Hidayah emphasized that the ministry was not involved in the official process leading to the MoU.[56] According to her, that kind of forum should have been held by the Department of Foreign Affairs or the Department of Manpower and Transmigration. On a similar note, Susilo pointed out that, although the MoFA was involved through its Directorate General of Legal Affairs and International Treaties, the Indonesian delegation in the negotiation process was dominated by the staff of the MoMT.[57] Susilo also questioned the parliament's passive attitude toward the

53 Interview with Safitri, Salma on August 2, 2007. Based on Safitri's overall statement, her usage of the expression *jadi-jadian* seems to refer to how the NGOs felt that they had no knowledge and were not informed of the formulating process, and that the final document did not accommodate the inputs that they had given.

54 Interview with Hidayah, Anis on November 18, 2008.

55 Apparently Hidayah did not regard the workshop conducted by the SMoWE as a public consultation.

56 Interview with Hidayah, Anis on November 18, 2008.

57 Interview with Susilo, Wahyu on June 14, 2007.

2006 MoU since there were no immediate comments from the parliament on this agreement.[58]

The NGOs' campaigns for a MoU on domestic workers were conducted either by themselves or together with other migrant workers advocates. Migrant CARE, for example, on February 11, 2005 sent an open letter to President Susilo Bambang Yudhoyono highlighting that the MoU on the formal sector had not included those working as domestic workers and suggesting the President to meet Indonesian workers in Malaysia to hear their views in order to produce a MoU which actually provided protection for them.[59] Migrant CARE's actions show that although they were not involved in the official process, they made efforts to influence the government through open letters and media statements. Safitri mentioned SP's cooperation with the Women's Aid Organisation of Malaysia (WAO).[60] According to her, during the formulation process, the two organizations made and compared drafts for the MoU and then brought the drafts to their own governments.

The way the NGOs perceived the possibility for them to access the domestic and foreign policy-making process was not similar. Hidayah believed that the process of law-making was more accessible.[61] According to her, the MoU involved two countries and since politics in Malaysia was similar to Indonesia during the Suharto period, anti-democratic, it was difficult for NGOs to get involved. On the other hand, Zulbahary argued that, in terms of accessing the policy-making process, there was not much difference between domestic and foreign policies.[62] This statement and his other statement that SP did not have any problem in getting involved, requesting meetings with, and working with government elements most probably related to SP's reputation as an "older" or more established NGO and its more "benign" approach to the government. Nevertheless, as also stated by Zulbahary, similar to what happened in the domestic policy-making process, it was still difficult for SP to influence the content of the final product of the policy.

This section has shown the differences in the way the NGOs and the government perceived their interactions. Besides confirming that it was not possible for NGOs to be involved in the official process of making the MoU, the NGOs' nar-

58 There was no statement from the parliament in the media immediately after the MoU was signed. The call for amendment of the MoU from a number of parliament members only surfaced a couple of years later.

59 Cf. Migrant CARE 2005b, Suara Pembaruan, February 8, 2005.

60 Interview with Safitri, Salma on August 2, 2007. The WAO is a Malaysian NGO committed to confronting violence against women. Cf. Women's Aid Organisation of Malaysia 2009.

61 Interview with Hidayah, Anis on November 18, 2008.

62 Interview with Zulbahary, Thaufiek on November 19, 2008.

ratives also described how they had to find alternative channels to express their views. The next section will examine the situation after the MoU was signed. It will start by comparing the government and NGO points of view on the content of the MoU and then discuss NGO efforts and activities after the MoU was signed.

8.2 After the Signing of the 2006 MoU

8.2.1 The Government's and NGOs' Views on the MoU

After the MoU was signed, while the governments praised the signing of this MoU, the NGOs started to campaign against it. Thus, this section will look into the government's and NGOs' view on the content of the MoU, not as a document analysis, but rather as an examination of how some issues were negotiated before they were, or were not, finally included in the MoU.

The Government's Point of View

Official statements from both governments, immediately following the signing of the MoU, indicated their satisfaction with the MoU. Erman Suparno, the then Minister of Manpower and Transmigration, saw the potential for the MoU to provide a legal basis for the protection of Indonesian workers in Malaysia, help in preventing abuses against them and guarantee their rights.[63] Suparno also saw this MoU as proof of the intention of both governments to protect the rights of domestic workers. The Malaysian Internal Affairs Minister, Ahmad Mohd. Radzi, was also pleased with the agreement and said that "this MOU will provide standard protection for Indonesian domestic workers in Malaysia".[64] These statements in the mass media are quite general, leaving them open to various interpretations and debates. For example, what was meant by "standard protection" is unclear. Also the potential for the MoU to provide a legal basis is still debatable considering that a MoU does not have a strong binding power and its implementation depends largely on the willingness of the signing countries.

A slightly different opinion came from Agusman.[65] While acknowledging the MoU as a breakthrough, Agusman tried to explain its limited power. In what he

63 Cf. The Jakarta Post, May 15, 2006.

64 Ibid.

65 Interview with Agusman, Damos Dumoli on July 23, 2007. As mentioned earlier, Agusman was the Director of the Directorate of Economic and Socio-cultural Affairs of the

called an attempt to "reverse the pendulum to address the distortion", Agusman pointed out that public opinion forgets that protection does not lie with the MoU, but with the labor laws of each country.[66] Agusman also thinks that there was a public misunderstanding of the power of the MoU because migrant worker advocates such as HRW expected that it would create a space for the amendment of Malaysia's 1955 Labor Law. He considered that the faith placed in the MoU was "off target". This further shows the different perceptions between the government and migrant workers' advocates in the way they perceived the power of the MoU. Taking into consideration that a MoU has low binding power and the fact that the clauses of the 2006 MoU are more about conducting the placement and the protection of Indonesian workers in Malaysia in accordance with Malaysian Law, I would agree with Agusman that the power of the MoU is quite limited and it is unlikely that Malaysia would agree to a MoU, which would make it change its national law.

According to Agusman, a common MoU on labor is an administrative one such as the one signed with South Korea in July 2004.[67] In this type of MoU the two countries make an agreement which requires them to use their authority to conduct actions.[68] This is what Agusman considered as a "proper" MoU, while that with Malaysia was the only one of its kind in the world. Agusman also stated that a MoU is principally a contract between sovereign states; thus the rights, responsibilities, and obligations lie with the state. He argued that it should be binding upon the states, not upon subjects of the states such as the employers. There are a number of articles in the 2006 MoU which seem to directly deal with the subjects of the state such as requiring the agencies, employers, and domestic workers to comply with Malaysian law and the MoU. Agusman believed that the governments of Indonesia and Malaysia should be the ones to regulate the agencies, the employers, and the migrant workers, not the MoU. Based on this, he thought that the MoU represented an intrusion on Malaysia's sovereignty. This opinion is still debatable since the implementation of the articles in a MoU really depends on the willingness of each signing state. Thus, Agusman's opinion may

Directorate General of Legal Affairs and International Treaties, Indonesian Department of Foreign Affairs.

66 Agusman used Singapore as an example of a country not wanting to sign a MoU with Indonesia on the issue of migrant workers on the grounds of having a national law which adequately protects Indonesian workers.

67 Interview with Agusman, Damos Dumoli on July 23, 2007.

68 Ibid. As explained by Agusman, the MoU stipulates that those sent to South Korea must have certain qualifications and have to be healthy, and convinces them to come back to Indonesia after two years. South Korea has the responsibility to treat Indonesian migrant workers in accordance with their law and make sure that it's fair, and there is a clear right and obligation of both governments. Both governments, by virtue of their respective national laws, regulate people.

be true to the extent that the MoU is different from other existing MoUs because instead of only stating the rights and responsibilities of the signing states, it went into detail to stipulate matters such as employers', recruitment agencies', and domestic workers' responsibilities.

One of the NGOs' demands was the existence of a contract between migrant workers and their employers. According to Agusman, when this demand was brought into the negotiation, a Malaysian representative asked him whether he had a contract with his maid at home.[69] His "diplomatic" response was to argue that his maid is considered a part of his family and he does not make a contract with family members. This "part of the family" reasoning is commonly used to counter questions on why Indonesia is asking Malaysia to agree to do what Indonesia has not done for its citizens domestically. The NGOs are well aware of Indonesia's weak bargaining position when it comes to negotiating better conditions for its domestic workers with representatives from a receiving country like Malaysia. As already mentioned in Chapter 6, NGO activists like Anis Hidayah have been using this condition as a basis to argue for the passing of a national law on the protection of domestic workers. The fact that Indonesia does not have a law which regulates this type of work and protects the workers has been one of the weak points in Indonesia's diplomacy and negotiation with receiving countries. Indonesian NGOs have been campaigning for the passing of a law on domestic workers and Migrant CARE is involved in the collective campaign. However, as of the beginning of 2013, the bill for the protection of domestic workers was yet to be passed by the DPR.

The proposal for a minimum wage and a rest day in a week for migrant workers working in informal sector was denied by Malaysian representatives, who pointed out that they do not have these standards for local workers and they did not want to create discrimination between local and foreign workers.[70] As a result, the issues of a minimum salary and also of a rest day were not regulated in the body of the MoU, but became some of the issues which are included in the contract between the employer and the worker. Agusman argued that this was the right way to get more detailed demands, i.e. not by stating them in the body of the MoU but in a contract which bound the employer and the worker, a strategy which he said has been used by the Philippines to guarantee their workers' rights. Agusman heavily emphasized this point. He argued that the more detailed matters, which vary from one employment to another and result from an agreement between an employer and a domestic worker, such as amount of salary and rest day, should not be included in a MoU, which has more general coverage.

69 Interview with Agusman, Damos Dumoli on July 23, 2007.
70 Interview with Agusman, Damos Dumoli on November 6, 2008.

The government and the NGOs have different views on what should be perceived as an important issue. One of the issues that Agusman argued should get more attention is Malaysia's demand for direct recruitment,[71] which is not allowed by Indonesian law. He believed that such a practice would contribute to protection, presumably because if anything went wrong, it was possible to identify the agency accountable for the recruitment. Agusman explained that Indonesia finally "fenced" the issue by allowing the practice as long as it is conducted with the permission from and authorized by Indonesia.[72]

On the other hand, for the NGOs, issues like who should hold a migrant worker's passport, the employer or the migrant worker herself, is considered more major. NGOs have been urging the government to include a clause in the MoU stating that passports are to be held by the workers. In this case, Agusman argued for the opposite.[73] In a meeting with the NGOs after the signing of the MoU, while admitting that there were disadvantages and benefits in letting the employers hold the passport, he considered that this passport issue is not as crucial as other problems. He argued that, since there was a clause in the 2006 MoU which stated that passports are held by the employers, illegal status was no longer based on the fact that the migrant workers were not carrying a passport, and even if a migrant worker ran away from his/her employer, he/she did not need to prove that his/her passport was held by the employer because it was now a given condition. Agusman even challenged the NGOs to conduct research to confirm whether migrant workers had actually become "illegal" because their passports are held by their employers. He believed that what happened in the field was that if a woman domestic worker had been holding her passport and in a raid[74] she could

71 Interview with Agusman, Damos Dumoli on July 23, 2007. Malaysia's argument for this demand was that the close cultural relations between Malaysia and Indonesia and the personal contacts between their peoples should enable Malaysian employers to recruit Indonesian domestic workers without going through recruitment agencies. Indonesia refused, but Malaysia insisted that this practice was already happening.

72 The wording of Article 4 is: "Any Employer who wishes to employ a Domestic Worker without the service of MRA or through IRA must obtain prior approval from the relevant authorities in Malaysia. The relevant authorities shall, as soon as practicable, inform such approval to the Indonesian Mission." An understanding that can be drawn from this article is that approval comes from Malaysian authorities, while Indonesia is only informed through its mission. Thus, it does not reflect great control from the Indonesian side.

73 Interview with Agusman, Damos Dumoli on November 6, 2008.

74 Also know as *razia.* From time to time the police, or more often RELA (the special "voluntary" force formed to deal with the issue of illegal workers in Malaysia), conducts a raid to check foreigners' identification cards and detain foreign workers' who do not have any forms of identification.

not show her passport, she would be illegal.[75] But with the current clause in the MoU, if a domestic worker was asked for her passport by the police, the immediate answer would be that it was held by the employer. Thus, Agusman maintained that migrant workers were better protected if the passports were held by their employers.[76] Although Agusman seemed to be confident with the logic of how the arrangement under the MoU would work, there needs to be specific research to identify whether it is really effective in the field.

Agusman argued that he had "cleared the path" with Malaysia by securing the agreement that there had to be a contract between a domestic worker and her employer.[77] Thus, he urged the NGOs to work with the instrument made available by the MoU – the contract of employment – which he thought was more feasible, rather than continuing their campaigning on changing the body of the MoU. He asserted that, since a contract had private nature, there could be negotiation between the workers and their employers on what to include in it while a MoU should not include details due to its general application. In relation to his argument on the importance of a contract, Agusman put quite strong emphasis on the importance of improving the education, skills, and knowledge of Indonesian migrant workers so that the instruments provided by the MoU which had the potential to provide protection, such as the contract, could be effective.[78] Agusman believed that, ideally, protection would be higher if those workers knew their rights and responsibilities. However, he also admitted the existence of what he called a vicious circle (*lingkaran setan*) where those going to Malaysia are not educated and if they are educated, they do not want to go to Malaysia anymore. Thus, Indonesians going to Malaysia remain those who are not educated and/or trained.

Agusman criticized NGOs for their lack of knowledge on what a MoU is and that national law cannot be overruled by a MoU.[79] He claimed that he had to explain to the NGOs that Indonesia's ability to protect Indonesian migrant workers stops when they cross the border, Indonesia could not do policing action in Malaysia, and what Indonesia could do to provide protection was through interna-

75 The common practice is, although these workers entered Malaysia with proper documents, since they cannot show their passports during ID checks, they are accused of being undocumented or illegal and then sent to detention.

76 He even cited the example of the domestic workers of Indonesian diplomats whose passports are held by the diplomats.

77 Interview with Agusman, Damos Dumoli on July 23, 2007.

78 Agusman stated that, ideally, Indonesia should do what the Philippines are doing, that is sending domestic workers with a high school education, good mastery of English, and an understanding of what a passport is. He believes that the Philippine domestic workers understand the contract and can demand what should be included in it, including the rest day.

79 Interview with Agusman, Damos Dumoli on July 23, 2007.

tional law, using diplomatic protection and consular protection. He doubted that NGOs knew this and assumed that NGOs' basic assumption on protection of Indonesian migrant workers abroad was the same as protection of Indonesians in Indonesia. Thus, Agusman suggested that NGOs learn more about diplomatic and consular protection so their expectations could be more realistic.

This section has considered Agusman's view as a general reflection of the government's views on the 2006 MoU. The next section will look into the NGOs' views on this foreign policy instrument.

The NGOs' Point of View

The NGOs' criticisms of both the process of making the 2006 MoU and its content can be observed from the notes and statements they made after it was signed. In May 2006, immediately after the MoU was signed, SBMI, *Kopbumi*, and GPPBM produced a critical note on the MoU entitled 'Rejecting the Package of Modern Slavery'.[80] Their view on the MoU was that far from protecting the rights of migrant domestic workers, it contained basic elements which violated human rights principles, legitimized the trading of migrant workers, and enabled modern slavery. They also criticized the process of making this MoU for not being transparent, democratic, not based on human rights principles, and not reflecting the aspirations of migrant domestic workers. Thus, they recommended the Indonesian government not to become part of what they saw as human rights violation and immediately use article 15 of the MoU on the Amendment Procedure. The note was accompanied by a list of suggested amendments including changes to the title and a number of wordings such as "conveyance", "servant", and "offered",[81] which, according to them, made the MoU into a document that legalized the commodification of migrant workers. According to the note: the words "conveyance" and "offered" indicate that migrant domestic workers were perceived more as things or objects or trade commodities, not as human beings

80 Cf. Komnas Perempuan et al. 2006b.

81 The word conveyance is used in article 2: "The objective of this MoU is to develop the existing cooperation between the Parties for the purpose of strengthening the mechanism on the conveyance and recruitment of Domestic Workers from the Republic of Indonesia". The word servant is used in Article 1 to define a domestic worker as "[...] a citizen of the Republic of Indonesia who is contracting or contracted to work in Malaysia for a specified period of time for a specific individual as a domestic servant as defined in the Employment Act 1955, the Labour Ordinance Sabah (Chapter 67) and the Labour Ordinance Sarawak (Chapter 76)." The word offered is used in Article 6: "The Government of the Republic of Indonesia agrees to ensure that the Domestic Workers who are offered for selection by the employer to work in Malaysia shall satisfy the following conditions prior to entry into Malaysia[...]".

with dignity, conscience, and intelligence.[82] They further argued that the word "servant" potentially preserved a feudalistic rather than working relationship between employer and employees based on a contract of employment. The note also suggested some additions to Appendix A of the MoU, particularly in the sections on responsibilities of the employer and the domestic workers, to include and address issues such as minimum wage, holder of migrant workers' passports, religious sensitivity, rest day, living conditions and the right to marry. As explained in the previous section, according to Agusman, most of these issues were rejected by the Malaysian representatives.[83]

In June 2006, Salma Safitri, who was the Head of SP's National Executive Body, prepared a critical note for a discussion at SP's National Secretariat.[84] Besides adopting most of the content of the note prepared by the organizations above, this note also listed the violations of the rights of migrant domestic workers by the MoU including rights to rest, to marry, to reunite with their families, to hold their passports and the right to work of those infected by certain illnesses such as HIV/AIDS. This critical note also highlighted the ambiguities in the MoU, focusing on the non-reciprocal nature of some clauses which imposed restrictions and obligations on the migrant workers but not on the employers. The note concluded by stating SP's stand toward the MoU, rejecting clauses which did not protect Indonesian migrant workers' rights, urging the governments of Indonesia and Malaysia to review the content of the MoU and to revise it in order to protect migrant workers' rights, and inviting those concerned with the rights of migrant workers to work together.

On June 8, 2006, SP made a statement based on its critical analysis of the MoU.[85] Besides rejecting the non-protective clauses in the MoU and urging the government of Malaysia and Indonesia to review and revise the MoU, the statement also demanded that the governments of Indonesia and Malaysia allow space for civil society, especially women migrant domestic workers' organizations or migrant labor organizations, to be involved in and give inputs to the revision process to produce a MoU which is oriented to the needs of women migrant domestic workers. The statement also called on Indonesian and Malaysian NGOs to continuously campaign to change the MoU. On June 27, 2006, GPPBM also made a statement in a public opinion hearing meeting with Commission IX

82 Cf. GPPBM 2006. As stated in SP's critical analysis of the MoU, the word is understood as "*pengangkutan*" in Indonesian, which is more commonly used to describe an action of moving or carrying objects, things, or commodities. Cf. Safitri 2006. "Offered" is translated as "*ditawarkan*", commonly used in object trading.

83 Interview with Agusman, Damos Dumoli on November 6, 2008.

84 Cf. Safitri 2006.

85 Cf. SP 2006.

of the DPR.[86] This statement was based on the critical analysis made by the organizations in May 2006. Again, the main point of this statement was how the MoU legalized a practice of commodification and made Indonesian migrant domestic workers in Malaysia more vulnerable. The next section will look into NGOs' activities after the MoU was signed, particularly those aimed at campaigning for the revision of the 2006 MoU.

8.2.2 NGOs' Activism after the Signing of the MoU

In the view of Agusman, the meetings between the two governments on the implementation of the MoU have not been promising.[87] He saw them more as a forum where Indonesia conveyed complaints and then Malaysia explained why it happened, and after that everything continued as before. It can be assumed from Agusman's explanation that most matters brought to the joint working group's meetings were discussed but solutions were hard to achieve.

After the signing of the 2006 MoU, there was a meeting in Kota Kinabalu on the cost structure issue.[88] As mandated by the MoU, a joint working group which consists of officials from both governments was established to discuss any matter arising from the implementation of the MoU.[89] This meeting in Kota Kinabalu was the first for the joint working group and was aimed to discuss the cost structure matter and other issues, which included the Malaysian policy on the obligation for Indonesian workers to use Malaysian Airlines and to obtain Visas on Arrival, access to education for Indonesian workers' children, and deportation arrangements for illegal Indonesian workers. Just like the meetings for the formulation of the MoU, the meetings between officials from both countries to address the matters arising in the implementation of the MoU, these meetings remained limited to government representatives and inaccessible for the NGOs.[90] Thus, it seems that for NGOs to influence the implementation and/or to push for an amendment, they still needed to search for ways to channel their views. The following discussion will document NGO activities immediately after the MoU was

86 Cf. GPPBM 2006.
87 Interview with Agusman, Damos Dumoli on November 6, 2008.
88 Cf. Agusman 2006a, Interview with Agusman, Damos Dumoli on November 6, 2008. The cost structure constitutes the costs for the recruitment and placement of migrant workers, which are usually borne by employer and domestic workers. The debate has been going on about who should bear this cost and, if shared, who should bear the bigger portion, the Malaysian or Indonesian side.
89 Cf. The Government of Indonesia and The Government of Malaysia 2006.
90 With the exception of the meeting in 2007 in Surabaya, which, as explained later, Anis Hidayah from Migrant CARE could join as an observer.

signed and assess whether these activities have enabled them to gain more access to and influence the official process.

Zulbahary recalled that after the MoU was signed, SP was invited to a workshop by the SMoWE and met the lobbying team from the MoFA.[91] This workshop was conducted to gather inputs from stakeholders on the MoU. According to Zulbahary, the Indonesian delegation from the MoFA apologized for the bad MoU and made excuses by explaining that Indonesia could not intervene in Malaysia's legal system and that Malaysia did not need the MoU while Indonesia did.[92] Meanwhile, Agusman's explanation gave an impression that what he did in the workshop was more explaining to the participants what happened in the negotiation and "educating" them, particularly the NGOs, on what could and could not be discussed in the negotiation and included in the MoU because it might violate Malaysia's sovereignty.[93] This shows that although both the government and the NGOs acknowledged the interactions that existed between them, their views of the process were very different.

At the end of the workshop, it was agreed that the participants, NGOs, the SMoWE and the MoFA, would maximize the utilization of a clause which enables the amendment of the MoU.[94] For this purpose, a small monitoring team consisting of participants of the workshop, both from the government and NGOs, was formed. Unfortunately, as stated by Zulbahary, after the workshop, there was no further communication among the members of this team. Thus, although he considered their participation in the workshop as a form of SP's access to the process, in terms of influencing the content, he thought that their impact was negligible because their inputs tended to get drowned out.

91 Interview with Zulbahary, Thaufiek on May 16, 2007. This was confirmed by Agusman's previous explanation on his department's interactions with the NGOs. Interview with Agusman, Damos Dumoli on November 6, 2008.

92 Interview with Zulbahary, Thaufiek on November 19, 2008. Zulbahary's observation was that the team had low confidence and an inferiority complex because they were representing migrant domestic workers, while he believed that Indonesia should have had the upper hand because Indonesia can stop the sending of migrant workers anytime.

93 Interview with Agusman, Damos Dumoli on November 6, 2008.

94 Interview with Zulbahary, Thaufiek on July 9, 2007, on May 16, 2007, and on November 19, 2008. This refers to Article 15 of the MoU which states that "this MoU may be amended, modified, or revised by exchange of letters of mutual consent between the Parties through diplomatic channels. Such amendment, modification, or revision shall come into force on such date as may be determined by the Parties". The Government of Indonesia and The Government of Malaysia 2006. However, there is no explanation in the MoU of what conditions may lead to an amendment. As stated in article 13 of the MoU, national security, national interest, public order, or public health could be used as the reasons for each country to suspend temporarily either in whole or in part the implementation of the MoU. A suspension does not necessarily lead to an amendment of the MoU.

As for Migrant CARE, according to Hidayah, after the signing of the MoU, Migrant CARE and *Ecosoc* were invited to the Department of Manpower and Transmigration to listen to the explanation of why the MoU was signed and its content.[95] She suspected that this was another way to fulfill the requirement of involving civil society in the policy process because Indonesia was pressured by the UN to be transparent and conduct public consultation whenever a policy is launched. Hidayah argued that there was no point in holding the meeting because it took place after the MoU was signed. Hidayah stated that, after the MoU was signed and Migrant CARE got hold of a copy of the document, it wrote a complaint letter to the governments of Malaysia and Indonesia, asking why the MoU was signed despites its weaknesses and requesting that the implementation be postponed until the document was amended. However, there was no response from either government. Hidayah also described Migrant CARE's effort to have an audience with some opposition members of Malaysian parliament, made possible by the good relationship with these MPs of Alex Ong, Migrant CARE's country representative in Malaysia. One of the issues discussed was the MoU. Although this audience did not result in any significant change in Malaysia's policy, Hidayah believes that their effort had considerable impact, at least in terms of creating public awareness because they also involved the media.

Hidayah said that she had some hope when she was involved in the working group for the Presidential Instruction No. 6/2006.[96] As part of the working group, in 2007 she attended the bilateral meeting of the working group between Indonesia and Malaysia on the MoU in Surabaya. Although she could only be an observer, she considered it as a good chance to assess Indonesia's diplomatic power when facing Malaysia. With the advantage of inside observation, she was confident that it would enable her to give more informed inputs. The main point that she learned was that the Indonesian delegation did not have a strong enough bargaining power in the negotiation. Ideally, if this arrangement for NGO representatives to be observers could be made for a number of meetings between the two governments, it might help Indonesian NGOs understand the process and Indonesia's position better, thus helping them to provide more feasible suggestions.

In making their case against the MoU, Indonesian NGOs have also been citing the statements of actors with international recognition such as Jorge Bustamante, the then UN Special Rapporteur on the Human Rights of Migrants. Zulbahary from SP, for example, pointed out how Bustamante, after meeting with a number of NGOs, the government and other stakeholders, stated that the MoU between Indonesia and Malaysia violates "the international convention".[97] In the Report

95 Interview with Hidayah, Anis on November 18, 2008.
96 Ibid.
97 Interview with Zulbahary, Thaufiek on May 16, 2007.

of the Special Rapporteur on the Human Rights of Migrants, Bustamante stated that the article which stipulates the retention of migrant workers' passport by the employer without any receipt was a provision that "contravenes" the International Convention on the Protection of Migrant Workers and Members of their Families, to which Indonesia is a signatory.[98] Furthermore, according to him, based on the Vienna Convention on the Law of Treaties, although Indonesia had not ratified the convention, it was, being a signatory, "obliged to refrain from acts which would defeat the object and purpose of a treaty". As documented in a number of media reports, the NGOs have been citing Bustamante's statements and reports to support their case. Susilo also underlined the importance of regional and international instruments and figures.[99] He gave as an example that, together with HRW and Tenaganita, Migrant CARE had briefed the UN Special Rapporteur on Human Rights of Migrants, Jorge Bustamante. Susilo believes that their joint advice had significantly influenced Bustamante's statement that the MoU has the potential to violate human rights, something that could have not been done if they only depended on advocacy at the national level.

In June 2009, after a number of cases of abuse of migrant workers in Malaysia were again published by the media and protested by migrant workers' advocates, Indonesia imposed a moratorium or temporary ban on the sending of migrant workers to Malaysia.[100] This moratorium was used to put pressure on Malaysia to accept Indonesia's demand for negotiating the revision of the 2006 MoU on informal workers. This can be perceived as an improvement in the way the government of Indonesia negotiates with the government of Malaysia because Indonesia generally had a weaker bargaining position and could not put pressure on Malaysia. Nevertheless, it was still done in a cautious manner so as not to put the relationship between the two countries at risk.

In August 2009, both countries began the negotiation on the revision of the 2006 MoU.[101] During the negotiation the issue of cost structure again became a cause of deadlock. There were different views on who should bear the placement cost[102] and the Indonesian government wanted the cost structure to be adjustable, depending on the origin areas.[103] Meanwhile the talk on minimum salary was

98 Cf. Bustamante 2007. Particularly article 21, which states that confiscation of documents authorizing entry to or stay, residence, or establishment in the national territory or work permits shall involve a detailed receipt.

99 Interview with Susilo, Wahyu on November 7, 2008.

100 Cf. The Jakarta Post, March 15, 2010.

101 Cf. Kompas, February 11, 2010.

102 The suggested schemes were: 75 percent by Malaysia and 25 percent by Indonesia, 60 percent by Malaysia and 40 percent by Indonesia, or 100 percent by Malaysia. Cf. Koran Tempo, March 12, 2010.

103 Naturally, the recruitment and placement costs are different depending on origin areas due to factors such as local costs and distance.

dropped to avoid a deadlock.[104] Hidayah criticized Indonesia's poor negotiation skills, which, according to her, caused the failure in negotiating a minimum salary standard.[105]

Although it is rather difficult to prove, it can be said that the NGOs played a role in exposing the abuse cases which led to the negotiation for the revision of the MoU. However, NGOs like Migrant CARE were not optimistic about the result. Hidayah doubted the implementation of the MoU if it was not going to be supported by the establishment of a mechanism for law enforcement by the Malaysian government and open access for Indonesian migrant workers to seek justice.[106] A pessimistic view also came from Susilo, who considered that the new MoU would only meet the minimum needs for the protection of Indonesian migrant workers.[107] According to him, there are some points that should have been noted in the MoU such as the right of migrant workers to organize themselves. He also wanted a deliberation process which involves the parliament and civil society organizations.

The signing of the revised MoU was postponed several times. In May 2011, the two governments finally signed the Protocol Amending the MoU Indonesia-Malaysia 2006. Following the signing of the agreement, in November 2011, the leaders of the two countries met in Bali and agreed on eleven points:[108]

- Passport has to be held by migrant workers;
- one day off a week;
- Placement fee has to be in accordance with the cost structure,
- agreement on salary or payment;
- Salary has to be based on market mechanism and transferred through banks;
- standardized work contract signed by the worker and the employer;
- Both governments only recognized agencies which have agreements with the governments;
- Workers have to go through 200 hours of training;

104 Cf. The Jakarta Post, March 15, 2010.
105 Cf. ibid.
106 Cf. ibid.
107 Cf. Koran Tempo, March 12, 2010.
108 Cf. Buruh Migran 2011.

- Malaysia will stop the Journe Performance Visa;
- Conflicts will be resolved through a committee established by both countries;
- Direct recruitment has to be done in accordance with Indonesian laws and the placement of domestic workers will be reviewed in a certain period of time.

The agreement can be considered as an improvement since it accommodates some of the points that have been demanded by migrant workers' advocates. Nevertheless, the revision negotiation process indicates that there is no significant change in terms of how the negotiation was conducted and who was involved. There was still minimum civil society involvement during the revision negotiations and the draft was not made public.

8.3 Conclusion

This chapter has examined the process of making a foreign policy on migrant workers, as instanced by the 2006 MoU between Indonesia and Malaysia on the Recruitment and Placement of Indonesian Domestic Workers. The discussion in this chapter has indicated that NGOs' involvement in the process of making the 2006 MoU was quite limited. There was only two occasions mentioned where government representatives met the stakeholders, including NGOs, one to discuss inputs for the MoUs and another one after the MoU was finally signed.

In a domestic policy-making process, democratization, and good governance principles recommend policy-makers to apply mechanisms which enable the involvement of civil society through events such as public hearing meetings, audiences, and others. Although the effectiveness of these mechanisms in channeling civil society's inputs is still debatable, at least there are official forums which are intended to gather inputs from related stakeholders, including civil society organizations. When it comes to making a foreign policy in the form of agreements with other countries, NGOs tend to be more remote from the process. The government's main reason for this is usually that it is a government-to-government arrangement and involvement of other entities, including NGOs, is regarded as illegitimate. Consequently, it is extremely unusual for other stakeholders such as NGOs to be involved or even present in the meetings concerning the MoUs. The experience of Anis Hidayah from Migrant CARE, who was present as an observer at one of the meetings can be considered a rare exception.

The discussion in this chapter has confirmed the argument in the previous chapter that relations have improved between the NGOs and several state entities, in the MoU case the SMoWE and the MoFA. Nevertheless, the discussion in this chapter shows that, although most NGOs consider the MoFA as one of the more cooperative and accommodative ministries, the interviews revealed that there were differences in the way they perceived and described their interactions and relationship. The discussion also illustrates that even the relationship between NGOs and the Ministries they considered more accommodative such as the MoFA was quite volatile, depending on the circumstances. Meanwhile, the NGOs' relationship with the main ministry responsible for the issue of migrant workers, the MoMT, remains distant.

In terms of the formulating process, besides showing that there was some interaction between the government and the NGOs before the formulation process, the interviews with both the government and the NGOs also confirm that most stages of the formulating process were not public and were not accessible by the NGOs. Thus, it was not possible for them to directly influence the content of the MoU while it was being written. This tendency repeats during the negotiation process for the revision of the 2006 MoU that began in 2009.

The discussions on the domestic and foreign policy-making processes in Chapters 6 and 8 have shown that NGOs were involved at the initial stage, before the official process began. They were asked to give inputs and they were acknowledged for this. However, this is as far as they could go because they could not formally be involved in the official process and influence the content of the final document. Moreover, while NGOs could still monitor and make attempts to lobby the parliament member during the process of making Law No. 39/2004, the negotiation process of the 2006 MoU was limited to government representatives, making it almost impossible for the NGOs to monitor the process, let alone influence it. Since the MoU process involved two countries, the NGOs had to interact with actors different from the ones they interacted with for the domestic policy lobbying. Also their limitation as local NGOs, which cannot operate beyond Indonesia's territory, had pushed them to seek various ways to achieve their goals, exposing them to various forms of collaboration. One way is through expanding their network, which will be part of the discussion in the next chapter that looks into the NGOs' efforts since the MoU was passed, putting it within the context of globalization.

9. Strengthening Influence on Policy: Working Regionally and Internationally Within the Context of Globalization

The previous chapter, Chapter 8, concentrated on the efforts made by NGOs directly aimed at influencing foreign policies on migrant workers. It provided a parallel with the NGOs' less than successful attempt to obtain an effective national law on migrant workers, discussed in Chapter 6. As in Chapter 7, this chapter will cover the NGOs' other activities which contribute to and strengthen their efforts to improve policies for migrant workers, but while Chapter 7 covered activities only within Indonesia's national borders, this chapter examines Indonesian NGOs' work overseas on this issue. Thus it investigates how the two NGOs researched, SP and Migrant CARE have been taking up the opportunities brought by globalization through their transnational activism, the difficulties they encounter in doing so and the efforts they have made to overcome the difficulties. This chapter focuses on the activities of the NGOs since Indonesia signed MoUs with Malaysia both on workers in formal (2004) and informal (2006) sectors. Similar to Chapter 7, this chapter aims to answer the main question of how the NGOs strengthen their influence on changing existing policy by answering the following questions: How have the NGOs continued their work? And how do they reflect on what they have done to assist them in moving forward?

The chapter is divided into three sections. The first two sections discuss key activities that the NGOs researched have been conducting at the regional and international levels: building cooperation and employing existing international instruments. These activities are considered to be the NGOs' responses to the transnational nature of the issue of migrant workers, which requires them to search for ways to extend their operations across national borders and employ regional and international instruments which have the potential to address problems faced by the migrant workers. The third section then assesses whether there have been any self-evaluation and/or learning processes arising from the NGOs' transnational efforts.

Works on Asian labor migration have highlighted the transnational nature of labor migration issue and the transnational activism conducted by local NGOs in responding to states' frequently weak or lack of policies on labor migration.[1] Building on these works, this chapter focuses on the efforts made by the NGOs researched.

1 Cf. Piper 2003, Ford 2005, Hugo 2005, Yamanaka and Piper 2005.

9.1 Building Cooperation

As identified by Keck and Sikkink through their concept of "boomerang pattern", NGOs' transnational activism is commonly motivated by their experience of an authoritarian political system at home, and is an effort to build pressure from the outside.[2] On a similar note, the efforts made by the NGOs researched to build regional and international cooperation are partly motivated by the difficulty in influencing Indonesian government policies through national pressures. Anis Hidayah from Migrant CARE, for example, believes that internationally acknowledged organizations like the U.S.-based HRW create greater impact when they launch their reports or statements and have a greater chance of being heard by the government and by international institutions like the UN.[3] Thus, by working with these organizations, the NGOs expect to attract more attention to the issue of temporary labor migration from Indonesia. This section discusses the regional and international cooperation that the NGOs have attempted to build to gauge its significance for their activism and the challenges that have arisen during the cooperation.

9.1.1 Networking

Similar to domestic cooperation with other NGOs, a transnational network connects the members and facilitates the exchange of resources and joint planning and conduct of activities such as public relations.[4] Furthermore, the NGOs' choices of which network to join at the regional and international level also to an extent reflect their organizational characteristics and the issue they are focusing on. SP is involved in regional and international networks such as CARAM Asia, GAATW, APWLD, MFA, and Women's Empowerment in Muslim Contexts (WEMC).[5] Migrant CARE has worked with organizations such as IPMWC, ASEAN Migrant Centre, MFA, and Global Call to Action against Poverty.[6]

Keck and Sikkink have underlined the importance of information mobilization between the actors of transnational advocacy networks in putting new issues on the public agenda, and in persuading, pressuring, and gaining leverage over international organizations and governments.[7] Indeed short to this, the most common reason for the NGOs researched to be involved in regional and international

2 Cf. Keck and Sikkink 1998, pp. 12-14.
3 Interview with Hidayah, Anis on June 15, 2007.
4 Cf. Keck and Sikkink 1998, pp. 6-7.
5 Interview with Safitri, Salma on June 6, 2007, and on August 2, 2007.
6 Interview with Hidayah, Anis on May 26, 2007, and on June 15, 2007.
7 Cf. Keck and Sikkink 1998, pp. 2-3.

networks derives from a general view of Indonesian migrant workers advocates that pressures from outside the country often have more impact on the government than pressure from inside. As argued by Thaufiek Zulbahary from SP, it is more effective to apply pressure from outside because at times the government listens more to voices from outside the country.[8] As an illustration, Zulbahary explained how SP, as a part of CARAM Asia, presented the situation in Indonesia at a regional consultation with the UN Special Rapporteur, in the belief that the latter could use the information effectively to put pressure on the Indonesian government through his recommendation. Zulbahary also pointed out how actions made or events occurring outside the country often have greater impact than if they occur inside the country. As an example, a demonstration conducted by Indonesian migrant workers in Hong Kong could push the Indonesian government to cancel the implementation of a policy.[9] Zulbahary believes that it would be different if the demonstration was conducted in Indonesia. He also pointed out that the Presidential Instruction No. 6/2006 on the Policy for the Reform of the Placement and Protection System of Indonesian Workers Overseas was made after President Susilo Bambang Yudhoyono came back from a meeting with migrant workers abroad. Therefore, as Zulbahary maintained, the NGOs have continued to use the strategy of putting the government under the international spotlight for violation of human rights through its migration system.

Similarly, Wahyu Susilo from Migrant CARE argued that even if there were changes in policies toward migrant workers in Indonesia, they would be more likely to be triggered by pressure from the society or from outside the country.[10] He even regarded the improved attention toward the elimination of trafficking as an "order" (*pesanan*) from the U.S.. This statement illustrates how even the agenda for NGO activism in the south is very much influenced by the flow of agendas formulated in the north – an example of how globalization of ideas occur within civil society and focus of activism is greatly determined by the global trend.

Anis Hidayah from Migrant CARE also considered the effort to gather support and coordinate outside pressures as a strategy to push the government of Indonesia to act.[11] She believed that Migrant CARE could gain support to push the Indonesian government to ratify the 1990 ICRMW through its involvement in regional and international networks of NGOs such as IPMWC.

8 Interview with Zulbahary, Thaufiek on November 19, 2008.

9 The policy required migrant workers to report to their agents before working for a new employer.

10 Interview with Susilo, Wahyu on June 14, 2007.

11 Interview with Hidayah, Anis on June 15, 2007.

Besides building pressure on the government from the outside, as explained above, the staff of both SP and Migrant CARE interviewed for this research also acknowledged the following reasons for their organizations' continuous engagement in regional and international networks. *Firstly*, as asserted by Hidayah, regional and international networks allowed the NGOs to gain wider acknowledgment and reputation, which could assist them in elevating the issue they are concerned with to supranational levels.[12] This was confirmed by Zulbahary, who believed that SP had benefited from its involvement in regional and international networks because, the participatory approaches commonly used in the networks allowed the voices of migrant workers to be heard at regional or international levels.[13] He explained that one of the activities within the networks is mapping problems faced by migrant workers through reports from each country which can later be used as a basis for building solidarity and joint strategies and eventually support national advocacy. *Secondly*, as stated by Risma Umar from SP, the networks allow the NGOs to extend their influence to reach the governments of each member of the networks, including those of receiving countries.[14] *Thirdly*, NGOs involvement in a network can strengthen their capacities because it can become a forum for sharing between them on matters such as strategies, knowledge, creativities, skills, and how to build joint advocacies.[15] *Fourthly*, the NGOs can gather support and assistance from the network for advocating issues, such as the issue of HIV/AIDS among migrant workers advocated by SP[16] and for handling cases.[17] As also stated by Susilo in commenting on the increased initiative of Indonesian NGOs to get involved in international networks, the initiative should have happened much earlier and not only to apply pressure, which would be aimed back at the government but also most importantly to handle transnational cases.[18]

The types of activity that the two NGOs conduct through their cooperation at the regional and international level are very similar. For SP, it involves

- sharing information and knowledge, including data on the situation in each country;
- building strategy;

12 Ibid.
13 Interview with Zulbahary, Thaufiek on May 16, 2007.
14 Interview with Umar, Risma on August 8, 2007.
15 Interview with Safitri, Salma on August 2, 2007, with Umar, Risma on August 8, 2007, and with Zulbahary,Thaufiek on May 16, 2007.
16 Interview with Safitri, Salma on August 2, 2007.
17 Interview with Hidayah, Anis on June 15, 2007.
18 Interview with Susilo, Wahyu on June 14, 2007. This point can be seen as a reflection of how case handling is given a degree of priority in Migrant CARE.

- strengthening analytical capacity;
- using the network to campaign on the problems faced by Indonesian migrant workers;
- conducting research;
- simultaneously lobbying the governments in both sending and receiving countries;
- conducting joint advocacy activities.[19]

As for Migrant CARE, it involves

- exchange of information and mutual support;
- making joint statements;
- jointly responding to an issue, raising public awareness;
- building international solidarity;
- conducting research;
- widening their network and speeding up information flow.[20]

Gathering, exchanging, and sharing information constitute an important part of the interactions within the networks. As Keck and Sikkink have emphasized, the ability of networks' members such as NGOs to "generate information quickly and accurately and deploy it effectively" becomes their "most valuable currency".[21]

To gain an understanding of Indonesian NGOs' involvement in the network and how they are perceived by the partners, I interviewed Cynthia Gabriel, the Regional Coordinator of CARAM Asia, a network that SP is involved in. Gabriel's explanation of the activities of CARAM Asia as a network of NGOs,[22] which include building better coordination between its partners in Indonesia and

19 Interview with Safitri, Salma on June 6, 2007, with Umar, Risma on August 8, 2007, and with Zulbahary, Thaufiek on May 16, 2007. Some examples of activities conducted through networks, given by Zulbahary, are the joint statement between SP and Tenaganita on the MoU between Indonesia and Malaysia and the regional advocacy effort against the mandatory HIV/AIDS tests, based on the research in 14 countries coordinated by CARAM Asia. Interview with Zulbahary, Thaufiek on September 24, 2007.

20 Interview with Hidayah, Anis on June 15, 2007.

21 Keck and Sikkink 1998, p. 10.

22 In general, there are three aspects of CARAM Asia's work: *Firstly*, action research where they work with their partners to reach the migrant communities and incorporate their experiences and their feedback into their research and publications, *secondly*, capacity building, where they organize specific programs to strengthen the different skills of the partners and the different perspectives that they need, and *thirdly*, advocacy which is organizing their own program to target stakeholders like ASEAN, parliamentarians, intergovernmental agencies, UN agencies and others. Interview with Gabriel, Cynthia on August 13, 2007.

Malaysia (SP and Tenaganita), illustrates the activities of the NGOs within their network. When the MoU was signed between Indonesia and Malaysia, CARAM Asia had both partners issue statements about it.[23] Gabriel saw this as CARAM Asia's effort to strengthen its partners and the grassroots work that they do, and to take their voices up to the regional level to develop responses there. She emphasized the importance of grassroots work, without which responses at the regional level will be quite groundless. CARAM Asia has also conducted capacity building activities for its partners in Indonesia, including SP. An example is the development of a campaign tool kit on foreign domestic workers in 2007, which covers a whole range of issues and concerns on foreign domestic workers and looks at the different conventions internationally and the different laws that those who work on the issue of foreign domestic workers need to know about.[24]

The NGOs' involvement in regional and international networks is also used to build and support their existing cooperation with NGOs in receiving countries, which is valuable because most Indonesian NGOs do not have any branches or representatives there. As explained by Safitri, SP has worked with Tenaganita, a leading Malaysian NGO on the issue of migrant workers and the WAO in planning campaigns on the MoU between Indonesia and Malaysia.[25] Safitri asserted that for SP, when migrant workers face problems in receiving countries, advocacy should be conducted by local NGOs there in accordance with the law in that country. Opening a branch in the receiving countries is not a strategic choice because of the high cost and their limited knowledge of the area. As already identified by Keck and Sikkink, posting staff in other countries is not something most NGOs can afford.[26] They may occasionally send staff, but this is not practical for maintaining continuous flow of information. Therefore, these authors suggest that NGOs should create international links to get and send out information. In Migrant CARE's case, it may have Alex Ong as the country representative in Kuala Lumpur but he still cooperates with Tenaganita.[27] However, Indonesian

23 Cf. SP 2006, Tenaganita 2006, Interview with Gabriel, Cynthia on August 13, 2007.

24 Interview with Gabriel, Cynthia on August 13, 2007. CARAM Asia also provides what they call action tools to assist trainers including training sessions for foreign domestic worker communities. According to Gabriel, one of their main objectives is to strengthen the organization of foreign domestic workers themselves so that, in the long run, they will be able to present their own issues and won't have to depend on other people speaking on their behalf.

25 Interview with Safitri, Salma on August 2, 2007.

26 Cf. Keck and Sikkink 1998, p. 22.

27 Interview with Hidayah, Anis on June 15, 2007, and Ong, Alex on August 16, 2007. According to Alex Ong, he also communicates with the Malaysian trade union, MTUC, the WAO, and other Malaysian NGOs. In Singapore, Migrant CARE worked with Transient Workers Count Too (TWC2). When Migrant CARE wanted to hold a public discussion in Singapore which involved Indonesian migrant workers, the Indonesian embassy, and oth-

NGOs cannot entirely depend on the NGOs in receiving countries, particularly in Malaysia, because they have their own limitations and challenges. As explained by Gabriel few NGOs in receiving countries work on migrant labor because other issues are of higher priority for the civil society there.[28] According to her, Malaysia has a small NGO community due to the repressive nature of the government which is very conscious and very nervous about too many NGOs getting registered. She compared Malaysia's situation to Indonesia during the New Order where there was limited space for NGOs, determined by the government.

The above explanations have shown how for Indonesian NGOs their networking efforts would be most valuable for capacity building and leveraging the issues faced by Indonesian migrant workers to the regional and international level. As for joint actions, they are limited to making statements and building public opinions. Also, just as in the national network of NGOs, there are various challenges in conducting activities within regional and international networks, such as limited resources, distance, and difficulties in coordinating actions. As expressed by Irene Fernandez from Tenaganita,

> "There's been very much and more on the level of sharing information. I would actually like to see ... joint advocacy work going on and there's a major gap in that. The tendency is that they do their advocacy there, we do our advocacy here. But it has to be much more planned, strategized, and how do we get both governments accountable..."[29]

Although Fernandez acknowledged the information that they have received from Indonesian NGOs like Migrant CARE, she also argued that information sharing is not enough. "Joint" and "together" are some of the words that the NGOs have been using to describe their activities within the networks. Nevertheless, as highlighted by Fernandez, there are difficulties in conducting related activities focusing on certain issues because coordination is still a challenge, not only between Indonesian NGOs and NGOs from other countries, but also among Indonesian NGOs themselves, as illustrated by the failure of *Kopbumi*.

Lack of coordination and consolidation of different activities among the NGOs was also felt by Gabriel.[30] She regarded lack of real consolidation of efforts as part of the problem and regretted that it existed when democratization was occurring in Indonesia, there were so many more NGOs and the president had taken steps such as allowing the visit of the special rapporteurs and creating

ers who were concerned with the issue, they needed to work with TWC2, particularly to get the permit, since it was not easy to get a permit to conduct activities there.

28 Interview with Gabriel, Cynthia on August 13, 2007.

29 Interview with Fernandez, Irene on August 15, 2007. Direct transcription of the interview.

30 Interview with Gabriel, Cynthia on August 13, 2007.

a special institution directly under his office (the BNP2TKI). Gabriel observed that, while the president had played his public relation role very well, the NGOs had not really maximized all the opportunities and were not assertive enough in getting some standard demands met by the Indonesian government. Gabriel argued for greater consolidation between Indonesian NGOs and better coordination and relations between NGOs in Indonesia and Malaysia that work on migrant workers.

There is also a question as to how the Indonesian NGOs perform at the regional and international networks or forums. Gabriel considered there were improvements although they might not be good enough.[31] Inevitably, she compared Indonesian civil society organizations with the Philippine ones, which, according to her, had advantages, such as good mastery of English, which enabled them to articulate their concerns at the regional level. Nevertheless, she insisted that the language barrier or possibly the cultural values which may prevent Indonesians being more assertive should not be an issue for Indonesian NGOs, because the more urgent need was the consolidation of strategies for Indonesian NGOs, which she thought was not really happening. She believed that better consolidating and strategizing would help Indonesian NGOs to emerge from the back seats that they usually took in the regional platform. Gabriel applied similar comparisons to the governments of Indonesia and the Philippines. She argued that the Indonesian government must play a stronger role in protecting the rights of its own citizens as the Philippine government has done by insisting that their workers must be paid a minimum wage. Thus, while the NGOs expect to build the capacity of their staff through their involvement in the networks, they also need to acquire adequate skills so that they can participate actively in the networks and optimize their benefit of joining.

Recommendations for Indonesian NGOs to extend their activities beyond the national borders and engage in regional and international networks also came from some government officials. Ade Adam Noch from the BNP2TKI, for example, expected Indonesian NGOs to voice their demands toward the receiving countries, not just meddle domestically and blame the Indonesian government.[32] Damos Dumoli Agusman from the MoFA also expected the NGOs to direct their protests more toward receiving countries like Malaysia, build a type of regional network similar to the ASEAN network, and understand the law of each receiving country.[33] Agusman also suggested that Indonesian NGOs should build a

31 Ibid.

32 Interview with Adam Noch, Ade on September 4, 2007.

33 Interview with Agusman, Damos Dumoli on July 23, 2007. Agusman claimed that they (the MoFA) have opened the path by taking the initiative with the Philippines to create a regional convention on migrant workers within the ASEAN framework. He wants Indonesian NGOs to build a network with NGOs from other sending countries such as the

network with Malaysian NGOs. His statement reveals that the government has limited knowledge of what a number of Indonesian NGOs have been doing with Malaysian NGOs and their regional networks, considering that the cooperation between Indonesian NGOs and Malaysian NGOs, such as Tenaganita, started at least in the 1990s. Alternatively, it may show that what the NGOs have been doing has not been considered significant by the government.

This section has shown that the main reasons for the NGOs to engage with regional and international networks are similar to why they participate in domestic networks, as discussed in Chapter 7: to strengthen their activism and build stronger pressure on the government. The main challenges they are facing are also similar, consolidating and coordinating actions among the members. Nevertheless, although the NGOs have started to realize the relative power of international pressure on the national government, they opt to sustain their involvement in the regional and networks for other benefits that they still gain such as capacity building and issue leveraging.

9.1.2 ASEAN

Some NGO activists have pointed out the importance of using ASEAN as a multilateral regional organization to promote the protection of the rights of migrant workers. Since its establishment, Migrant CARE has made ASEAN one of its advocacy targets. As stated by Hidayah, for this purpose they joined MFA.[34] Their goal was that in six years, there would be an ASEAN declaration or convention on the protection of migrant workers. Thus, they aimed at lobbying the ASEAN Secretariat to not only concentrate on politics and the economy, but also to make migrant workers part of their political agenda. Obviously, the NGOs cannot directly participate in this governmental organization. Thus, as asserted by Hidayah, their action took the form of urging the government of Indonesia to build coalitions with other sending countries and create bilateral or multilateral policies on the protection of migrant workers at the ASEAN level.[35] Susilo also pointed out that they have pushed the Indonesian government to propose the

Philippines and Vietnam, to put pressure on Malaysia so that Malaysia will position itself as a good receiving country by enacting a law which will include domestic workers. Agusman also stated that, although the NGOs have been shouting for a rest day in a week, if they do not understand that the local law does not allow this, there is no point in doing so. Agusman explained that he stopped negotiating for the one rest day a week when he learned that Malaysian law does not regulate this because there was no point in forcing it.

34 Interview with Hidayah, Anis on May 26, 2007.

35 Ibid.

formulation of the declaration on the protection of migrant workers.[36] On January 13, 2007, members of ASEAN finally signed the ASEAN Declaration on the Protection and Promotion of the Rights of Migrant Workers in Cebu, Philippines. Hidayah saw this as a tool for Indonesia to push receiving countries in ASEAN, particularly Malaysia. Although she realized that ASEAN instruments are considered "soft law" without any legal power to provide legal sanctions, she expected that political sanction and "shame mobilization" could build pressure on governments.

Hidayah admitted that they were not significantly involved in ASEAN's processes and mechanisms,[37] and her use of the words "urging", "pushing", and "monitoring" to describe their activities at the ASEAN level further highlights their dependence on the government to carry their voices into the organization's decision-making process. Nevertheless, recent changes have brought a degree of hope for greater influence of civil society on ASEAN. Tati Krisnawaty pointed to important developments at the ASEAN level, particularly with the effort to make ASEAN a "caring and sharing community", which indicates a more positive attitude toward human rights related issues.[38] She further emphasized the role of the SAPA Working Group on Migration and Labor,[39] which shadows ASEAN meetings. She also regarded as positive developments the changes of leaders of ASEAN governments to those who are more concerned about human right issues, NGOs' engagement, and the international development of a human rights paradigm.

The NGOs' involvement at the ASEAN level can also be observed from the activity of the networks that they join. In SP's case, it is CARAM Asia's activity. As explained by Gabriel, CARAM Asia did a lot of work with ASEAN.[40] Although it has been difficult to make ASEAN members commit to anything concerning human rights, in 2007 besides signing the declaration as mentioned above, ASEAN also established a committee for the promotion and protection of the rights of migrant workers. Because it is possible that this may end up as something "symbolic with no depth in it", Gabriel believed that it was their job as a regional organization to make sure they provided depth by making recommendations about what the committee needs to do. For this reason, CARAM Asia was involved in a task force which was established by the ASEAN Secretary General to develop a multilateral framework for the protection of migrant

36 Interview with Susilo, Wahyu on November 7, 2008.

37 Interview with Hidayah, Anis on September 14, 2007.

38 Interview with Krisnawaty, Tati on November 7, 2008.

39 SAPA was established at a regional consultation in Bangkok, February 3-4, 2006, attended by more than 50 participants representing about 30 civil society organizations from the Asian region.

40 Interview with Gabriel, Cynthia on August 13, 2007.

workers where CARAM Asia attempted to insert some specific rights for domestic workers and women migrants.

Although ASEAN has no binding power over its members, the fact that it is virtually the only regional organization in which both sending and receiving countries, particularly Indonesia and Malaysia, are members, has made it the most rational channel for the NGOs to push for a regional agreement on protection of migrant workers. The changes within ASEAN toward greater attention toward human rights issues makes NGOs' advocacy at this level worth continuing. This section again shows that when it comes to dealing with the government, or in this case a regional governmental organization, NGOs' effort alone may not be enough to initiate change. The effort needs to be supported by increased attention toward the issue among the members of the organization, which is more likely to be generated by changes in global norms.

9.1.3 UN Bodies

Although the NGOs researched have in various ways interacted with UN bodies, cooperation with the main body concerned with labor issues, the ILO, including its representative in Jakarta, is not very significant. According to Hidayah, the ILO cooperated more with migrant workers unions rather than with NGOs, presumably because of its mandate, which is to work with employer and labor organizations and governments.[41] Nevertheless, Albert Yosua Bonasahat from the ILO's Jakarta office[42] stated that, although traditionally the ILO's main civil society partners would be trade unions, the ILO realized that in the case of migrant workers, trade unions are quite slow in entering the arena and advocating for Indonesian migrant workers because they are more focused on national labor issues.[43] There may be increased attention among trade unions toward the issue but there are still more NGOs working on it. Bonasahat mentioned Migrant CARE

41 Interview with Hidayah, Anis on June 15, 2007. The cooperation between the government of Indonesia and the ILO is confirmed by the explanation given by Ferry Adamhar from the Department of Foreign Affairs that his department cooperated with the ILO, including on a project aimed at developing Indonesian diplomats. Interview with Adamhar, Ferry on July 6, 2007. According to Adamhar, Indonesian diplomats are now trained by the ILO to conduct their protecting functions. In the official training given to Indonesian diplomats they are informed about standard setting and standard norms of what they should do and how to do it if Indonesian migrant workers face problems overseas.

42 Bonasahat was the national coordinator for a program on the eradication of forced labor and trafficking on Indonesian migrant workers in the ILO's Jakarta office.

43 Interview with Bonasahat, Albert Yosua on July 11, 2007.

and *Kopbumi* as two of the ILO's partners.[44] However, he stated that their interaction with Migrant CARE was limited to involving it in some meetings, not in implementing programs. With SBMI, however, the ILO had programs at the grassroots level. According to Bonasahat this was due to SBMI's capacity, as compared to Migrant CARE, which is more focused on activities such as research and policy analysis at the national level. At the time the research for this book was conducted, it seems that the ILO tended to choose working with SBMI and *Kopbumi* or other organizations which have activities and networks at the grassroots level. As reflected in Bonasahat's explanation and the review documents of the ILO projects aimed at protecting Indonesian migrant domestic workers,[45] the ILO tends to work more with the government in advocating the policy and their protection programs were directly aimed at migrant worker communities in the origin areas and receiving countries, although it was stated that the implementing partners were those from the government, federations of workers, employers' organizations, and NGOs.[46] This explains the ILO's preference to work with migrant workers organizations and NGOs with stronger grassroots affiliation, which largely rules out the two NGOs researched.

Bonasahat also explained that the ILO's cooperation with its partners had a reciprocal nature where the ILO provided them with technical support and the partners gave the ILO information that they gathered. According to him, the latter was not actually a requirement for their cooperation but usually the partners provided the information voluntarily. In terms of the possibility for the partners to use the ILO as a channel to put pressure on the government or to influence the policies, he explained that the office in Jakarta worked on projects rather than on policy advocacy.[47] However, he said that it was possible that during discussions

44 In terms of choosing partners to work with, Bonasahat stated that they seek organizations which have good track records and experience in handling migrant worker cases. Interview with Bonasahat, Albert Yosua on July 11, 2007. The form of partnership is also determined by the partners' capacities, so that there is a degree of guarantee that the program will be sustainable, even when later on the ILO will no longer provide technical assistance. Also decisions are made based on proposals submitted by the partners, considering whether the resources are effectively utilized. The initiative for a programm can come from either the ILO or its partners.

45 This project, which covered Indonesia, Philippines, Malaysia, Singapore, and Hong Kong, was divided into two phases. Cf. Kejser 2007. The first phase in 2004-2006 was titled the ILO Project Mobilizing Action for the Protection of Domestic Workers from Forced Labour and Trafficking in Southeast Asia. The second phase in 2006-2008 was titled the ILO Project Combating Forced Labour and Trafficking of Indonesian Migrant Workers.

46 Cf. Kejser 2007.

47 Bonasahat explained that the ILO does not conduct direct policy advocacy: rather, its programs assist the development of their partners' capacities so they can provide services, conduct advocacies or campaigns. Interview with Bonasahat, Albert Yosua on July 11,

with partners from civil society the need for ratifying the international convention was raised and it was then channeled or forwarded through the ILO's meetings with its government partners. From Bonasahat's explanation, it appears that the NGOs cannot use the ILO as a direct channel to put pressure on the government to influence the policy process because certain protocols prevent the ILO from meddling in Indonesia's policy process. However, the NGOs can expect the ILO to provide them with support to strengthen their actions. Bonasahat also assumed that the partners benefited from their association with the ILO. At least, if they are known to have good cooperation with an international body, they may be considered cooperative and responsible organizations. Thus, when they work with the government there is some trust and acknowledgment of their capacities.

I also interviewed Riana Puspasari of the UNIFEM office in Jakarta.[48] According to her, UNIFEM facilitated a number of meetings such as those discussing the MoU between Indonesia and Jordan and best practice among recruitment agencies at the regional level where a code of ethics and corporate social responsibility were on the agenda. She also mentioned that UNIFEM had facilitated the travel of Salma Safitri from SP to a UN meeting, and cooperated with SP in relation to the implementation of CEDAW with the aim of informing people about CEDAW and about what the government had done and had yet to do, which led to a demand that the government ratify the 1990 ICRMW. However, she pointed out that the office in Jakarta is a small project office with a very limited budget, making them frequently unable to fulfill funding requests from NGOs.[49]

2007. This applies to all the ILO's partners, which include the government, civil society groups, and business groups, and can take the forms of research, training, or other technical assistance. According to Bonasahat, it is possible for the ILO to be involved in a policy process if, for example, there is a formal request from the government, through the parliament or one of its departments to advice on a bill for a law. This request would then be forwarded to the ILO's head office and its legal team would formulate their observations and recommendations. If no request is forthcoming, the ILO cannot directly involve itself; rather, it will help strengthen the positions of its partners when they interact with the government or the parliament by providing services such as conducting seminars. The results will then be brought into the process by the partners, not by the ILO.

48 Interview with Puspasari, Riana on August 10, 2007. Puspasari was the National Project Coordinator for the Migrant Worker Project at UNIFEM's Jakarta office. Before working for UNIFEM, she worked on the issue of migrant workers through other grant institutions such as The Asia Foundation and Yayasan TIFA.

49 Puspasari argued that UNIFEM is different from other grant institutions. Interview with Puspasari, Riana on December 11, 2008. According to her, usually UNIFEM has already formulated its program and focus, and then they will find the right partners for the program. She believes better results are achieved if the issue has been made specific from the start. In other institutions, based on her experience in the Asia Foundation and Yayasan TIFA, grants are awarded based on proposals that come in under certain wide categories such as human rights. Puspasari sees this as similar to a supermarket, implying that these institutions will support various trainings, seminars, media campaigns which are very di-

This brief explanation of the cooperation between two UN bodies, the ILO, and UNIFEM, with the NGOs has shown that it tends to be limited to "facilitating" certain activities which are related to influencing policy. This usually means funding a one-off activity such as training sessions or seminars or funding an activist's trip to a UN meeting. The UN bodies seem to work more with other organizations, which are formed by migrant workers and/or have strong grassroots base due to reasons such as their original mandate, as in the case of the ILO, and their shifting focus to the grassroots level. This can be considered as a challenge for the NGOs to adapt to the changing trend in the way these UN bodies work.

9.2 Employing Existing International Instruments

In terms of complying with international agreements, Indonesia has ratified international conventions such as CEDAW, the Convention against Torture and Other Cruel, Inhuman or Degrading Treatment or Punishment (CAT), and the Convention on the Elimination of All Forms of Racial Discrimination (CEAFRD). However, Indonesia has yet to ratify the ICRMW, which could be considered as a milestone in the international efforts of protecting the rights of migrant workers.

The work of Nicola Piper and Robyn Iredale has identified and analyzed the reasons why some main sending and receiving countries in Asia-Pacific had not signed and ratified the ICRMW.[50] One of the points that they made was that there was a lack of understanding within the governments on what ratification entailed and what they could gain or lose by it. As also described by Safitri, some government elements, for example those from the Department of Health and the Department of Education, thought that ratification would burden them with the obligation to guarantee the provision of health and educational services for expatriates in Indonesia, who are already well off.[51]

On September 22, 2004, the Indonesian government, represented by the then Minister of Foreign Affairs, Hassan Wirajuda, signed the ICRMW.[52] Wirajuda asserted that this showed the Indonesian government's commitment to provide protection for its workers and their families overseas. As mentioned earlier, In-

verse and the results tend to be sporadic. Puspasari believes that UNIFEM's way is more measurable because they can identify changes that occur during the program, who actually contributes to the changes, the dominant factors, the challenges, and whether the activities were effective or not because the actors involved are limited.

50 See Nicola Piper and Robyn Iredale 2003.

51 Interview with Safitri, Salma on August 2, 2007.

52 The signing was conducted during the UN Annual Treaty Event in the 59th meeting of the General Assembly.

donesia finally ratified the convention on April 12, 2012, almost eight years after signing it. By 2013, the parliament and the government are still working on revising Law No. 39/2004 which is expected, particularly by migrant workers' advocates, to adopt the principles of the convention.

In the period before Indonesia ratified the convention, interviewees from both SP and Migrant CARE explained that besides continuing to voice their demands for ratification, their NGOs made efforts to employ other existing regional and international instruments. SP, for example, had used CEDAW to promote the rights of Indonesian women migrant workers. With a number of other NGOs, SP wrote a shadow report on the implementation of CEDAW by the government of Indonesia, in which SP concentrated on the issue of trafficking of migrant workers.[53] The shadow report which highlighted the government's low commitment was submitted to the CEDAW committee and publicized through a press conference. However, according to Safitri, only a small number of people, whether in the government, the NGOs or the media understood the importance of CEDAW.[54] As also argued by Puspasari, although there were a number of articles from CEDAW that could be used to address the issues faced by Indonesian women migrant workers, the number of people who knew and understood this was limited.[55]

The views from the government side on the importance of regional and international instruments are quite varied. Noch, for example, considered the ASEAN declaration and UN convention as influential documents.[56] According to him, when an agreement was made at the regional or international level, there was an obligation to implement it and each government had to adopt it into their policies. A different opinion came from Agusman from the MoFA who argued that the NGOs should concentrate more on pushing for a regional convention rather than on ratification of the 1990 ICRMW because according to him there was a bigger possibility to engage Malaysia in a regional agreement.[57]

Similar to the NGOs' initiative to work with regional and international organizations, it is still debatable whether the effort to employ existing international instruments is effective in putting more pressure on the Indonesian government and influencing their policies. After all, the organizations are the government's domain and the implementation of conventions really depends on the government's political will and consent. Furthermore, in stating the objectives of their networking efforts the NGO activists tend to emphasize more on building re-

53 Interview with Umar, Risma on August 8, 2007, and with Zulbahary, Thaufiek on May 16, 2007.

54 Interview with Safitri, Salma on August 2, 2007.

55 Interview with Puspasari, Riana on August 10, 2007.

56 Interview with Noch, Ade Adam on September 4, 2007.

57 Interview with Agusman, Damos Dumoli on July 23, 2007.

gional and international pressures to influence Indonesian domestic policies and rarely articulate an aim of influencing policies of the receiving countries, most probably because the NGOs realize that their activism is limited by the borders and sovereignty of the state. Nevertheless, the transnational nature of the labor migration issue, and the fact that the policies of the receiving countries have not provided adequate protection for migrant workers while they are working there, have made it significant for the NGOs to make influencing policies of receiving countries as one of the priorities in their agendas. This may be a challenging task considering the NGOs' limitations, but it is attainable considering they have already joined regional and international networks and cooperated with receiving countries' NGOs. As shown in this chapter, the challenge is to sustain the cooperation and improve coordination among them.

9.3 Learning and Self-Evaluating

The learning process of NGOs should involve identification, understanding, and responding to the changes that occur around them, which may include changes within the organizations themselves. A step taken by the NGOs which is clearly based on a lesson learned is the tactic of building pressure outside the country, aimed at influencing and pushing the government to take certain actions. Susilo considered that a significant change has occurred inside the NGOs, shifting from merely working on cases to activities such as using regional and international instruments to strengthen their efforts of promoting and protecting human rights.[58] Most Indonesian migrant workers advocates have experienced difficulties in exerting influence inside the country. Thus, many tried to get involved with regional and international networks, mainly expecting that pressure and humiliation from outside would exert appreciable influence on the government.

Umar also argued that there has been a change in the strategies and work patterns of NGOs since the New Order Era.[59] According to her, SP is now aware that the issue of migrant workers is not merely about government policy but also about other factors that influence that policy. The reflection had made SP realize that advocacy should be aimed at both the government and the public and that it could not work alone and needed the support of networks. This is reflected in SP's decision to work with Tenaganita, which, according to Umar, was based on the consideration that it is an NGO in Malaysia, a receiving country, which has worked on the issue of migrant workers for a long time and like SP, it is part of the network CARAM Asia. Through its involvement in the team of civil society

58 Interview with Susilo, Wahyu on November 7, 2008.
59 Interview with Umar, Risma on August 8, 2007.

organizations that prepared and submitted the shadow report to the CEDAW committee, SP also learned how international humiliation can push the government to act or make a commitment. Although the implementation is still questionable, in the meeting with the CEDAW committee, the Indonesian government representatives made a commitment to ratify the ICRMW and evaluate Law No. 39/2004.

As discussed earlier in this chapter, international effort was initially aimed at building pressure to influence policies inside the country. Through time, the NGOs have come to learn that there is no guarantee for this, and even if the government had made a commitment in a regional and international forum, it did not necessarily translate into immediate implementation. As admitted by Hidayah, Migrant CARE's involvement with regional and international networks and forums has not resulted in significant influence in Indonesia.[60] She said that the benefit was more for widening their network, speeding up information and building public opinion, which she considered as relatively easy to conduct compared to activities such as initiating migrant workers' organizations. Hidayah's statements indicate a shift from the initially strong belief that international pressure would bring considerable impact on the national government. They also indicate that while there are joint activities which are relatively easier to perform within the networks such as making statements, other activities which demand more synchronizing of actions, time, and resources are difficult to implement. Hidayah further argued that outside pressures need to be combined with increased domestic lobbying, not just of individual members of parliament but of the parties which have more power in the parliamentary process.[61] This indicates that the NGOs have further learned the importance of combining their domestic, regional and international activism.

9.4 Conclusion

NGOs' disappointment with the content of the MoU between Indonesia and Malaysia, the fact that it took Indonesia quite a while to ratify the 1990 ICRMW, and the reality that the NGOs' efforts to influence policy-making have not been very successful had motivated Indonesian NGOs to build cooperation with partners at the regional and international levels and use other international instru-

60 Interview with Hidayah, Anis on September 14, 2007.

61 Interview with Hidayah, Anis on November 18, 2008. While admitting that the parties still have weaknesses, including not having strong platforms, since most of them are still dominated by "the old generation", Hidayah observes younger people entering certain parties, such as PDI-P, which she expects to bring changes.

ments as alternative ways to achieve their goal of promoting the rights of migrant workers. The NGOs' initiative of going transnational is mainly motivated by their frustration with their inability to put enough pressure on the government through domestic activism. Throughout the process, the NGOs have benefited from their engagement with regional and international partners, particularly through activities such as capacity building, case handling, information exchange, and issue leveraging.

However, as argued in Chapter 7, through the process, the NGOs have also learned that potential alternatives may turn out to have their own weaknesses. The networking experience at the regional and international levels further proves that coordinating activities within a network and sustaining cooperation can be quite challenging when it involves different characteristics, visions, and priorities, as well as locations separated by national borders in the case of regional and international networks.

Again, it is still too early to claim that there is a strategizing process going on. The difficulties involved in coordinating actions between the NGOs and their partners in the receiving country and within the networks have prevented the shift toward a more strategic partnership and establishment of strategies and long-term commitments and plans. However, the regional and international activism has taught the NGOs some lessons. On realizing the weakness of domestic pressure on the government they turned to regional and international forces, expecting that these forces would be able to bounce their agenda back into the country to create a greater impact. Then when it was proven that the regional and international engagements and instruments also had limited influence on the government, the NGOs learned that eventually their transnational efforts needed to be supported by equally strong activism at home. Although the learning process has again been a matter of trial and error, it has signified the importance of balancing domestic and international activism in responding to both democratization and globalization, which simultaneously affect a transnational issue like labor migration.

10. Conclusion: Emerging Strategies?

This book is based on a study of the activism of two Indonesian NGOs on the issue of women migrant workers, particularly since *Reformasi* occurred in Indonesia in 1998. The analysis, which concentrates on their efforts to influence a domestic and a foreign policy concerning migrant workers, has been framed by democratization and globalization processes which occur simultaneously and affect virtually all aspects of life within the country and the concept of transnational activism, which reflect their efforts to engage powerful actors outside the country. Since the research was conducted a decade after the fall of the New Order regime, it goes beyond discussing how NGOs become agents of democratization. Assuming that democratization and globalization have created opportunities for civil society elements to develop and improve their activism, it assesses how NGOs have been taking up these opportunities, the challenges they encounter in doing so, and the efforts they have made to overcome the difficulties.

A number of studies have investigated Asian government policies on migrant workers, including Indonesia's. Accepting their argument that the policies do not provide enough protection for migrant workers and need to be improved, this book has focused more on how migrant worker advocates, particularly NGOs, attempt to influence the making of the policies. In 2004, the government passed Indonesia's first law on labor migration, Law No. 39/2004 on the Placement and Protection of Indonesian Workers Overseas and in 2006 Indonesia signed a MoU with Malaysia on the Recruitment and Placement of Indonesian Domestic Workers. Claimed by the government as part of their achievements and criticized by migrant worker advocates as not providing the needed protection for migrant workers, these two policy instruments have been the focus of this book.

In summarizing the findings and concluding the analysis of the research, this chapter is divided into four sections. The first section briefly summarizes the chapters of this book. The second and third sections conclude analyses of the NGOs' responses to democratization and globalization process, including how they take up the opportunities and overcome the challenges. The fourth section identifies the NGOs' current role and what can be done to improve it, which is significant for envisaging the future direction of NGO activism on the issue of women migrant workers in Indonesia as a sending country. The main aim is to identify whether there have been any strategies emerging.

10.1 Summary of the Chapters

The research topic was introduced in Chapter 1, and the consulted literature was reviewed in Chapter 2. The rest of the book was then divided into three parts and concluded in this chapter, Chapter 10. Part one, which consists of Chapters 3, 4, and 5, set the context of this research. Problems occur at every stage of the migration process and a well-established body of literature has documented these problems. Chapter 3 briefly discussed some of the main problems faced by Indonesian women migrant workers, showing how they are interconnected and which stakeholders are involved. As commonly acknowledged by the government, migrant workers advocates and scholars, 80 percent of the problems occur even before the workers leave Indonesia and many of the problems experienced abroad are rooted in bad management of the migration system at home. The condition is worsened by the fact that Indonesia's labor migration system is not supported by effective laws and regulations and suffers from corruption, bad and illegal practices, and a lack of protective mechanisms.

The Indonesian government has generated a number of policies and efforts to improve the regulation and management of overseas labor migration. Chapter 4 examined some of these efforts. In general, the government's policies and actions in the last decade on this issue tend to be reactions to a range of frequently contradictory pressures. On one hand, economic and unemployment pressures have caused the government to continue to promote and to facilitate the sending of Indonesians to work abroad. On the other hand, pressure from migrant workers' advocates has forced the government to take measures to address the issue. Pressures also came from events such as the 1998 *Reformasi,* the Asian financial crisis, and mass deportations of migrant workers from Malaysia. This chapter highlighted how different elements of the state are responsive to different types of pressures.

The failure of a government in providing services to its citizens, which may be due to its limited capabilities, capacities and coverage, leaves room for the increased involvement of other stakeholders, including NGOs. Thus, Chapter 5 gave a brief overview of Indonesian NGOs after *Reformasi* and then discussed briefly how those concerned with the issue of women migrant workers began to take up the issue, try to organize themselves, and adapt to the new political environment. It then introduced the two NGOs researched, SP and Migrant CARE, pointing out their similarities and differences which are significant in understanding their responses and approaches toward government policies and actions they choose to make, as discussed in parts two and three of this book.

Part two examined the NGOs' responses to democratization by looking, in Chapter 6, at how they attempted to influence the process of making a domestic policy, Law No. 39/2004 on the Placement and Protection of Indonesian

Workers Overseas, and, in Chapter 7, at their other activities which are directed, one way or another, to support their policy advocacy efforts. Chapter 6 described how a coalition of Indonesian NGOs tried to push for a law on migrant workers at the time when *Reformasi* occurred in Indonesia and every element of the state was in the process of redefining its position and role within the new system. The law may have not turned out completely as they expected, but most NGOs admit that it is better to have a law than no law at all since there are clauses that can still be used in their efforts to improve the protection of migrant workers. Also, despite NGOs' disappointment with the law, the interactions between NGOs and state entities throughout the law-making process illustrates improvement in their relationship. This chapter showed how all stakeholders involved, including the government, the parliament and the NGOs, underwent a process of learning how to interact with each other within the new political system and environment.

After the law was finally passed, the learning process continued. The NGOs had to redefine their strategies to adjust to the new situation where there is now a law on the placement and protection of migrant workers. This period after the law was passed was covered in Chapter 7, which highlighted the NGOs' efforts to seek and employ alternative ways to influence policies on migrant workers by utilizing other laws and regulations, engaging cooperative entities in the government and parliament, and building cooperation to put pressure on the government. In this search for alternatives, the NGOs learned, for example, that networking can be quite challenging to sustain when the entities involved have quite varied characteristics, visions, priorities and resources and there are competitions among them on matters such as funding. As for a strategizing process, the better established NGOs like SP may have developed more structured program planning, but decisions on what to focus on greatly depend on the current conditions and trends of labor migration and the available funding.

International labor migration, a major feature of globalization in recent decades, challenges national NGOs to respond to a transnational issue. Part three of the book focuses on the NGOs' responses toward globalization with Chapter 8 examining the NGOs' efforts to influence a foreign policy, the 2006 MoU between the governments of Indonesia and Malaysia on the Recruitment and Placement of Indonesian Domestic Workers, and Chapter 9 assessing the NGOs' activities at the regional and international levels which are intended to support their policy advocacy. The discussion of the MoU indicated that, while in a domestic policy-making process there is a degree of increased involvement of civil society, when it comes to the making of agreements with other countries NGOs tend to be more remote from the process. While they could still monitor the making of Law No. 39/2004, the process of negotiating the 2006 MoU was limited to government representatives, making it almost impossible for the NGOs to monitor the process, let alone influence it. A positive outcome of this limitation is that it pushed the NGOs to seek various ways to channel their voices which led them to various forms of collaboration through national, regional, and international networks, as discussed in Chapter 9.

Chapter 9 again highlights a learning process where initially the NGOs turned to transnational activism with the expectation of building more powerful pressures on the Indonesian government from outside the country. They then learned that just like what happens domestically, coordinating, and sustaining international cooperation are challenging tasks and that outside pressures still need to be complemented by domestic ones.

10.2 Responding to Democratization

The democratization process associated with the Reform Era in Indonesia has brought changes that create both opportunities and challenges for the NGOs. As noted in works on Indonesian NGOs, the transition toward a more democratic society has allowed the NGO sector to grow,[1] including those concerned with the issue of women migrant workers. Another significant change is the greater freedom for civil society, including NGOs, to express their views. Conducting demonstrations in front of state institutions and receiving countries' embassies in Jakarta and making statements on national and international media have become parts of the NGOs' routines in campaigning for the rights of migrant workers.

Another feature of the more democratic Indonesia is the increased freedom of the press and the NGOs' activism has benefited from the more articulate media in the Reform Era. The mutually beneficial relationship between the media and NGOs involves the latter as alternative sources of data for the media and the media as a channel for NGOs to voice their demands, raise public awareness, and build pressure on the government. Although some government critics have suggested the NGOs seek publicity merely to satisfy their donors, NGOs have continued to build their media profile and utilize it to support their activism.

A discussion of NGOs within a context of democratization will definitely include, if not center on, NGOs' interactions with the state and their involvement in the political process. This research focuses on the first decade after 1998, when both the state and civil society elements were in the process of redefining their positions and roles within the new system and finding a feasible form of engagement between them. In the introduction to this book I stated that the analysis of NGOs' involvement in the policy process and their relationship with decision-makers is considered as a way of assessing democratization in Indonesia. Discussions of the interactions between NGOs and the state in various parts of

1 Cf. Hadiwinata 2003, Antlöv et al. 2006.

this book have shown that they are both still adjusting to their new roles and environment, and they are still learning how to build more productive interactions which definitely involve negotiations and adjustments. This learning stage can create both opportunities and challenges with varied results depending on the actors and matters involved.

The discussions on NGOs' interactions with state institutions in this book demonstrate the accommodative attitudes of certain government institutions. NGOs' participation in workshops, seminars, and public hearings aimed at gathering policy inputs can also be considered as an indication of their improved involvement in the policy-making process. Nevertheless, despite the common government rhetoric that it is open to work with elements of civil society, the book has also shown how among state institutions and officials, the degree of acceptance of NGOs' involvement varies greatly. Dissimilarities can also be observed in the NGOs' attitude to state institutions. Thus, in understanding NGOs' influence on policies concerning labor migration, generalizations are not only difficult to make but would not do justice to the stakeholders' varied stances, perceptions and attitudes toward each other which are important in explaining the varied forms of interaction and degree of cooperation between them and the difficulties in making comprehensive policies to address the problems faced by women migrant workers. Since the NGOs' relationship with the MoMT, the main ministry responsible for the issue of migrant workers, remains sour – with the NGOs criticizing most policies and actions made by this ministry and the ministry tending to take a defensive stance and limit its interaction with them – the NGOs have tried various ways to improve their access to and influence on the policy-making process, including approaching members of parliament and government entities who are more sympathetic toward their cause. They expect the more accommodative state institutions such as the MoFA, the SMoWE, and the DPR could become their "alternative channels" into the policy process. Nevertheless, cooperation with these bodies has not significantly improved the NGOs' access to the policy process, because the partners have their own limitations and are not influential enough in the process of making Indonesian policies on labor migration. Thus, there is an urgent need for the NGOs to re-strategize their alignment efforts. While approaching certain supportive individuals in the government and parliament may be more feasible considering the NGOs' limited resources, aiming for party commitment on the promotion of migrant workers' rights may result in a greater influence on the policy process. Although there is still an absence of a clear and strong party platform among Indonesia's political parties, a number of parties, particularly PDI-P and PKB, have shown their inclination to support policies which provide better protection for women migrant workers.

Referring to the concept of the policy cycle, the NGOs have had a significant role at the agenda-setting stage in pushing the government and the parliament to formulate a law on migrant workers through their campaigns. An improvement may also be observed at the policy formulation stage with the government and the parliament claiming that they had obtained policy inputs from various stakeholders, including NGOs. Also the fact that NGOs can now be present as observers in some of the parliament's deliberation meetings and can make attempts to influence the process through their allies in the parliament, can be seen as further progress in Indonesia's democratization process. The NGOs have also tried to improve their monitoring roles during the policy implementation stage by gathering data on the problems faced by migrant workers and the bad practices within the labor migration system. The challenge now is how the NGOs can channel their findings back to the government as part of the "policy evaluation" stage. This is a challenge that the NGOs need to answer immediately because of the government's stated intention to revise Law No. 39/2004. The NGOs' disappointment with the content of Law No. 39/2004, which, according to them, does not provide adequate protection for migrant workers, has also motivated them to campaign for and employ other related policies to address some of the problems faced by migrant workers. While calling for the revision of Law No. 39/2004, the NGOs have been using other existing laws and regulations such as the much praised law on trafficking.

This book has also set out to examine the NGOs' relationship with other related stakeholders. The NGOs have made some efforts to improve their interaction with their allies by engaging them through networks, forums, collaborations, and other forms of cooperation. At the same time, the cooperation effort also exemplifies another important lesson learned by the NGOs: that some potential alternatives turn out to have their own weaknesses. Initially considered as a solution, to the limitations of individual NGOs, networking proved to be challenging, particularly in coordinating activities and sustaining cooperation. Competition among network members has sometimes prevented the development of productive collaboration. Thus, although a more democratic environment has allowed more freedom for NGOs, as part of civil society, to conduct their activism and collaborate in doing so, they still have to address a number of internal factors which may hinder the development of the much-needed joint and coordinated actions to influence policies. Furthermore, as noted in Chapter 7, interaction with labor agencies is still minimal and the relationship with certain migrant workers' unions tends to be more competitive than cooperative.

Another challenge for NGOs is to maintain their credibility. The research has shown that their independent and non-governmental status remains an important concern among the NGOs. While seeking a more cooperative relationship with the state, the NGOs tend to cautiously keep distance from state institutions and avoid too close an association with political parties. In the context of a more democratic Indonesia, as argued by Eldridge, the challenge is for the NGOs to find a balance between engaging with and withdrawing from political parties and the government.[2] Furthermore, to maintain their credibility, NGOs need to be accountable. As highlighted by Hadiwinata one of the challenges for Indonesian NGOs is to maintain the trust of their beneficiaries, donors, and the public, which, according to him, requires the NGOs to improve their accountability system and provide transparent information to their target groups, donors, government and the general public.[3] The NGOs researched have tried to be accountable by making regular reports on their activities and funding. However, these reports are directed more toward their donors, members (for SP), and the public rather than towards their beneficiaries, because given the location of the latter and their indirect relationship, it is quite difficult to create a mechanism which allows the NGOs to be directly accountable to them.

On the topic of accountability, Antlöv et al. argued that it requires two preconditions: for funding agencies to see accountability not merely as accounting but more as public accountability and for civil society organizations to be more independent from foreign funds.[4] As discussed in this book, both NGOs researched are still quite dependent on foreign funding agencies. Some activists outside the NGOs that I interviewed emphasized the need to make funding accountability more about how a project affects and actually helps the community rather than how much assistance was given to how many persons. There were also suggestions for the NGOs to conduct activities to raise their own funding, an idea which is still rejected by most NGOs since it would put their non-profit status at risk. So far, as admitted by a number of NGO activists, this tendency to take up the "more likely to be funded" activities has contributed to the competition among organizations working on the issue of migrant workers and the difficulties for them to share roles and coordinate actions within their networks. Migrant CARE, with its high-media profile, has little difficulty in finding funding sources for its activities. As for SP, obtaining funding is not an issue either but since it has other issues of concern besides migrant workers, the funding allocation for their migration programs greatly depends on the priorities set in the members' congress, and whether the organization can secure significant funding which is specifically allocated for these programs.

As democratization may take a long time to bring significant and tangible results, Hadiwinata anticipated that a major transformation will not be something

2 Cf. Eldridge 2005, pp. 150-51.
3 Cf. Hadiwinata 2003, pp. 114 and 119.
4 Cf. Antlöv et al. 2006, p. 162.

that the NGOs can immediately create.[5] The challenge here is for the NGOs to preserve their interest, energy, and resources to sustain their activism. If not, the risk will be that NGOs may jump from one issue to another depending on the possibility of providing immediate results and attracting funding. NGOs are also vulnerable to fatigue, which is already sensed by some of the senior activists in this area. Sustainability of NGOs' activism requires stamina. Susilo argues that while at the beginning of the reform era there was euphoria when civil society had high expectations, ten years later it is clear that reforms could not be achieved immediately.[6] Susilo believes that this has brought the NGOs to the point where they started to get tired. On a similar note, Albert Yosua Bonasahat, argued that sustainability depends on the resilience of migrant worker advocates.[7] He suggested that migrant workers advocates should be able to control the rhythm by creating moments and activities which continuously highlight what is still needed for the protection of migrant workers. Thus NGOs need to come up with innovative ideas, not merely following the trend or the programs of donor institutions. In other words, the NGOs need to be strong enough to ride the wave of globalization, instead of being dragged along by it.

Another form of dependency that the NGOs need to be aware of is their reliance on certain senior or high profile activists. As observed and argued by Puspasari, many organizations have collapsed because of this.[8] This "over-reliance" on certain individuals can also be observed from the NGOs' approach toward certain accommodative individuals in the government, parliament, and political parties. While a close relationship with key figures, such as Abdurrahman Wahid, may have assisted the NGOs in achieving their short term goals such as handling cases, in the long run they need to aim for a wider and more sustainable network of collaboration to create a significant impact.

One of the main objectives of this book is to capture the shift of NGOs' activism in responding to the changes occurring in Indonesia during the transition from the New Order to the Reform period. The most obvious shift is the trend to adopt advocacy work, particularly for Jakarta-based NGOs. Although the NGOs researched still deliver services, mainly in the form of handling cases, both stated that policy advocacy is their main activity. SP claims that case handling is no longer its main activity and that the cases they tackle are chosen for their significance in supporting a bigger campaign. It is quite different with Migrant CARE which still handles most cases that come to it.

5 Cf. ibid., p. 254.
6 Interview with Susilo, Wahyu on November 7, 2008.
7 Interview with Bonasahat, Albert Yosua on July 11, 2007.
8 Interview with Puspasari, Riana on December 11, 2008.

In the 1990s, Eldridge had observed the trend for development NGOs to start talking about democracy and public participation and for human rights NGOs to embrace social and economic issues.[9] Parts of this book have shown that a decade later in the Reform Era, this cross-issue trend continues to develop since more NGO activists realize the complex and cross-sector nature of the issues they are working on require cross sectoral efforts to address them. The NGOs' efforts to work and build cooperation with other NGOs and stakeholders which do not necessarily make migrant workers their main concern, including religious organizations, is an example that the barriers have become more permeable.

Another part of the democratization process that the NGOs had to respond to was Indonesia's decentralization policy which transferred considerable administrative and financial power to local governments. This has determined the NGOs' decision to conduct some activities at the local level, particularly at the migrant workers' origin areas. The main reason for doing so may have been to empower migrant workers and their families by helping them to organize themselves through migrant workers' organizations. However, since their policy advocacy efforts at the national level have not brought satisfying results, and realizing that local governments and parliaments now have the authority to make policies which may address some of the problems at the earlier stage of labor migration, the NGOs have engaged local governments and parliaments, educated them on the issue and even assisted them in drafting policies. This signifies the NGOs' ability to comprehend and make the most of the shift in Indonesia's power structure after the reform. The challenge for them now is to make sure that this advocacy at the local level results in policies which actually address the problems faced by women migrant workers and that this effort can be sustained and scaled up to reach more local governments in Indonesia.

This book has shown how the NGOs' activities are determined by the existing political space and how they have tried to extend it. Although the political system has become more open and accommodative, it is still a half-opened window of opportunity which requires the NGOs to force a bigger opening by building pressure through national and international networking. This activity, coupled with efforts such as lobbying certain supportive individuals in the parliament and the government can be considered as the NGOs' attempt to expand their political space. Their assistance in forming migrant worker organizations can also be considered as a way to claim space for the community. Shigetomi only mentions the state and the community as determinants of NGOs' political space,[10] but in the context of labor migration, labor agencies also have strong influence on policies, and thus also influence the political space available for NGOs. Unfortunately, as

9 Cf. Eldridge 1995, p. 1.
10 Cf. Shigetomi 2002, p. 12.

also shown by the absence of discussion of the business actors in this book, i.e. labor agencies, the NGOs have minimal, if no, interaction with them.

There is still room for NGOs to further shape the political context, and the challenge now is for them to formulate a comprehensive strategy, which may involve opening themselves to new forms of engagement with new partners, whether from the government, the business, or other civil society elements. Although it may be difficult when some actors have not changed their perceptions and attitudes, there needs to be a continuous effort from all stakeholders to break down their stereotyped views of each other and open up to the possibility of working with stakeholders who may be ready to take a fresh approach.

10.3 Responding to Globalization

The concept of globalization features in this research because the issue of labor migration itself involves crossing national boundaries and engaging with different environments, authorities, jurisdictions, governments, and policies. In relation to this, NGOs concerned with the issue of migrant workers, including Indonesian NGOs, have admitted the need to make their activism transnational as a way of strengthening their activism at home and putting pressure on the government. Thus this book is concerned with how NGOs have been conducting their transnational activism and whether it has actually strengthened their position at home.

As discussed in part three of this book, the NGOs' response to globalization is reflected in their efforts to influence a foreign policy, the 2006 MoU between the governments of Indonesia and Malaysia. A MoU with a receiving country is considered as a potential means of protecting Indonesian migrant workers during their employment abroad. Because the NGOs are unable to extend their activism across national boundaries into a receiving country, influencing the content of the MoU has become a significant part of their transnational activism. However, accessing the MoU formulation process has been difficult for the NGOs, let alone influencing the content. Their experience in advocating for the formulation and later the revision of this MoU has led the NGOs to admit that they had a better chance of accessing a domestic policy-making process than a foreign policy one which is restricted to government representatives. Thus, while globalization has made national boundaries more permeable, it has not eliminated the separation of roles between state and non-state actors. Nevertheless, the discussion did confirm the improved relations between the NGOs and a number of state institutions such as the State Ministry of Women's Empowerment and the Ministry of Foreign Affairs.

The NGOs' transnational activism is motivated by factors such as their disappointment with the content of the MoUs with receiving countries, the fact that it took Indonesia quite a while to ratify the 1990 International Convention on the Protection of the Rights of All Migrant Workers and Members of Their Families and their inability to build strong enough pressure on the government through domestic activism. These transnational efforts involve activities such as cooperating with receiving country NGOs and other actors at the regional and international levels and utilizing regional and international instruments. The cooperation has assisted Indonesian NGOs in bringing the issues faced by Indonesian migrant workers to the regional and international levels and helped them in coordinating efforts during case handling. Also, participation in regional and international forums has allowed the NGOs to build the capacities of their staff.

With the increased efforts of NGOs to build cooperation both inside and outside the country, comes the challenge of managing and sustaining it. Jordan and Tuijl have questioned NGOs' ability to effectively manage relationships across sectors, levels and borders and argued that to maintain even a simple information exchange requires resources.[11] For the same reason, and more, Chapters 7 and 9 have also questioned the effectiveness of the NGOs' network and coalition building. Differences among the members and limited resources are among the factors that have prevented more coordinated actions. Hidayah mentioned problems such as bureaucracy and lack of shared platforms within the NGO community as challenges that need to be addressed.[12] She believes that NGOs' advocacy will be stronger if it is done by a coalition, but fragmentation, which is reflected through the disagreements and rivalries among NGOs, has prevented this from occurring. As expressed by the respondents from receiving countries' NGOs and regional networks who have worked with the NGOs researched, over time the level of cooperation tends to diminish to certain activities such as case handling.

This is due to the difficulties involved in coordinating efforts and timing activities such as campaigns. Again, the issue of consolidation and coordination among the NGOs arises. Jordan and Tuijl have warned that NGOs run the risk of becoming "entangled in conflicting alliances" as they expand their networking.[13] Although the NGOs researched claimed that they are careful to cooperate with actors and join networks and coalitions which are aligned with their principles, as they continue to expand their cooperation there will come a time when interests conflict. In fact, the demise of certain networks and/or cooperation proves that conflicts do exist among them. The absence of coordination and consolidation within the NGO community has made it difficult for them to come up with a

11 Cf. Jordan and Tuijl 2002, p. 117.
12 Interview with Hidayah, Anis on May 26, 2007.
13 Cf. Jordan and Tuijl 2002, p. 117.

common voice, a challenge that they need to overcome if they plan to continue their efforts to influence policies on migrant workers. Moreover, there are capacity issues that the NGOs need to address. Compared to NGO activists from other sending countries like the Philippines, Indonesian NGO activists have been less active in international forums, presumably due to challenges such as language mastery, experience, capability, and skill. An improvement in this area would definitely improve their participation in regional and international forums.

One of the key lessons learned by the NGOs through their activism at the regional and international levels is that for transnational activism to bring significant impact on domestic policies on migrant workers and the national labor migration system, it needs to be coupled with equally strong activism at home – something which the Philippine NGOs learned much earlier. The NGOs researched have been involved in the campaign to push for the passing of a national law on the protection of domestic workers, with the argument that the passing of such a law will give legitimacy for Indonesia's demand that the receiving countries protect its domestic workers. To date, Indonesia's requests for minimum wage and rest days have been refused by Malaysian authorities who question the fact that Indonesia itself does not have a law which stipulates those points. Consequently, the campaign for an Indonesian national law on the protection of domestic workers needs to be a significant part of the NGOs' activism on women migrant workers. This recent development signifies the urgency of close cooperation between Indonesia's labor NGOs and NGOs' concerned with the issue of migrant workers, because the effort to address a domestic labor issue has the potential to strengthen Indonesia's bargaining position in negotiating the protection of its workers overseas. Thus, while authors such as Keck and Sikkink underline the importance of transnational activism as an effort to build pressure from the outside through what they call the "boomerang pattern",[14] I argue that, based on this research on the NGOs activism on the issue of Indonesian labor migration, transnational activism can be aimed toward both home government and those hosting Indonesian workers. In other words, it can be used as a boomerang and an arrow. There is also a need to strengthen domestic policy advocacies which may amplify the effects of the transnational activism and strengthen negotiations with receiving countries.

In relation to the above, during the course of the research I have started to question the effectiveness of both national and international networking. Networking may have worked for information sharing, capacity building and addressing individual cases, but it is less effective for coordinating actions big enough to put pressure on the government and create significant impacts. Although the NGO staff interviewed insisted on the importance of their transnation-

14 Cf. Keck and Sikkink 1998.

al activism, they were not confident enough to claim that it has strengthened their activism at home. Their view concerning the advantages of conducting transnational activism generally includes cooperation in exposing and handling cases, learning from other NGOs, and increasing their reputation as an organization. As for building pressures strong enough to influence government policies, their transnational activism is still challenged by lack of coordination and resources. Thus, while I began my research agreeing to the proposition put forward by authors like Ford for NGOs to increase their transnational activism, in line with Piper and Uhlin, who refuse the expectation for transnational activists to replace the state,[15] I argue that the better approach is what they call "synergy" between both actors. Therefore, I prefer not to adopt Ford's line of argument which tends to draw a rather solid line separating state and elements of civil society such as NGOs and put them in opposing positions. I would rather argue for increased cooperation between them.

The NGOs' transnational activism in the context of responding to globalization has confirmed that they are still learning how to utilize it more effectively. It may have brought significant benefits for the NGOs in overcoming their limitations and developing their activism, but again the challenge is how they can sustain and improve it to bring a more significant and lasting impact.

10.4 Carving out an Influential Role

In examining whether NGOs have been able to carve out a distinctive role within Indonesia's labor migration system, this research highlights the importance of perceptions of both the NGOs and other stakeholders as to what the NGOs' role is and how it has been played. The main debate about the appropriate roles of NGOs revolves around whether they should be handling cases or advocating policy. Although most opinions tend to support the NGOs taking both roles, they disagree about which role the NGOs should prioritize. Some, like Indra Piliang, believe that it is more productive for NGOs to focus on handling cases which he thinks will eventually lead to policy advocacy.[16] Although Piliang admitted that it was possible for NGOs to work on regulations through lobbying, he doubted the capacity of NGOs working on the issue of migrant workers to lobby the government and the parliament. Wahyu Susilo, on the other hand, argued for NGOs taking active roles in both policy advocacy and case handling simultaneously.[17] A different opinion comes from Riana Puspasari from UNIFEM, who argued

15 Cf. Piper and Uhlin 2004a.
16 Interview with Piliang, Indra on September 3, 2007.
17 Interview with Susilo, Wahyu on November 7, 2008.

that Jakarta-based NGOs should decrease their case-work and focus on policy.[18] She believes that letting those at the grassroots level try handling the cases first as much as they can will benefit the empowering effort.

It appears that NGO activists prefer to keep their options open by not limiting their roles to only handling cases or advocating policies. Although their immediate answer when asked what role they are focusing on would be policy advocacy, they continue handling cases which may boost their media profile but at the same time take up a significant amount of their resources. I concluded in favor of the role sharing view. The more democratic environment in Indonesia's Reform Era has allowed greater opportunities for the NGOs to choose from a wider range of roles. The challenge for the NGOs now is more about choosing the most suitable roles and sharing roles amongst themselves according to their specialties, a choice which, according to Piliang, should be genuinely based on whether a particular NGO actually fits that role, not based on availability of projects.[19] For Jakarta-based NGOs like the two researched, a more suitable scheme is to focus on policy advocacy and limit their handling of cases to those which may significantly support their policy campaigns, an approach which SP claimed to have been doing. While this may appear to discriminate against the handling of cases that are not judged "significant" for the NGOs' campaign, ideally the role sharing and networking among NGOs should provide a solution by allowing the referral of some cases to other NGOs which focus more on case handling.

Such role sharing may be difficult to implement because some roles do not attract significant media spotlight and funding sources for the NGOs. At present many NGOs tend to assume as many roles as they can, despite the contradictory nature of the roles or their limited resources for doing so. Alternatively, a number of NGOs take up the same roles, leaving other tasks undone. As maintained by Safitri it has been difficult for NGOs to share and divide the work among them due to factors such as donor preferences and the NGOs' determination to be seen as the best.[20] Safitri admitted that NGOs prefer to choose work that will get ample publicity. This is worsened by the fact that most donors prefer to fund activities which will expose their names in various publications. As a result, while some tasks are untouched, others are duplicated. Safitri believed that this occurs among both NGOs and government authorities. However, since the NGOs have begun a degree of specialization by concentrating on a specific sector where they have greater capability and at the same time have conducted cross-sectoral cooperation, there is still a chance for role-sharing among NGOs to occur.

18 Interview with Puspasari, Riana on December 11, 2008.
19 Interview with Piliang, Indra on September 3, 2007.
20 Interview with Safitri, Salma on August 2, 2007.

In terms of advocating policy, there are also different opinions on how the NGOs should conduct this role. NGO activists such as Susilo are keen to take the monitoring role where they observe and judge the implementation of Law No. 39/2004, identify whether there have been any significant changes since the law was passed and whether the mandates of the law have been implemented.[21] On the other hand, although many government officials and parliament members agree in valuing the role of NGOs in providing inputs into policy, they are divided about the monitoring role. Only a few like Tatang B. Razak suggested that the NGOs should monitor any misconduct or deviance and alert the government when it happens.[22] Razak also emphasized the need for NGOs to complement the government's policies, a view shared by most government officials who welcome NGOs' active role as long as they cooperate with the government. It is quite obvious that while the NGOs and the government agree on the NGOs taking the role of input provision, they have different views on what role can the NGOs play at other stages of the policy cycle, with the NGOs seeking a more active role including in monitoring and evaluating the government's policies. Meanwhile, just as in many other cases of NGO involvement, it seems that NGOs' roles are most welcomed by the government in areas where it has least resources or interest.

For the NGOs to be able to carve out an influential role in the management of labor migration from Indonesia they need to work on a number of issues. *Firstly*, they need to be able to evaluate their own capabilities and capacities to determine their strength as an organization and their main goals. *Secondly*, they need to be able to determine which specific roles they are going to prioritize based on whether the role reflects their cause and suits their capabilities and resources. *Thirdly*, the NGOs need to practice role sharing among themselves. If an NGO takes on too many roles, it will eventually exhaust itself and a comprehensive, solid and widespread activism by civil society will continue to be difficult to achieve. If the NGOs can at least work on the above matters, there will be more chance that they can put stronger pressure on the government and convince them to accept more active roles of the NGOs in the management of labor migration. In short, for the NGOs the chance to develop their roles is determined both by their environment and their own efforts.

21 Interview with Susilo, Wahyu on November 7, 2008.
22 Interview with Razak, Tatang B. on August 14, 2007.

10.5 Conclusion

The research for this book has examined the role of two Indonesian NGOs, SP and Migrant CARE, in influencing government policies on migrant workers in a changing context of democratizing Indonesia and globalizing world by focusing on a domestic and foreign policies on migrant workers. Although it has set out to focus on Indonesian women migrant workers in the informal sector, particularly domestic workers, since the existing government policies do not address the gender issue separately, a significant part of this book had to refer to migrant workers in general. There may also be opinions, even from NGOs activists, that since the majority of migrant workers are women, in most instances when the words "*buruh migran*" or migrant workers is used, it automatically refers to women migrant workers. However, after going through the existing policies, problems, and efforts made to address the problems, I still believe that there are aspects of female labor migration that need to be addressed separately due to the commonly informal nature of their job and the private nature of their workplace, which have continuously excluded them from both labor laws and the labor movement.

Securing access to the policy-making process is both important and challenging for the NGOs. The discussion of their efforts to influence policies has shown a degree of increased NGO involvement in the policy process, at least at the initial stage of the policy cycle – agenda setting and policy formulation. It is not possible to present measurable proofs to a claim that the recent changes in Indonesia's government policies on migrant workers, such as the passing of Indonesia's first law on labor migration and the signing of MoUs with receiving countries have been a result of NGOs' activism. However, it can be safely argued that the NGOs' campaigns since the 1990s and their efforts to expose the problems faced by Indonesian women migrant workers in the media have brought the issue to the surface, formed public opinion and put enough pressure on the policy-makers to include the issue of migrant workers in their agenda. At the policy formulation stage, NGOs have also been more involved, whether formally through the input gathering forums or informally through their personal lobbying. However, the NGOs' involvement virtually stops at this point since policy formulation is still mostly a closed process. As for the policy implementation stage, although the NGOs attempted to conduct monitoring activities, they have not been able to channel their feedback, let alone push for the revision of the law with which they are dissatisfied. Thus, the research has confirmed my initial assumption that the main concern has shifted from whether NGOs are involved in the policy process to whether their inputs actually make a difference to the policies, because there is a tendency that the involvement of civil society is welcomed more as an effort to fulfill a requirement for a so-called democratic policy-making process than as a genuine effort to listen to and accommodate the voices of the people.

Evidently NGOs' access to policy process differs between domestic and foreign policies. With the democratization process and the demand for good governance, the involvement of civil society has become a necessity, however limited it is. However, when it comes to the formulation of a foreign policy, particularly when it is an agreement which involves other countries like the MoU between Indonesia and Malaysia on domestic workers, the government-to-government nature prevents NGOs' involvement in the negotiation process.

This book also shows how both the government and the NGOs have gone through a learning process of how to interact with each other within the new policy environment which involves negotiations and adjustments on both sides. With Indonesia's current stage of democratization the ideal condition of cooperative relationships between the two actors is proven to be challenging to achieve. Since the Indonesian democratization process is still at an early stage, in order to sustain it both the state and the NGOs need to continue, and if possible accelerate this learning process. However, there are indications of improved relationships between some elements of state and civil society. Furthermore, while a closer relationship between the government and the NGOs may allow a dialogue which results in better policies on migrant workers, there is still an issue of how close can these two entities be before the NGOs start to lose their "non-governmental" status and be questioned for doing so. In this case, placing the relationship within a continuum context where both the NGOs and the government can position themselves within an acceptable proximity seems to be the feasible action.

One of the important questions asked in the research is whether NGOs have been able to change along with the changing political context. I would argue that the NGOs have made considerable efforts to adapt to the new environment while addressing their weaknesses and limitations. One instance of this adaptation is the NGOs' constant search for alternative channels to influence the policies on migrant workers, overcome their limitations as organizations and put pressure on the government. Some of the NGOs' alternatives include using other laws and/or regional and international instruments, engaging and working with accommodative entities in the government and parliament and expanding their national, regional and international network. In fact, the increased effort to build cooperation with any potential partners to support their cause has become one of the distinctive features of NGO activism on the issue of migrant workers in Indonesia's Reform Era. Nevertheless, along with the wider and more complex network of cooperation comes the challenge of sustaining the cooperation which has been proven to be hard to do, due to factors such as differences and competition among the members and difficulties in coordinating and sharing roles, whether it is at the national, regional, or international level.

As for the NGOs' transnational activism, although the NGOs claim that they have benefited from it, there is little evidence that it has actually strengthened the policy influencing efforts at home, the initial reason for conducting it. The success of this transnational activism is more tangible in case-handling efforts. On rare occasions the government may seem to have made an action as a response to a joint effort of the NGOs and their international network to expose certain cases faced by migrant workers. However, a long term commitment to such activism is harder to establish. Indonesian NGOs' contribution to the network is also limited due to their limited resources and their staff's limited capabilities as compared to NGOs from some other sending countries like the Philippines.

Conducted more than a decade after Indonesian NGOs began their activism on the issue of migrant workers and the reform era began in Indonesia, the research for this book is concerned with whether the NGOs have been able to carve out a significant role in the management of labor migration from Indonesia. While in practice there are NGOs that are still trying to play several roles at a time, most NGO activists have admitted that in order to optimize their performance, NGOs need to limit themselves to the roles they are good at and there needs to be role sharing among them. With the NGOs' limited resources and the complexity of the issue of labor migration, it seems that a more feasible option is for the NGOs to choose a role based on the resources, skills, and knowledge that they have and continue to develop this role. Although it has proven difficult for the NGO community to do role-sharing among them, it is still an ideal path to take if the aim is to comprehensively address the issue of migrant workers at every level.

The NGOs' choices of how to conduct their activities, who to work with, and what to focus on have, to a certain degree, been the results of a self-evaluation and a learning process. In some instances, it may seem that there have been no changes since the NGOs still generally take a stance as opponents of the government, they still frequently resort to methods of "shame mobilization", and although they claim to focus more on policy advocacy, they still do case handling and are often preoccupied by it. Therefore, regarding the question of whether there is any strategizing process going on, my answer has to be that it is still too early to claim that there is one happening since there is no solid evidence which indicates its occurrence, the learning process is still dominated by trial and error, and the NGOs have not formulated a comprehensive long term strategy. However, as the democratization and globalization processes are ongoing, the learning process is too. For the present, the best way of looking at the NGOs' learning process is as a continuum where the changes are made in accordance with the needs and the existing political context.

In answering the main question of the research, I would argue that the NGOs have succeeded in putting the issue of women migrant workers on the governments' policy agenda. As for influencing the process of making the policies and their contents, the NGOs' influence is very limited. While the NGOs have been more involved in the process of making a domestic policy, as can be seen in their involvement in input gathering meetings prior to the deliberation process of Law No. 39/2004, their presence as observers in the parliamentary meetings, and their personal lobbies on certain members of parliaments, their involvement in the process of making a foreign policy is close to nil. Nevertheless, more importantly, the years of campaigning for policies which protect the rights of women migrant workers have provided the NGOs with valuable knowledge and experience to build their future work on. Although limited, they have also built the foundation for furthering their activism which involves wider networks, increased capabilities, and better understanding of the policy context. There is a great possibility for the NGOs to deepen their influence on the policies, particularly with their constant effort to search for alternative channels and methods such as shown in their involvement in the campaign for laws on trafficking and on protection of domestic workers.

To conclude, the body of this book has substantiated my claim that, as represented by the two NGOs researched, although there may be differences in the degree to which they have gained access to the domestic and foreign policy-making process, Indonesian NGOs concerned with the issues of women migrant workers have been able to carve an influential role in the management of labor migration from Indonesia. Changes in the policy context, changes within state institutions, more accommodative attitude from key stakeholders, and the NGOs' effort to change along with the changes around them have gained them wider political space to conduct their activism. The NGOs may still be dissatisfied with the policy products but since the democratization and globalization processes are ongoing, the government of Indonesia has stated its intention to revise the policies and the NGOs are still the leading civil society organizations in the activism on behalf of migrant workers, changes and more satisfactory results can be expected to result from improved NGO activism based on the lessons they have learned so far.

References

Abelson, Adam (2003). NGO Networks: Strength in Numbers? Office of Private and Voluntary Cooperation, Bureau of Democracy, Conflict, and Humanitarian Assistance, U.S. Agency for International Development.

Adamhar, Ferry (July 6, 2007). Interview by author. Jakarta.

Agusman, Damos Dumoli (2006). Buruh Migran Perempuan (BMP), Migrasi Internasional, dan Permasalahan Standar Perjanjian Kerja. In: Naovalitha, Tita/Trimayuni, Pande Ketut (eds.). Seminar dan Lokakarya Perlindungan Sosial Untuk Buruh Migran Perempuan. Jakarta: The World Bank and Kementerian Koordinator Bidang Kesejahteraan Rakyat Republik Indonesia, pp. 30-34.

Agusman, Damos Dumoli (2007). Perlindungan TKI di Luar Negeri oleh Pemerintah RI "Peranan dan Batasan". Jakarta: Ministry of Foreign Affairs.

Agusman, Damos Dumoli (July 23, 2007). Interview by author. Jakarta.

Agusman, Damos Dumoli (November 6, 2008). Interview by author. Jakarta.

Anggraeni, Dewi (2006). Dreamseekers: Indonesian Women as Domestic Workers in Asia. Jakarta: Equinox Publishing, International Labour Organization.

Antara News (September 13, 2009). KBRI Tetap Pertahankan Gaji PRT 600 Ringgit.

Antara News (November 23, 2009). DPR Akan Godok UU PRT.

Antlöv, Hans/Ibrahim, Rustam/Tuijl, Peter van (2006). NGO Governance and Accountability in Indonesia: Challenges in a Newly Democratizing Country. In: Jordan, Lisa/Tuijl, Peter van (eds.). NGO Accountability: Politics, Principles, and Innovations. London: Earthscan, pp. 147-66.

Aspinall, Edward (2004). Transformation of Civil Society and Democratic Breakthrough. Stanford: Stanford University Press.

Badan Eksekutif Nasional Solidaritas Perempuan (2008). Laporan Pertanggungjawaban Badan Eksekutif Nasional Periode 2004-2007 Solidaritas Perempuan. Jakarta: Solidaritas Perempuan.

Ball, Rochelle/Piper, Nicola (2006). Trading Labour-Trading Rights: The Regional Dynamics of Rights Recognition for Migrant Workers in the Asia-Pacific. In: Hewison, Kevin/Young, Ken (eds.). Transnational Migration and Work in Asia. New York: Routledge, pp. 213-34.

Bambang S, Eko (May 25, 2004). Komnas Perempuan Desak Masalah PRT masuk MOU Indonesia–Malaysia. In: Jurnal Perempuan. www.jurnalperempuan.com, accessed June 18, 2007.

Bambang S, Eko (September 27, 2004). Aksi Tolak RUU Buruh Migran Kali ini Serentak di Seluruh Indonesia, Pembahasan di DPR Jalan Terus. In: Jurnal Perempuan. www.jurnalperempuan.com, accessed June 18, 2007.

Bambang S, Eko (September 28, 2004). Jacob Nuwa Wea: "LSM itu Omong Kosong, Buat Apa Melibatkan Mereka". In: Jurnal Perempuan. www.jurnalperempuan.com, accessed June 18, 2007.

Bambang S, Eko (September 29, 2004). RUU PPTKILN Disahkan Menjadi UU, Aktivis Buruh Migran Bentangkan Spanduk Keprihatinan. In: Jurnal Perempuan. www.jurnalperempuan.com, accessed June 18, 2007.

Bambang S, Eko (October 28, 2004). Hasballah M Saad: "UU PPTKILN Tidak Berperspektif HAM". In: Jurnal Perempuan, www.jurnalperempuan.com, accessed June 18, 2007.

Bayliss, Paul/Ibrahim, Rustam (1996). The Indonesian NGO Agenda: Toward the Year 2000. Jakarta, CESDA-LP3ES.

Bebbington, Anthony/Hickey, Samuel/Mitlin, Diana C. (2008). Can NGOs Make a Difference? The Challenge of Development Alternatives. London: Zed.

Beittinger-Lee, Verena (2005). Civil Society in Indonesia-Concepts and Realities. In: Wessel, Ingrid (ed.). Democratisation in Indonesia after the Fall of Suharto. Berlin: Logos, pp. 93-117.

BNP2TKI (2010). www.bnp2tki.go.id, accessed February 12, 2010.

BNP2TKI (2013). Penempatan Berdasarkan Jenis Kelamin (2006-2012). www.bnp2tki.go.id/statistik-mainmenu-86/penempatan/6758-penempatan-berdasarkan-jenis-kelamin-2006-2012.html, accessed February 20, 2013.

Bonasahat, Albert Yosua (July 11, 2007). Interview by author. Jakarta.

Buruh Migran (2011). Indonesia-Malaysia Sepakati 11 Butir Kesepakatan Penempatan TKI. www.buruhmigran.or.id/2011/12/24/tki-malaysia-buruh-migranindonesia-malaysia-sepakati-11-butir-kesepakatan-penempatan-tki/, accessed April 17, 2013.

Bustamante, Jorge (2007). Report of the Special Rapporteur on the Human Rights of Migrants, Jorge Bustamante, Addendum, Mission to Indonesia. Human Rights Council, United Nations. www.universalhumanrightsindex.org/documents/852/1080/document/en/doc/text.doc, accessed June 18, 2007.

Caraka (August 2008). PRT Indonesia di Malaysia Paling Diminati, Paling Murah. Kuala Lumpur.

Chant, Sylvia (1992). Conclusion: Towards a Framework for the Analysis of Gender-Selective Migration. In: Chant, Sylvia (ed.). Gender and Migration in Developing Countries. London: Belhaven Press, pp. 197-206.

Chin, Christine B. N. (1997). Walls of Silence and Late Twentieth Century Representations of the Foreign Female Domestic Worker: The Case of Filipina and Indonesian Female Servants in Malaysia. In: International Migration Review, Vol. 31, No. 2, pp. 353-85.

Choi, Alex H. (2006). Migrant Workers in Macao: Labour and Globalization. In: Hewison, Kevin/Young, Ken (eds.). Transnational Migration and Work in Asia. New York: Routledge, pp. 144-65.

Clarke, Gerard (1998). The Politics of NGOs in South-East Asia: Participation and Protest in the Philippines. London: Routledge.

Clear, Annette (2005). Politics: From Endurance to Evolution. In: Bresnan, John (ed.). Indonesia: The Great Transition. Lanham: Rowman and Littlefield Publishers, pp. 137-88.

Cohen, Robin (2006). Migration and Its Enemies: Global Capital, Migrant Labour and the Nation-State. Hampshire: Ashgate Publishing Limited.

Debrah, Yaw A. (2002). Migrant Workers in Pacific Asia. London: F. Cass.

Departemen Keuangan Republik Indonesia (2010). Data Pokok APBN 2005-2010. www.depkeu.go.id/ind/Data/Berita/data_apbn.pdf, accessed January 25, 2010.

Deplu (2007). Tentang Deplu. www.deplu.go.id, accessed December 17, 2007.

Deplu (2010). Organisation. www.deplu.go.id/Pages/AboutUs.aspx?IDP=1&l=e, accessed March 15, 2010.

Depnakertrans (2004a). Pandangan Menakertrans Soal Perlindungan TKI. In: Majalah Nakertrans, Edisi 03, Th. XXIV, Juni 2004.

Depnakertrans (2004b). RI-Malaysia Tandatangani MoU Tentang Penempatan TKI di Malaysia. In: Majalah Nakertrans, Edisi 02, Th. XXIV, Maret 2004.

Depnakertrans (2007). BNP2TKI Badan Nasional Penempatan dan Perlindungan Tenaga Kerja Indonesia Buka Peluang Baru TKI. Nakertrans.

Depnakertrans (2008). www.nakertrans.go.id/, accessed September 28, 2008.

Depnakertrans (2010), www.nakertrans.go.id/, accessed March 20, 2010.

Depnakertrans (2013). www.pusdatinaker.balitfo.depnakertrans.go.id/katalog/download.php?g=2&c=17, accessed April 5, 2013.

DPR (2008). Proses Pembuatan Undang-Undang. www.dpr.go.id/tentang/proses.php, accessed May 10, 2008.

Edwards, Michael (2008). Have NGOs 'Made a Difference?' From Manchester to Birmingham with an Elephant in the Room. In: Bebbington, Anthony/Hickey, Samuel/Mitlin, Diana C. (eds.). Can NGOs Make a Difference? The Challenge of Development Alternatives. London: Zed, pp. 38-54.

Edwards, Michael/Hulme, David (2002). NGO Performance and Accountability: Introduction and Overview. In: Fowler, Alan/Edwards, Michael (eds.). The Earthscan Reader on NGO Management. London: Earthscan, pp. 187-203.

Eldridge, Philip John (1995). Non-Government Organizations and Democratic Participation in Indonesia. Kuala Lumpur: Oxford University Press.

Eldridge, Philip John (2005). Nongovernmental Organizations and Democratic Transition in Indonesia. In: Weller, Robert P. (ed.). Civil Life, Globalization,

and Political Change in Asia: Organizing Between Family and State. London: Routledge, pp. 148-70.
Embassy of the Republic of Indonesia Kuala Lumpur Malaysia (2008). Home Staff. www.kbrikl.org.my/, accessed August 29, 2008.
Fernandez, Irene (August 15, 2007). Interview by author. Kuala Lumpur.
Friedrich-Ebert-Stiftung (FES) (2010). www.fes.or.id/profile.php?lang=1, accessed March 11, 2010.
Fisher, William F. (1997). Doing Good? The Politics and Antipolitics of NGO Practices. In: Annual Review of Anthropology, Vol. 26, No. 1, pp. 439-64.
Ford, Michele (2002). Responses to Changing Labour Relations: The Case of Women's NGOs in Indonesia. In: Gills, Dong Sook/Piper, Nicola (eds.). Women and Work in Globalising Asia. London: Routledge, pp. 90-111.
Ford, Michele (2004). Organizing the Unorganizable: Unions, NGOs, and Indonesian Migrant Labour. In: International Migration, Vol. 42, No. 5, pp. 99-119.
Ford, Michele (2005). Migrant Labour in South East Asia, Country Study: Indonesia. Friedrich-Ebert-Stiftung (FES): Project on Migrant Labor in Southeast Asia. www.fes.org.ph/pdf/FORD_Indonesia_final.pdf, accessed July 13, 2006.
Ford, Michele (2006a). After Nunukan: The Regulation of Indonesian Migration to Malaysia. In: Kaur, Amarjit/Metcalfe, Ian (eds.). Mobility, Labour Migration and Border Controls in Asia. Basingstoke: Palgrave Macmillan, pp. 228-47.
Ford, Michele (2006b). Migrant Labor NGOs and Trade Unions: A Partnership in Progress? In: Asian and Pacific Migration Journal, Vol. 15, No. 3, pp. 299-311.
Ford, Michele (2009). Workers and Intellectuals: NGOs, Trade Unions and the Indonesian Labour Movement. Singapore: Asian Studies Association of Australia in Association with NUS Press.
Gabriel, Cynthia (August 13, 2007). Interview by author. Kuala Lumpur.
Gills, Dong Sook (2002). Globalisation and Counter-Globalisation. In: Gills, Dong Sook/Piper, Nicola (eds.). Women and Work in Globalising Asia. London: Routledge, pp. 13-31.
Governments of Indonesia and Malaysia (2006a). Agreed Minutes of the First Joint Working Group Meeting for the Implementation of the Memorandum of Understanding Between the Government of the Republic of Indonesia and the Government of Malaysia on the Recruitment and Placement of Indonesian Domestic Workers, Kota Kinabalu, Malaysia, July 20-21, 2006. Kota Kinabalu: Indonesian Ministry of Foreign Affairs and Malaysian Ministry of Home Affairs.

Governments of Indonesia and Malaysia (2006b). Agreed Minutes of the Technical Committee Meeting on the Proposed Memorandum of Understanding Between the Government of the Republic of Indonesia and the Government of Malaysia on the Recruitment and Placement of Indonesian Domestic Workers, Yogyakarta, March 3-4, 2006. Yogyakarta: Indonesian Ministry of Foreign Affairs and Malaysian Ministry of Home Affairs.

Governments of Indonesia and Malaysia (2006c). Agreed Minutes Second Senior Official Meeting on the Proposed Memorandum of Understanding Between the Government of the Republic of Indonesia and the Government of Malaysia on the Recruitment and Placement of Indonesian Domestic Workers, Bogor, April 17, 2006. Bogor: Indonesian Ministry of Foreign Affairs and Malaysian Ministry of Home Affairs.

GPPBM (2006). Pernyataan Gerakan Perempuan untuk Perlindungan Buruh Migran (GPPBM) untuk Perlindungan Pekerja Rumah Tangga (TKW-PRT) Indonesia di Malaysia: MoU RI-Malaysia Melegalkan Praktek Komoditisasi dan Makin Merentankan TKW-PRT Indonesia di Malaysia. Rapat Dengar Pendapat Umum (RDPU) GPPBM dengan Komisi IX DPR-RI, Gedung Nusantara I Lt 1 DPR RI Jakarta.

Grugel, Jean (2004). State Power and Transnational Activism. In: Piper, Nicola/Uhlin, Anders (eds.). Transnational Activism in Asia: Problems of Power and Democracy. New York: Routledge, pp. 26-42.

Gumay, Hadar N. (2002). Assessing Democratic Evolution in Southeast Asia. Singapore: Institute of Southeast Asian Studies.

Gurowitz, Amy (2000). Migrant Rights and Activism in Malaysia: Opportunities and Constraints. In: The Journal of Asian Studies, Vol. 59, No. 4, pp. 863-88.

Hadiwinata, Bob Sugeng (2003). Politics of NGOs in Indonesia: Developing Democracy and Managing a Movement. London: RoutledgeCurzon.

Hadiz, Vedi R. (2005). Understanding “Democratic Transitions”: Some Insights from Gus Dur’s Brief Presidency in Indonesia. In: Shiraishi, Takashi/Abinales, Patricio N. (eds.). After the Crisis: Hegemony, Technocracy and Governance in Southeast Asia. Kyoto: Kyoto University Press and Trans Pacific Press, pp. 119-33.

Harun (August 16, 2007). Interview by author. Kuala Lumpur.

Hidayah, Anis (January 2, 2007). Email to author. Jakarta.

Hidayah, Anis (May 26, 2007). Interview by author. Jakarta.

Hidayah, Anis (June 15, 2007). Interview by author. Jakarta.

Hidayah, Anis (September 14, 2007). Interview by author. Jakarta.

Hidayah, Anis (September 15, 2007). Interview by author. Jakarta.

Hidayah, Anis (November 18, 2008). Interview by author. Jakarta.

Hidayat, Jumhur (July 30, 2007). Interview by author. Jakarta.

Howlett, Michael/Perl, Anthony/Ramesh, M. (2003). Studying Public Policy: Policy Cycles and Policy Subsystems. Ontario: Oxford University Press.

HRW (2004a). Help Wanted: Abuses Against Female Migrant Domestic Workers in Indonesia and Malaysia. Human Rights Watch. www.hrw.org/reports/2004/indonesia0704/indonesia0704full.pdf, accessed November 16, 2007.

HRW (2004b). Malaysia: Labor Accord Fails Indonesian Migrant Workers Bilateral Agreement Denies Basic Labor Protections, Excludes Domestic Workers. Human Rights Watch. www.hrw.org/english/docs/2004/05/11/malays8569.htm, accessed November 16, 2007.

Hugo, Graeme (1992). Women on the Move: Changing Patterns of Population Movement of Women in Indonesia. In: Chant, Sylvia H. (ed.). Gender and Migration in Developing Countries. London: Belhaven Press, pp. 174-96.

Hugo, Graeme (2005). Indonesian International Domestic Workers: Contemporary Developments and Issues. In: Huang, Shirlena/Yeoh, Brenda S. A./Rahman, Noor Abdul (eds.). Asian Women as Transnational Domestic Workers. Singapore: Marshall Cavendish Academic, pp. 54-91.

Hukumpedia (2010). Naskah Akademis. www.hukumpedia.com/index.php?title=Naskah_akademis_%28RUU%29, accessed April 1, 2010.

Hulme, David/Edwards, Michael (eds.) (1997). NGOs, States and Donors. London: Macmillan Press LTD.

Humaidah, Lisa Noor (July 12, 2007). Interview by author. Jakarta.

Humaidah, Lisa Noor (n/a). Catatan Ringkas Analisa Terhadap UU PPTKILN. Jakarta.

ILO (2006). Using Indonesian Law to Protect and Empower Indonesian Migrant Workers: Some Lessons from the Philippines. Jakarta: ILO Project on Mobilizing Action for the Protection of Domestic Workers from Forced Labour and Trafficking in Southeast Asia.

Indonesian Embassy in Kuala Lumpur (2007). Rekapitulasi Pekerja Asing di Malaysia 2003-2007. Kuala Lumpur: Indonesian Embassy in Kuala Lumpur.

Indonesian Peacebuilding Directory (2007). www.direktori-perdamaian.org/ english/org_detail.php?id=220, accessed October 16, 2007.

INFID (2009). Profile INFID. www.infid.org/newinfid/content.php?pci=2, accessed July 5, 2009.

Irewati, Awani (2003). Kebijakan Indonesia Terhadap Masalah TKI di Malaysia. In: Irewati, Awani/Inayati, Ratna Shofi/Pudjiastuti, Tri Nuke (eds.). Kebijakan Luar Negeri Indonesia terhadap Masalah TKI Ilegal di Negara-Negara ASEAN. Jakarta: Pusat Penelitian Politik LIPI.

Irewati, Awani/Inayati, Ratna Shofi/Pudjiastuti, Tri Nuke (eds.). (2003). Kebijakan Luar Negeri Indonesia terhadap Masalah TKI Ilegal di Negara-Negara ASEAN. Jakarta: Pusat Penelitian Politik LIPI.

Jemadu, Alex (2004). Transnational Activism and the Pursuit of Democratization in Indonesia: National, Regional and Global Networks. In: Piper, Nicola/Uhlin, Anders (eds.). Transnational Activism in Asia: Problems of Power and Democracy. New York: Routledge, pp. 149-67.

Jones, Sydney (2000). Making Money off Migrants: The Indonesian Exodus to Malaysia. Hong Kong: Capstrans and University of Wollongong.

Jordan, Lisa/Tuijl, Peter van (2002). Political Responsibility in Transnational NGO Advocacy. In: Fowler, Alan/Edwards, Michael (eds.). The Earthscan Reader on NGO Management. London: Earthscan, pp. 100-22.

Katjasungkana, Nursyahbani (July 6, 2007). Interview by author. Jakarta.

Kaur, Amarjit (2004). Wage Labour in Southeast Asia Since 1840: Globalisation, the International Division of Labour and Labour Transformation. Hampshire: Palgrave Macmillan.

Kaur, Amarjit (2006). Managing the Border: Regulation of International Labour Migration and State Policy Responses to Global Governance in Southeast Asia. Paper presented at the 16th Biennial Conference of the Asian Studies Association of Australia. Wollongong.

Keck, Margareth E./Sikkink, Kathryn (1998). Activists Beyond Borders: Advocacy Networks in International Politics. Ithaca: Cornell University Press.

Kejser, Lotte (2007). ILO Migrant Workers Project 2006-2008 in Indonesia, Philippines, Malaysia, Singapore, Hong Kong SAR. Project Advisory Committee Meeting.

Kerr, Joanna/Sweetman, Caroline (2003). Editorial. In: Kerr, Joanna/Sweetman, Caroline (eds.). Women Reinventing Globalisation. Oxford: Oxfam GB, pp. 3-14.

Khusnaeny, Asmaul (September 24, 2007). Interview by author. Jakarta.

Komnas Perempuan/GPPBM/HRWG/KOPBUMI/LBH Jakarta/SBMI/Solidaritas Perempuan (2006a). Sia Sia, Reformasi Dibelenggu Birokrasi, Catatan Hasil Pemantauan Awal Terhadap INPRES No. 06/2006 Tentang Kebijakan Reformasi Sistem Penempatan dan Perlindungan Tenaga Kerja Indonesia. Jakarta: Komnas Perempuan.

Komnas Perempuan/HRWG/SBMI/KOPBUMI/GPPBM (2006b). Menolak Paket Perbudakan Modern, Catatan Kritis atas Memorandum of Understanding Antara Pemerintah Indonesia dan Pemerintah Malaysia Tentang Rekruitment dan Penempatan Pekerja Rumah Tangga Indonesia. Jakarta: Komnas Perempuan.

Komnas Perempuan/SP (2002). Indonesian Migrant Workers: Systematic Abuse at Home and Abroad. Jakarta: Komnas Perempuan and Solidaritas Perempuan/CARAM Indonesia.

Komnas Perempuan/SP (2003). Indonesian Migrant Domestic Workers: Their Vulnerabilities and New Initiatives for the Protection of Their Rights (Indonesian Country Report to the UN Special Rapporteur on the Human Rights of Migrants, 2003). Jakarta: Komnas Perempuan and Solidaritas Perempuan/CARAM Indonesia.

Kompas (August 15, 2002). DPR Akan Galang Bentuk Pansus TKI.

Kompas (June 5, 2004). Sila Kedua Pancasila Bagi TKI: Mana Itu.

Kompas (September 1, 2004). Konsep RUU PPTKILN Mulai Disandingkan.

Kompas (September 24, 2004). Meski Alot, DPR Akan Setujui RUU PPTKILN.

Kompas (October 30, 2004). Pemulangan TKI, Ujian Nyata 100 Hari Perubahan.

Kompas (February 11, 2010). Negosiasi Berlarut Picu TKI Ilegal.

Kompas (June 15, 2010). Perlindungan PRT Jadi Konvensi.

Koran Tempo (March 12, 2010). Mou Tenaga Kerja Akhirnya Tuntas.

Koran Tempo (May 10, 2010). Aktivis Desak UU PRT Disahkan.

Krisnawaty, Tati (November 7, 2008). Interview by author. Jakarta.

Lim, Astrid Felicia (2004). UU Perlindungan TKI Disahkan. www.detiknews.com/index.php/detik.read/tahun/2004/bulan/09/tgl/29/time/183053/idnews/216206/idkanal/10, accessed December 21, 2007.

Loveband, Anne (2006). Positioning the Product: Indonesian Migrant Women Workers in Taiwan. In: Hewison, Kevin/Young, Ken (eds.) Transnational Migration and Work in Asia. Abingdon: Routledge, pp. 25-89.

Lyons, Lenore (2004). Organizing for Domestic Worker Rights in Southeast Asia: Feminist Responses to Globalisation. Paper presented at 15th Biennial Conference of the Asian Studies Association of Australia. Canberra.

Mahkamah Konstitusi Republik Indonesia (2005). Putusan Nomor 019-020/PUU-III/2005. Jakarta.

Mahkamah Konstitusi Republik Indonesia (2007). Putusan Nomor 028-029/PUU-IV/2006. Jakarta.

Media Indonesia (2004). LSM Akan Ajukan RUU PPTKILN ke Mahkamah Konstitusi.

Menteri Luar Negeri Indonesia (2003). Pernyataan Pers Menteri Luar Negeri RI, Refleksi Tahun 2002 dan Proyeksi Tahun 2003. Jakarta: Ministry of Foreign Affairs.

Menteri Luar Negeri Indonesia (2005). Pernyataan Pers Tahunan Menteri Luar Negeri Republik Indonesia. Jakarta: Ministry of Foreign Affairs.

Menteri Luar Negeri Indonesia (2008). Pernyataan Pers Tahunan Menteri Luar Negeri Republik Indonesia Kilas Balik 2007 dan Proyeksi 2008. Jakarta: Ministry of Foreign Affairs.

Migrant CARE (2004). Laporan Tahunan 2004. Jakarta.

Migrant CARE (2005a). Laporan Tahunan 2005. Jakarta.

Migrant CARE (2005b). Surat Migrant CARE untuk SBY menjelang Kunjungan ke Malaysia: Perjuangkan Hak-Hak Buruh Migran Indonesia di malaysia !!!. Jakarta.

Migrant CARE (2006). Organisation Profile, Migrant CARE Indonesian Association for Migrant Workers Sovereignty. Jakarta.

Migrant CARE (2007). Hasil Monitoring Terminal III Bandara Soekarno Hatta Tahun 2007. Jakarta.

Migrant CARE (2008). Summary of Funding Sources. Jakarta.

Muchtar (2005). Permasalahan Tenaga Kerja Wanita Indonesia: Study Kasus di Singapura. In: Nuryana, Mu'man (ed.). Permasalahan Sosial Tenaga Kerja Wanita Indonesia. Jakarta: Departemen Sosial RI, Badan Pelatihan dan Pengembangan Sosial, Pusat Penelitian Permasalahan Kesejahteraan Sosial.

Munck, Ronaldo (2009). Globalisation, Governance and Migration: An Introduction. In: Munck, Ronaldo (ed.). Globalisation and Migration: New Issues, New Politics. Third World Quarterly, special issue, Vol. 29, No. 7, pp. 1227-46.

Nagib, Laila (2001). Studi Kebijakan Pengembangan Pengiriman Tenaga Kerja Wanita ke Luar Negeri. Jakarta: Kantor Menteri Negara Pemberdayaan Perempuan and Puslitbang Kependudukan dan Ketenagakerjaan Lembaga Ilmu Pengetahuan Indonesia.

Noch, Ade Adam (September 4, 2007). Interview by author. Jakarta.

Nuwa Wea, Jacob (September 29, 2004). Sambutan Pemerintah pada Sidang Paripurna DPR-RI atas Persetujuan Rancangan Undang-Undang Republik Indonesia Tentang Penempatan dan Perlindungan Tenaga Kerja Indonesia di Luar Negeri. Jakarta: Ministry of Manpower and Transmigration.

Nyman, Mikaela (2006). Democratising Indonesia: The Challenges of Civil Society in the Era of Reformasi. Copenhagen: Nordic Institute of Asian Studies (NIAS).

Ong, Alex (August 13, 2007). Interview by author. Kuala Lumpur.

Ong, Alex. (August 16, 2007). Interview by author. Kuala Lumpur.

Organizing Committee (2006). Kerangka Acuan Semiloka Membangun Kerangka Perlindungan Buruh Migran Perempuan - Pekerja Rumah Tangga (BMP-PRT) Indonesia di Malaysia. Cisarua. January 23-25, 2006. Draft 03/01/06.

Parlemen.net (2010). Bagaimana Undang-Undang Dibuat. www.parlemen.net/site/ldetails.php?docid=bagaimana, accessed April 2, 2010.

Pigay, Natalis (2005). Migrasi Tenaga Kerja Internasional: Sejarah, Fenomena, Masalah dan Solusinya. Jakarta: Pustaka Sinar Harapan.

Pikiran Rakyat (2002). Muhaimin Iskandar, "Mungkin DPR Bentuk Pansus TKI". Soal TKI Mencapai Ambang Batas Kritis.

Piliang, Indra (September 3, 2007). Interview by author. Jakarta.

Piper, Nicola (2002). Gender and Migration Policies in Southeast Asia - Preliminary Observations from the Mekong Region, Southeast Asia's Population in a Changing Asian Context. Bangkok: Siam City Hotel.

Piper, Nicola (2003). Feminization of Labor Migration as Violence Against Women: International, Regional, and Local Nongovernmental Organization Responses in Asia. In: Violence Against Women, Vol. 9, No. 6, pp. 723-45.

Piper, Nicola (2004a). Gender and Migration Policies in Southeast and East Asia: Legal Protection and Sociocultural Empowerment of Unskilled Migrant Women. In: Singapore Journal of Tropical Geography, Vol. 25, No. 2, pp. 216-31.

Piper, Nicola (2004b). Rights of Foreign Workers and the Politics of Migration in South-East and East Asia. In: International Migration, Vol. 42, No. 5, pp. 71-97.

Piper, Nicola (2005a). Gender and Migration. www.test.gcim.org/attachements/TP10.pdf, accessed July 25, 2006.

Piper, Nicola (2005b). A Problem by a Different Name? A Review of Research on Trafficking in South-East Asia and Oceania. In: International Migration, Vol. 43, No. 1-2, pp. 203-33.

Piper, Nicola (2005c). Transnational Politics and Organizing of Migrant Labour in South East Asia - NGO and Trade Union Perspectives. In: Asia-Pacific Population Journal, December 2005, pp. 87-110.

Piper, Nicola (2006). Gendering the Politics of Migration. In: International Migration Review, Vol. 40, No. 1, pp. 133-64.

Piper, Nicola (2009). Feminisation of Migration and the Social Dimensions of Development: The Asian Case. In: Munck, Ronaldo (ed.). Globalisation and Migration: New Issues, New Politics. Third World Quarterly, special issue, Vol. 29, No. 7, pp. 1287-1303.

Piper, Nicola (2010). Temporary Economic Migration and Rights Activism: An Organizational Perspective. In: Ethnic and Racial Studies, Vol. 33, No. 1, pp. 108-25.

Piper, Nicola/Iredale, Robyn (2003). Identification of the Obstacles to the Signing and Ratification of the UN Convention on the Protection of the Rights of All Migrant Workers, The Asia Pacific Perspective. International Migration and Multicultural Policies Section, UNESCO. www.portal.unesco.org/shs/fr/file_download.php/09ea2df029c0f73876051ce2648028dfasia_pacific_full_report.pdf, accessed July 15, 2006.

Piper, Nicola/Uhlin, Anders (2004a). New Perspectives on Transnational Activism. In: Piper, Nicola/Uhlin, Anders (eds.) Transnational Activism in Asia: Problems of Power and Democracy. New York: Routledge, pp. 1-25.

Piper, Nicola/Uhlin, Anders (eds.) (2004b) Transnational Activism in Asia: Problems of Power and Democracy. New York: Routledge.

Poeloengan, Lisna Y. (2006). Standar Biaya Penempatan Yang Terjangkau. In: Naovalitha, Tita/Trimayuni, Pande Ketut (eds.). Seminar dan Lokakarya Perlindungan Sosial Untuk Buruh Migran Perempuan. Jakarta: The World Bank and Kementerian Koordinator Bidang Kesejahteraan Rakyat Republik Indonesia.

Pramodhawardani, Jaleswari (2006). Batam, Buruh Migran Perempuan dan Persoalan "Budaya". In: Pramodhawardani, Jaleswari (ed.) Kesetaraan dan Keadilan Gender Dalam Budaya Patriarkhi: Kasus Tenaga Kerja Perempuan di Luar Negeri. Jakarta: LIPI Press, pp. 43-77.

Presiden Republik Indonesia (October 23, 2000). Undang-Undang Republik Indonesia Nomor 24 Tahun 2000 tentang Perjanjian Internasional. Jakarta: Sekretaris Negara Republik Indonesia.

Presiden Republik Indonesia (October 18, 2004). Undang-Undang Republik Indonesia Nomor 39 Tahun 2004 Tentang Penempatan dan Perlindungan Tenaga Kerja Indonesia di Luar Negeri. Jakarta: Sekretaris Negara Republik Indonesia.

Pusat Pengkajian Pengolahan Data dan Informasi (2008). RUU TKI di LN 2004. Jakarta: Bidang Arsip dan Dokumentasi, Sekretariat Jenderal Dewan Perwakilan Rakyat Republik Indonesia.

Puspasari, Riana (August 10, 2007). Interview by author. Jakarta.

Puspasari, Riana (December 11, 2008). Interview by author. Jakarta.

Razak, Tatang B. (August 14, 2007). Interview by author. Kuala Lumpur.

Riker, James V. (1995a). Contending Perspectives for Interpreting Government-NGO Relations in South and Southeast Asia: Constraints, Challenges and the Search for Common Ground in Rural Development. In: Heyzer, Noeleen/Riker, James. V./Quizon, Antonio B. (eds.). Government-NGO Relations in Asia: Prospects and Challenges for People-Centred Development. Kuala Lumpur: Asian and Pacific Development Centre, Macmillan Press and St. Martin's Press, pp. 15-55.

Riker, James V. (1995b). From Cooptation to Cooperation and Collaboration in Government-NGO Relations: Toward an Enabling Policy Environment for People-Centred Development in Asia. In: Heyzer, Noeleen/Riker, James. V./Quizon, Antonio B. (eds.). Government-NGO Relations in Asia: Prospects and Challenges for People-Centred Development. Kuala Lumpur: Asian and Pacific Development Centre, Macmillan Press and St. Martin's Press, pp. 91-130.

Riker, James V. (1995c). Reflections on Government-NGO Relations in Asia: Prospects and Challenges for People-Centred Development. In: Heyzer, Noeleen/Riker, James. V./Quizon, Antonio B. (eds.). Government-NGO Relations in Asia: Prospects and Challenges for People-Centred Development.

Kuala Lumpur: Asian and Pacific Development Centre, Macmillan Press and St. Martin's Press, pp. 194-96.
Riker, James V. (1998). The State, Institutional Pluralism, and Development from Below: The Changing Political Parameters of State-NGO Relations in Indonesia. Cornell University.
Robinson, Kathryn (2000). Gender, Islam, and Nationality: Indonesian Domestic Servants in the Middle East. In: Adams, Kathleen M./Dickey, Sara (eds.). Home and Hegemony: Domestic Service and Identity Politics in South and Southeast Asia. Ann Arbor: University of Michigan Press, pp. 249-82.
Rumansara, Augustinus (1996). INFID's Experience in Advocacy and International Collaboration. In: Ibrahim, Rustam (ed.). The Indonesian NGO Agenda, Toward the Year 2000. Jakarta: CESDA - LP3ES.
Safitri, Salma (2006). Catatan Kritis Solidaritas Perempuan Terhadap MoU RI-Malaysia tentang Penempatan TKW PRT di Malaysia: MoU Melegalkan Praktek Komoditisasi dan Semakin Merentankan TKW-PRT Indonesia ke Malaysia.
Safitri, Salma (June 6, 2007). Interview by author. Jakarta.
Safitri, Salma (August 2, 2007). Interview by author. Jakarta.
Safitri, Salma (February 11, 2008). Email to author. Jakarta.
Safitri, Salma (May 14, 2008). Email to author. Jakarta.
Sakai, Yumiko (2002). Indonesia, Flexible NGOs vs Inconsistent State Control. In: Shigetomi, Shinichi (ed.). The State and NGOs, Perspective from Asia. Pasir Panjang: Institute of Southeast Asian Studies, pp. 161-77.
Santoso, Widjajanti M. (2006). Hubungan Antar Lembaga di Dalam Masalah Perlindungan Tenaga Kerja. In: Pramodhawardani, Jaleswari (ed.). Kesetaraan dan Keadilan Gender dalam Budaya Patriarkhi: Kasus Tenaga Kerja Perempuan di Luar Negeri. Jakarta: LIPI Press, pp. 17-42.
SBMI (2009). Siapa SBMI. www.infosbmi.blogspot.com/2007/07/pernyataan-sikap-serikat-buruh-migran.html, accessed June 2, 2009.
Seknas Kopbumi (2005). Legal Analysis Undang Undang No. 39/Tahun 2004 Penempatan dan Perlindungan Tenaga Kerja Indonesia di Luar Negeri. Jakarta: Seknas Kopbumi.
Setiabudi, Safruddin (June 19, 2007). Interview by author. Jakarta.
Shigetomi, Shinichi (2002). The State and NGOs, Issues and Analytical Framework. In: Shigetomi, Shinichi (ed.). The State and NGOs, Perspective from Asia. Pasir Panjang: Institute of Southeast Asian Studies.
Sijabat, Ridwan (September 19, 2007). Interview by author. Jakarta.
Sinaga, Ramiany (August 31, 2007). Interview by author. Jakarta.
Sinar Harapan (2004). UU PTKILN Akan Matikan Penempatan TKI Formal.
Soetrisno, Tuti L. (July 17, 2007). Interview by author. Jakarta.

SP (2006). Solidaritas Perempuan's Statement on Memorandum of Understanding Between the Government of the Republic of Indonesia and the Government of Malaysia on the Recruitment and Placement of Indonesian Domestic Workers. Jakarta.

SP (2007a). Program. www.solidaritas-perempuan.org/ sp_ind/, accessed December 28, 2007.

SP (2007b). Sejarah SP. www.solidaritasperempuan.org/sp_ind/index.php? option=com_frontpage&Itemid=71, accessed December 28, 2007.

State Ministry of Women's Empowerment/SP (2006a). Draft Kesepakatan Pembagian Kerja. Jakarta.

State Ministry of Women's Empowerment/SP (2006b), Kerangka Acuan Semiloka Membangun Kerangka Perlindungan Buruh Migran Perempuan - Pekerja Rumah Tangga (BMP-PRT) Indonesia di Malaysia Cisarua. January 23-25, 2006. Draft 03/01/06.

Suara Pembaruan (October 1, 2004). UU bagi Buruh Migran Disetujui, Akankah Nasib Mereka Berubah?

Suara Pembaruan (February 8, 2005). Tekan Malaysia agar Fair.

Susilo, Wahyu (2005). Partisipasi atau NonPartisipasi? Catatan tentang Pengalaman Advokasi Buruh Migran. In: Bahagijo, Sugeng/Tagaroa, Rusdi (eds.). Bunga Rampai Partisipasi. Jakarta: Penerbit Perkumpulan PraKarsa.

Susilo, Wahyu (June 14, 2007). Interview by author. Jakarta.

Susilo, Wahyu (May 26, 2008). Email to author. Jakarta.

Susilo, Wahyu (November 7, 2008). Interview by author. Jakarta.

Susilo, Wahyu (February 11, 2010). Personal communication with author. Jakarta.

Sustikarini, Amalia (2004). Dual Track Diplomacy Government-NGO: Solusi Alternatif Dalam Masalah Pelindungan TKI di Malaysia. In: Jurnal Global, Departemen Hubungan Internasional Fakultas Ilmu Sosial dan Ilmu Politik, Universitas Indonesia, Vol. 13.

Sutaat (2005). Permasalahan Sosial Tenaga Kerja Wanita dan Implikasi Terhadap Program Pelayanan Sosial. In: Nuryana, Mu'man (ed.). Permasalahan Sosial Tenaga Kerja Wanita Indonesia. Jakarta: Departemen Sosial RI, Badan Pelatihan dan Pengembangan Sosial, Pusat Penelitian Permasalahan Kesejahteraan Sosial.

Sutaat/Nuryana, Mu'man (2005). Masalah Sosial Pekerja Migran Indonesia di Shelter KBRI Kuala Lumpur. In: Nuryana, Mu'man (ed.). Permasalahan Sosial Tenaga Kerja Wanita Indonesia. Jakarta: Departemen Sosial RI, Badan Pelatihan dan Pengembangan Sosial, Pusat Penelitian Permasalahan Kesejahteraan Sosial.

Tempo Interaktif (September 14, 2004). Koalisi Masyarakat Minta Tunda RUU Buruh Migran.

Tempo Interaktif (September 16, 2004). Koalisi Buruh Protes RUU Perlindungan TKI.
Tempo Interaktif (September 17, 2004). Depnakertrans Bantah RUU Perlindungan TKI Mengukuhkan Trafficking.
Tempo Interaktif (January 26, 2010). Migrant CARE Minta Terminal Khusus TKI Segera Ditutup Penuh.
Tenaganita (2006). Tenaganita's Critique of the Memorandum of Understanding on Domestic Workers Signed by the Malaysian and Indonesian Governments on May 13, 2006. Kuala Lumpur.
The Government of Indonesia/The Government of Malaysia (2006). Memorandum of Understanding between the Government of the Republic of Indonesia and the Government of Malaysia on the Recruitment and Placement of Indonesian Domestic Workers. Bali.
The Jakarta Post (September 14, 2002). Malaysia and Indonesia Both Exploit Workers.
The Jakarta Post (September 30, 2004). House Endorses Bill on Migrant Worker Protection.
The Jakarta Post (April 17, 2006). NGOs Fault MOU on Migrant Workers.
The Jakarta Post (May 15, 2006). RI, Malaysia Ink MOU on Protection of Migrant Workers.
The Jakarta Post (March 15, 2010). Doubts Remain in Place Despite Migrant Protection Deal.
The World Bank (2010). Remittances Data. www.econ.worldbank.org/WBSITE/EXTERNAL/EXTDEC/EXTDECPROSPECTS/0,,contentMDK:21352016~pagePK:64165401~piPK:64165026~theSitePK:476883,00.html, accessed February 11, 2010.
Tirtosudarmo, Riwanto (2007). Mencari Indonesia: Demografi-Politik Pasca-Soeharto. Jakarta: Yayasan Obor Indonesia and LIPI Press.
Umar, Risma (August 8, 2007). Interview by author. Jakarta.
Wawa, Jannes Eudes (2005). Ironi Pahlawan Devisa: Kisah Tenaga Kerja Indonesia dalam Laporan Jurnalistik. Jakarta: Kompas.
Wessel, Ingrid (2005). The Impact of the State on the Democratisation Process in Indonesia. In: Wessel, Ingrid (ed.). Democratisation in Indonesia after the Fall of Suharto. Berlin: Logos, pp. 5-26.
Wirajuda, Hassan (2004). Keynote Speech Dr. N. Hassan Wirajuda Menteri Luar Negeri R.I Dialog Nasional Membangun Sinergitas Kebijakan Lokal, Nasional dan Internasional Bagi Penegakan HAM Buruh Migran Indonesia. Kerjasama Komnas Perempuan dan Departemen Luar Negeri. Jakarta.
Women's Aid Organisation of Malaysia (2009). About us. www.wao.org.my/#, accessed March 15, 2009.

Yamanaka, Keiko/Piper, Nicola (2005). Feminized Migration in East and Southeast Asia: Policies, Actions and Empowerment, www.unrisd.org/unrisd/website/document.nsf/462fc27bd1fce00880256b4a0060d2af/06c975dec6217d4ec12571390029829a/$FILE/OP11%20web.pdf, accessed July 30, 2006.

Young, Ken (2006). Globalization and the Changing Management of Migrating Service Workers in the Asia-Pacific. In: Hewison, Kevin/Young, Ken (eds.). Transnational Migration and Work in Asia. Abingdon: Routledge, pp. 15-36.

Ziegenhain, Patrick (2008). Indonesian Parliament and Democratization. Singapore: Institute of Southeast Asian Studies.

Zulbahary, Thaufiek (May 16, 2007). Interview by author. Jakarta.

Zulbahary, Thaufiek (July 9, 2007). Interview by author. Jakarta.

Zulbahary, Thaufiek (September 24, 2007). Interview by author. Jakarta.

Zulbahary, Thaufiek (March 11, 2008). Email to author. Jakarta.

Zulbahary, Thaufiek (November 19, 2008). Interview by author, Jakarta.